Shipwr...
Pirates & P... ...s:
Sunken Treasures of the
Upper South Carolina Coast, 1521-1865
by
Dr. E. Lee Spence
(marine archeologist, cartographer, and historian)

Over 300 documented shipwrecks!

This book covers the area from Bulls Island to the South Carolina - North Carolina line. It includes the rich waters of Myrtle Beach, Georgetown, Cape Romain, McClellenville, Santee River, Pee Dee River, Black River, Waccamaw River, Winyah Bay, South Island, North Island, DeBordieu Island, Pawleys Island, the Grand Strand, Huntington Beach, Long Bay, Cherry Grove, and Little River, South Carolina.)

Library of Congress Card Catalog Number: 95-69597
ISBN: 1-886391-06-8 (hardcover) $19.95
ISBN: 1-886391-07-6 (paperback) $12.95

Suggested Classifications: archeology; blockade runners; diving; pirates; privateers; salvage; shipping; shipwrecks; South Carolina history; Spence, Edward Lee; Spence's List; treasure trove; underwater archeology; wrecks

ALL RIGHTS RESERVED

This book, *Shipwrecks, Pirates & Privateers: Sunken Treasures of the Upper South Carolina Coast, 1521-1865*, has been copyrighted by the author, Edward Lee Spence, for both compilation and composition. All rights reserved. No part of this work may be reproduced or transmitted in any form or by any means, electronic or mechanical, including photocopying and recording, or by any data base, storage, or retrieval system, except as may be expressly permitted by the 1976 Copyright Act or in writing by the author. *SL Codes*™ are the exclusive property of the author, but may be used for limited citation purposes, when such use is not otherwise in violation of the 1976 Copyright Act. Compilation of the data contained in this book took over twenty-five years and cost many thousands of dollars. To protect that investment in time and money, actual and punitive damages, etc., will be sought in the event of any copyright infringement. All correspondence and inquiries should be directed to Narwhal Press, 1629 Meeting Street, Charleston, South Carolina 29405 or to Dr. E. Lee Spence, Underwater Archeologist, P.O. Box 211, Sullivan's Island, South Carolina 29482.

(Trademark notice: SL Codes and Spence's List are exclusive trademarks owned by Edward Lee Spence.)

Front Cover: The author surfacing with silver sugar tongs and ornate brass lamp from shipwreck. Photo by Kevin Rooney. Small photo shows gold thimble found on the Cape Romain pirate wreck, by and courtesy of Shipwrecks Inc.

Back Cover: Binnacle lamp from the wreck of the *Regina*. Photo by Charles King. Small photo of the author by Merrily de Lignières.

Title Page: The author taking measurements of an anchor found in fifty feet of water. Photo by and courtesy of Shipwrecks Inc.

Published by Narwhal Press, 1629 Meeting Street, Charleston, South Carolina 29405

First Edition
© Copyright 1995, by Edward Lee Spence

The author (to left) with the late Ron Gibbs of the National Park Service, after a dive on a Civil War wreck. Note artifacts on deck. 1967 photo by Pat Gibbs.

Shipwrecks, Pirates & Privateers:

The author holding a rare Civil War cannon ball in front of musket balls, etc., he found while diving in a shallow creek. 1968 photo by Pat Gibbs.

Concretion containing ballast rock, 2 silver wedges, 2 silver balls, and 72 pieces-of-8. Photo by the author.

Sunken Treasures of the Upper SC Coast, 1521-1865

TABLE OF CONTENTS

Divers in South Carolina can expect to find a wide range of rare china while diving the State's many shipwrecks. Photo by the author.

The Research/Salvage vessel 'Fathom II,' at dock in Charleston, South Carolina, was used by the author for his 1972 expedition.
Photo by and courtesy of Jo Pinkard.

This book is dedicated to my friend
"Pirate Jim" Batey
(master diver and fisheries biologist)
with special thanks for his having twice saved my life.

It is also dedicated to my "pirate" ancestors,
Sir Francis Drake and Sir John Hawkins.

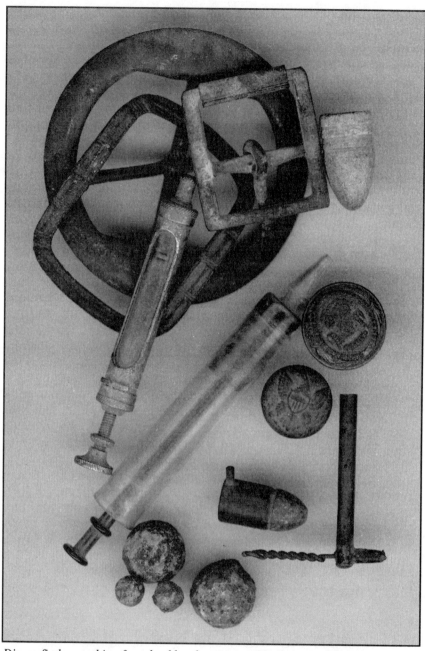

Divers find everything from buckles, buttons, and bullets to syringes while exploring South Carolina's many shipwrecks. The brass tube with the twisted wire is a friction primer and would have been used to ignite the powder in a cannon. Photo by Charles King.

CREDITS & ACKNOWLEDGMENTS

I would like to acknowledge and thank the late Howard I. Chapelle, the late William E. Geoghegan, and Mendel L. Peterson, all formerly of the Smithsonian Institution, for their early encouragement of my research on shipwrecks.

The National Endowment for the Humanities, the South Carolina Committee for the Humanities, the Savannah Ships of the Sea Museum, the College of Charleston, and the Nielsen Electronics Institute, all have my appreciation for their financial support.

Persons at the National Archives who provided invaluable help have included Kenneth R. Hall, Larry MacDonald, Teresa F. Matchette, Mike Meier, Rick Peuser, Constance Potter, Bill Sherman, and John K. VanDereedt.

Edwin Bearss, George Fisher, the late Ron Gibbs, and the late Harold Peterson, all then with the United States National Park Service, also helped spur me onward.

The late Harold Edgerton of M.I.T., and the late Edwin Link of Harbor Branch Foundation, the late George Bond of Sea Lab, each loaned me equipment for my searches, and each offered extensive encouragement and fatherly advice.

Archeologists, George Bass, Robert F. Marx, Duncan Mathewson, Ivor Noel-Hüme, Stan South, the late Peter Throckmorton, and Gordon Watts, all helped in developing my appreciation of shipwrecks as an archeological resource.

Historians/archeologists Elizabeth Andrews, Ed Beacham, the late Elias Bull, Priestly Coker, Mal Collet, the late Tom Dickey, Bob Gibson, Harlan Green, Steve Hoffius, Bob Holcombe, Charles King, Carter Leary, Pat Mellen, Wayne Neighbors, Percy Petit, Paul Reitzer, Wayne Strickland, Jack Thompson, and Mark Wilde-Ramsing each assisted me, and their help continues to be appreciated.

James Dawson and R.C.E. Lander of Lloyd's of London, and D.J. Lyon of the National Maritime Museum in London opened many of their records to me.

Admiral Chris Andreasen, Meg Danley, Chuck Ellis, George Mastrogianis, Mark Friese, Steve Verry, at NOAA, have all aided me in my cartographic searches.

The long roll of divers who have helped me in various ways includes Bill Alge, Jim Batey, John Berg, Frank and Paul Chance, Clifton Doyle, John Coleman, Jerry Crosby, Bob Densler, Ted Dhooge, Mark Dougherty, Erin Efird, Mel Fisher, Ray Forker, Joe Froelich, Mike Freeman, Skipper Keith, Val Gruno, Vic Heyward, Steve Howard, Randy Lathrop, Del Long, Ray Lunsford, Jim

Shipwrecks, Pirates & Privateers:

Maranville, Pat McCarthy, Mick McCoy, Charles Moore, Hugh Myrick, Bill Neville, Charles Peery, E. Phillips, the late Ron Renau, Tom & Sally Robinson, Rick Rogers, Kevin Rooney, Drew Ruddy, Hampton Shuping, Steve Swavely, Dan Thomson, Dave Topper, Gene West, Ralph Wilbanks, "Wet Willie", and Jack Williamson.

Books prepared by Bruce Berman, the late Forrest R. Holdcamper, Dave Horner, and Bob Marx have been of immense use to me in my work, and have been referenced frequently herein.

Special thanks to the Atlantic Marine Insurance Companies of New York who allowed me access to their marine disaster files.

Thanks also go to individuals like Joe Bolchoz, Stan Fulton, the late Beverly Grizzard, Norwood Marlow, the late Hank O'Neal, Bud Parker, Jo Pinkard, Stan Nielsen, Tom O'Rourke, Ned Sloan, Rev. James Storm, Whit Tharin, Buddy Truett, and Roland Young, who have encouraged and/or supported my work in various ways.

I have been helped by numerous commercial fisherman, including Walter O'Neal, Jr. and Sr., the entire Magwood family, Joe Porcelli (who also dives), and Wally Shaffer.

I would like to especially thank the late Fred Hack of Hilton Head Island; the late Mills B. Lane of Savannah; and Robert R. Nielsen Sr. for supporting my research and explorations.

The following corporations have assisted me on my various underwater archeological projects: Allis Chalmers; Barringer Research; Bendix; EG&G; Fisher Research Laboratories; Gulf Oil; Ingersoll Rand; J.W. Fisher; Klein Associates; McKee Craft; Mercury Motors; Orca Industries; Rolex Watch Co.; Seagram's Classic Wines; Seahawk Deep Ocean Technology; Trimble Navigation; White's Electronics; and Zodiac (rubber boats).

Collectively, the help provided by these people, has ranged from moral and financial support to tending my air hoses. Unfortunately, there is no practical way that I can list all of those who deserve recognition and thanks.

Many of the distinguished people listed above have doctorates and other degrees, for simplicity and the fact that I don't know everyone's correct titles, I have not shown degrees. I hope they will understand. For those people who I have inadvertently left out, I still extend my best wishes and thanks.

E. Lee Spence

These artifacts (sword hilt, butt plate, trigger guard, haversack hooks, etc.) were recovered from an unidentified shipwreck off Cherry Grove, South Carolina.. Photo by Charles King.

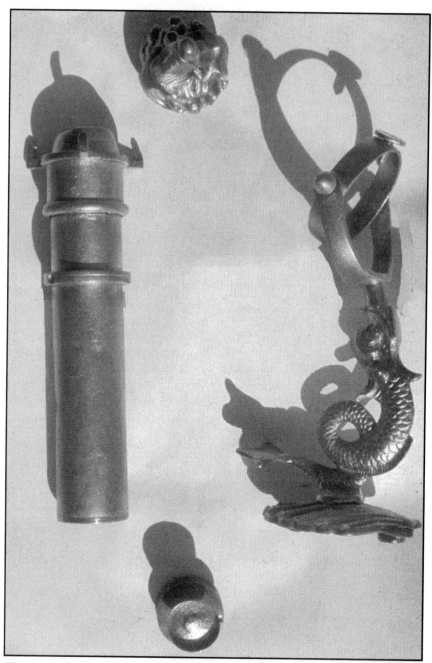

This ornate lamp (shown cleaned and disassembled) was salvaged from a Civil War era wreck. When found, it still contained some of the wax from its candle. Photo by the author.

CHAPTER ONE
Introduction & Overview

The upper coast of South Carolina, which includes much of Long Bay and runs from just below Cape Romain (McClellanville) to Little River (the North Carolina line), does not strike most people as a likely spot to search for shipwrecks and sunken treasure until they realize that it was once part of Colonial Spanish Florida.

Once the Spanish galleons had passed Cape Canaveral, Cape Romain was the most significant hazard on the entire east coast of Colonial Spanish Florida. Despite its relatively small size, Cape Romain was as great a danger as Cape Canaveral. Cape Romain is located on the route that was followed by most of the Spanish fleets returning to Spain with gold and silver mined in the New World. The Spanish fleets actually sailed directly for this point, which is located at latitude 33°, and used it as a check point. Once they had spotted it, they would turn their ships due east and sail along the 33rd parallel heading for the next check point, the Bermuda Islands.

Cape Romain's extremely shallow shoals extend well past the three mile jurisdiction of the South Carolina state government. Cape Romain has always been remote. Until the founding of Charleston in 1670 it was over 100 miles to the nearest European settlement (both the Spanish and French built forts in the vicinity of present day St. Helena, South Carolina). Nearby Georgetown wasn't settled until 1732 (the year both George Washington and the famed Swamp Fox, Francis Marion, were born).

Even today there are no roads, causeways or bridges going to the islands which make up the cape. This means that, if and when there were wrecks, anyone who survived wrecking on the outer shoal of the cape and managed to make it to Cape Island, had little chance of getting to safety without being captured by cannibal Indians who lived between Cape Romain and St. Helena.

Undoubtedly, many of those who did get to shore would have been so afraid of capture that they would have hidden out until they eventually died of thirst, starvation, exposure, or disease. Because of these and other factors, detailed reports of wrecks at this location during the Spanish and French colonial period would have been quite rare. Even when accurately reported in a timely manner, the remoteness would have added to the difficulty of salvage.

Several years ago the Federal Court officially recognized my discoveries and rights on the outer shoal (and thus potentially the most lucrative portion) of Cape Romain and I am once again engaged in salvaging those discoveries. However, my research has led me to realize that some of the vessels that hit on this shoal didn't immediately sink and could have come to rest far past their original striking point at Cape Romain. Such drifting derelicts could have sunk anywhere in the Long Bay formed by the coast between Cape Romain and Cape Fear. Some of the Spanish coins picked up by tourists along DeBordieu Island, Pawley's Island, Huntington Beach and Myrtle Beach undoubtedly came from such wrecks.

Shipwrecks bring thoughts of pirates, sudden death, and instant wealth. But, in a broader sense, shipwrecks have affected, or are capable of affecting, virtually every aspect of life in South Carolina.

Part of South Carolina's resources include the thousands of uncharted virgin wrecks lying in her rivers, bays, and shallow coastal waters. These shipwrecks contain literally hundreds of millions of dollars in treasure, history and artifacts. They can be a boon to school children, fishermen, salvors, historians, archeologists and the tourist industry. They are a resource that could furnish dozens of museums and thousands of classrooms with display and study material.

The artifacts contained in these wrecks are not only treasures in the form of gold, silver and precious jewels. They are also the five and dime variety goods which were brought in from all over the world to be sold in South Carolina's markets. Many of these are items which on land would have been totally destroyed simply through use, lack of proper care and disinterest. Yet, they are of immense interest and value to today's historians, archeologists and collectors.

For over four hundred and fifty years the siren call of South Carolina's beautiful shoreline has repeatedly lured the ships of unlucky mariners to a watery grave. Although most of South Carolina's shipwrecks are concentrated around Charleston, at least a thousand took place in the area covered by this book. These ships carried everything from gold to guano.

This book lists over 300 separate wrecks, relatively few of which have been found, and most of those only in the last few years. Some of the recently discovered wrecks have already yielded cannon, coins, cutlasses and china.

One of North America's first recorded shipwrecks was that of a Spanish vessel belonging to Don Lucas Vasquez de Ayllon. It took place in 1521 on what is now Cape Romain, South Carolina. No lives were lost, but the ship and its cargo were quickly buried in the sand where they could not be salvaged and, undoubtedly, remain to this day.

The author examining the remains of a crate of dinner plates on a shipwreck.
Photo by Ray Lunsford.

These modern looking, bullet shaped objects are actually cannon "balls" from the time of the Civil War. Some cannon balls were solid while others were filled with gun-powder and armed with an explosive fuse.

Shipwrecks, Pirates & Privateers:

Barely five years later the Spanish Don lost another vessel. This one was a caravel of about one hundred tons. She was only fifty to fifty-five feet in length and sixteen to eighteen feet in beam. Many historians believe she was lost at the entrance to Winyah Bay. If they are correct, this wreck is probably fairly intact, as the area is given to rapid sanding and silting. The wreck was not salvaged at the time of its sinking, and the sand, mud and silt have very likely protected the ship and the artifacts on board.

Even a relatively thin layer of sand can protect artifacts from the voracious appetite of teredo navalis, a tiny sea worm that eats all exposed wood, cloth, and paper on a wreck. These worms are capable of reducing an uncovered wreck to a pile of ballast and rubble in a few years. The mud not only prevents the teredo, and other marine borers, from devouring the remains of the wreck, it is also capable of preserving such fragile items as books and delicate wineglasses.

This means that, if de Ayllon's ships are ever found, the public will have a unique historical treasure of immense educational value. These particular wrecks may even have carried large quantities of coins and precious jewels. The Spaniards recognized that a voyage to colonize a new land would mean that they would be gone for years and possibly the rest of their lives. They routinely took their wealth with them. But even the "lesser" items - the plates, cups, bowls, cooking utensils, arms, and ships fittings - tell a story that history books have left unwritten.

Vessels are sometimes reported as expected to be lost or as a "total loss" but are later saved, while others are expected to be saved, yet are lost. This book contains some of both.

Even small vessels such as canoes may have monetary and/or archeological importance.

In 1739, a Spanish canoe with twenty thousand pieces of eight aboard was captured by an American privateer and carried into Providence, Rhode Island. Although that incident did not take place in South Carolina, it does illustrate the fact that vessels should not be discounted as unimportant simply because of their size.

Ships were lost for many reasons. Some were lost as a result of negligence or storms. Others were scuttled to avoid capture, or even sent to the bottom in a blazing cannon duel with pirates.

By far the most unusual cause of a ship's loss had to have been dried peas getting wet, swelling, and bursting the hull of the schooner *Augustus Moore* while it was off Georgetown in 1855.

Fires are a significant cause of sailing vessels being lost. Surprisingly, cargoes of lime (the type used in mortar and plaster) getting wet and thereby generating enough heat to cause a fire, was a frequently cited cause of shipboard fires. A small sloop with a cargo of lime from Boston burned off Georgetown in 1811. In 1841 the schooner *Christopher Columbus*, which had just arrived at Georgetown from New York, took fire from her cargo of lime, and it was necessary to scuttle her.

Lightning frequently hit the tall masts of the sailing vessels and sometimes resulted in death and destruction.

Fires at dock-side were frequently attributed to arson.

Conflagrations aboard steam vessels were common as the burning ash dropped back down on the vessel.

The late summer and early fall of every year seemed to bring hurricanes and autumn storms. Most, if not all, caused at least some destruction among the shipping.

Major hurricanes have struck an average of every twenty to thirty years and have wrought untold wreck and ruin. Over the centuries these hurricanes have sunk thousands of ships in South Carolina's waters.

Vessels on the high seas which were struck by high winds and thrown on their "beam ends", were often reported in the papers. These vessels are not usually mentioned in the accompanying list because of their sheer numbers and the fact that they were frequently righted and saved. Although they may have originally been wrecked off the upper coast of South Carolina such wrecks might drift as derelicts for weeks or even months, carrying the vessel hundreds of miles from where the accident was originally reported.

Many of the ships lost in storms were afterwards described as ashore, or as "high and dry". To the average reader this might seem to mean that the combined force of the storm and the tide threw the vessel entirely clear of the water. Such an interpretation is certainly correct for some vessels, but, it probably more often meant that the vessel had been driven into water too shallow to float her even if she had remained intact.

Vessels which are reported aground are not necessarily up on the beach or even close to shore. A vessel drawing eighteen feet of water could easily "run aground" one, two or even three or more miles from the nearest land.

It may seem like a big ocean out there, but ships frequently run each other down. The steamer *North Carolina* was run afoul of by another steamer "25 to 30 miles Northward by Eastward of Georgetown."

Ships even wrecked on wrecks. In some locations the wreckage of numerous vessels has become mingled, making it virtually impossible to tell where one wreck stops and the next starts.

The fancy spike to the right of the French powder flask looks Prussian, but is actually from a U.S. Army helmet. The brass object at the bottom of the picture is part of a musket and held the ram rod in place. Photo by Charles King.

The very design of the vessel was sometimes cited as the cause for the loss. But, it is sometimes only through trial and error that a working solution to a problem can be achieved. The loss of these and other vessels and the lives of their various crews, over a period of time, slowly helped to improve ship design and construction, and thereby achieve both safety and efficiency.

One of the improvements, which came with great cost of human life and suffering, was the use of steam engines to power vessels. The use of steam meant that vessels were less dependent on the tide and the winds. Schedules could be kept. Trips were quicker. Perishable cargoes were able to reach a larger market, and overall service was improved. But, it was improved at a cost. Early steam engines designed for shipboard use were inadequate. Weight of metal sacrificed for reduced draft and increased speed made the engines more prone to breakdowns than their land based counterparts. The marine air environment attacked, rusted and corroded parts. The early engines were cost effective, but they took a terrible toll.

Boilers frequently burst sinking the ship and scalding to death or drowning many of the crew and passengers.

Another cause of loss of life and property, directly attributable to the use of steam engines, was the setting on fire of the vessel or its cargo by the ash from steamers' smokestacks. The ash was eventually reduced, but not eliminated, as vessels switched from wood burning to coal burning systems.

The early steam engines were so prone to problems that for at least the first fifty years of their existence insurance companies allowed the steamers a better rate if they were also equipped with sails to help them get back if their engines failed.

Although it was years after the period covered by this book, steam engines were eventually replaced with internal combustion engines, usually burning diesel or gasoline. While relatively safer than steam powered engines, internal combustion engines had their own problems. Both diesel and gasoline powered engines have played some role in the loss of vessels in our waters. Fires have occurred on both types, although gasoline is more volatile and therefore inherently more dangerous. A cup of gasoline spilled into the unventilated bilges of a small boat is said to have the explosive power of a stick of dynamite. Gas vapors can be set off by a simple spark from a loose or bare wire.

Diesel engines, especially on old, poorly kept-up fishing trawlers, have been known to have their governors fail, allowing them to turn at excessively high speeds. The engine then sucks up fuel and its own lubrication oil at a terrible rate and becomes virtually impossible to shut down. When this happens the engine is said to have "run away" and it can literally spin the engine through the bottom of a vessel.

Gasoline engines with their electrical ignition systems can be shut down at a moment's notice, but they are highly susceptible to problems caused by moisture, and they always seem to fail at the worst possible moment. Such engine failures have caused vessels to be lost when they otherwise would have been saved.

Ships were sometimes lost through acts of cowardice, ignorance, stupidity, and even foolish acts of bravado.

Sometimes the only way to insure that the people would not be washed off of the wreck they were clinging to for life, was for them to tie themselves to the wreckage.

In 1829, about the latitude of Huntington Beach, the captain of a brig saw a derelict schooner with a dead man lashed to her helm, but was unable to board the vessel which was scudding before the wind, as sort of a "Flying Dutchmen", sailing along with a dead crew.

Shipwrecks could also mean a gruesome death in the mouth of a shark and the old newspapers frequently described the sailors screaming as they were pulled to their deaths.

One authority in the 1700's credited South Carolina's booming rice culture as having been started from a packet of rice seed that washed ashore after a shipwreck.

Monkeys and parrots, which once populated some of the sea islands of South Carolina were said to have been introduced there by shipwrecks.

Our coast has been the scene of shipwrecks loaded with the ransom of nations and kings.

Don Angel Villafañe, a Spanish conquistador, who had been with Cortez in the sack of Mexico City, visited the South Carolina coast in the mid 1500's in search of sunken treasure. An entire Spanish fleet, loaded with tons of stolen gold and silver, had been wrecked in a hurricane. The survivors of the wreck and storm waded ashore only to be met by cannibal Indians. Villafañe returned to Mexico without finding the wrecks.

The fact that the Spanish treasure fleets routinely passed along this coast is not widely known, but in years past it was a common event.

Unlike Florida and other states, where the water is deeper closer to shore and where wrecks frequently took place close enough to shore that coins wash up on the beach during storms, relatively few coins have been found on the beaches of South Carolina. So, the really valuable wrecks have yet to be found. No one has ever located a wreck in Florida or anywhere else with even near the amount of gold that some of these Spanish ships apparently carried.

Spanish gold isn't the only treasure that lies off this coast. By 1704, coinage from Spain, Mexico, Peru, France, Portugal, Holland, and of course England was circulating in the English colonies to such an extent that set rates of exchange were already being published in the local newspapers. Money flowed in and out of the various ports of South Carolina on a regular basis.

In May of 1770, the flow of coinage out of South Carolina had reached such proportions that it was endangering the stability of the province. The outward flow was attributed to "the King's Duties being paid in Silver", "the Trade with the Northern Colonies", and to people leaving South Carolina for pleasure, health or educational purposes and carrying their money with them. Three thousand five hundred Guineas, "chiefly in Half Johannes and Dollars" reportedly was carried out of South Carolina in one month by just three families.

By November, 1770, the situation had reversed. Money was flowing from London to South Carolina in considerable quantities in consequence of a "Resolution of Non-Importation."

In 1866, the Savannah "Daily News and Herald" reported that gold was being shipped out of the United States at the rate of over ten tons per week. Ships of virtually all nations, carrying varying amounts of money, have been reported sunk all up and down the upper coast of South Carolina.

One tip-off, that a ship might have carried treasure, is when the records state that she was lost while traveling "in ballast". To travel "in ballast" means to travel without cargo. An ocean voyage necessitated both expense and risk, so ships seldom sailed without full cargoes, unless they had a definite reason. One reason was the carrying of large quantities of money. To ship money on a vessel loaded down with a heavy cargo made it more vulnerable to pirates or storms. A loaded vessel sat deeper in the water and traveled much slower. A ship traveling "in ballast" also had no cargo to trade for a return cargo, so money had to be carried to purchase cargo for the return voyage.

Money was also carried to pay the crew, purchase supplies, take care of repairs, pilotage, etc. Passengers also carried their own money. In some cases it amounted to their life savings, as some of the passengers were traveling to a new place with no intention of ever returning to their old home.

Although paper money was in existence in the 1700's, it was not widely trusted until this century. It was normally of value only in the city or region in which it was issued. Persons traveling outside of their home area would naturally convert much, if not all, of their paper money to hard cash, so they would not have to sell their paper money at greatly discounted prices when they arrived at their destination.

Shipwrecks with no basis in fact are sometimes reported either as having just taken place, or as having just been discovered. Among researchers these wrecks are known as the "ghost galleons."

Possibly the most famous ghost wrecks of South Carolina are the two wrecks which were reported by a diver in the 1970's as having been found in a river near Georgetown. The diver enticed greedy government officials, a gullible press and an eager public with detailed descriptions of two Spanish galleons loaded with treasure. But the diver, who later sold cars for a living, never produced the gold or the wrecks. Unfortunately, I got to know the man very closely, and there is no doubt whatsoever, the man simply lied. The whole story was pure guano.

Another ghost wreck was the brig *Nancy* reported to have sunk on the Georgetown Bar in 1817 while traveling "in ballast" with specie (coins). The original report which appeared in the "Charleston Courier" was complete with a wealth of details including an account of the heroic efforts of the crew to swim to shore. The story was discounted as an entire fabrication only days later.

All of the coins shipped aboard the brig *Lucinda*, which was lost in 1806 near the Santee River while traveling "in ballast", were saved at the time the wreck, as was the $52,000 in face value in coin shipped aboard the brig *Phoebe* wrecked near Georgetown in 1838.

Most people are aware that the majority of the ships carried merchandise or raw goods, rather than gold or silver. But, they frequently make the mistake of thinking that all vessels carried at least some sort of cargo which would have value commercial value today.

Some vessels carried cargoes consisting entirely of salt. Others, like carried cargoes of ice. It would be impossible to say which would be a bigger waste of time and money for someone just seeking treasure. However, those wrecks, and ones like them, are still of interest and importance to underwater archeologists who see the remains of the ship itself as a treasure.

Fine wines often made up sizable portions of the cargoes of ships sailing out of France, Portugal and Spain. Needless to say, many of these ships were wrecked along the South Carolina coast, and many still contain thousands of intact bottles. Wine connoisseurs are just now beginning to realize the potential that rests in these shipwrecks. The waters have kept the corks moist and allowed the contents to rest under temperatures considered in the ideal range for the aging of wine. Many of these wines are in perfect shape. The wines already recovered from some of these wrecks range from heady ports to fine blends from Madeira. Some have sold for thousands of dollars. The people buying the wine paid the price for the quality, and not just for the romance of its unique history. The man who found that wreck kept its location secret and took that secret with him to his grave.

Famous persons sailing from South Carolina ports never to be seen again included Thomas Lynch and the beautiful Theodosia Burr Alston.

Georgetown resident Thomas Lynch was only thirty-two years old and was traveling to Cuba for his health when his ship was lost. He had been a captain in the Provincial Militia in 1775 and in 1776 had been one of South Carolina's four representatives to Congress. He was a signer of the Declaration of Independence. Lynch's ship may have been sunk by a British privateer, or may have gone down in a storm.

Theodosia Burr Alston was the daughter of Vice President Aaron Burr and the wife of South Carolina Governor Alston. Theodosia sailed from Georgetown, South Carolina, on the schooner *Patriot* in 1812. The *Patriot* disappeared without a trace. Theodosia was said to have been murdered by pirates and the schooner scuttled. (Entry 125 in the shipwreck list deals with this loss.)

The mention of shipwrecks always bring to mind cannon. It is the discovery of these great guns which often pinpoint or date a wreck. Cannon remain long after the more perishable portions of a ship have disintegrated from the action of the sea.

In the early days of our country cannon were carried by merchant ships as well as pirates, privateers and government ships, so their presence doesn't necessarily mean that you are on a Spanish galleon.

Archeologists are able to use the ship's cannon to ease their search as the large amounts of iron in them are easily detected by remote electronics.

Once a wreck has been discovered the number and size of the cannon help the archeologist determine the age, size, and nationality of the vessel.

Cannon are occasionally brought to the surface in shrimp nets by large trawlers. In 1983, a small cannon came up in a net off Cape Romain, South Carolina.

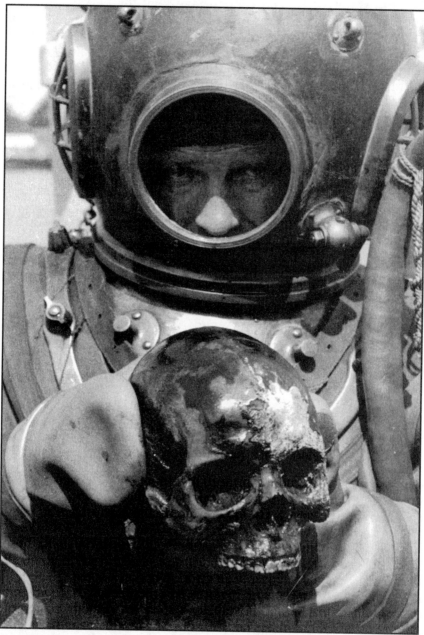

Despite what you might expect, human remains are rarely found on shipwrecks, but when encountered and recovered should always be treated with the utmost respect and properly buried. Some port cities have "stranger's graveyards" set aside solely for the burial of sailors who died at sea.
Photo courtesy of the Warship *Vasa* Museum.

Cannon are normally thought of just as the ship's armament but after they had worn out they were sometimes used as ballast.

Cannon were also an easily salvaged target and are frequently mentioned among the few items which were saved from a wreck.

Heavy guns lying on the sea floor, that are not in association with a shipwreck, frequently are the only evidence left of a ship that got away. They were often jettisoned by vessels attempting to outrun a more heavily armed attacker.

Cannon were sometimes pushed overboard in rough seas in an effort to save a slowly sinking ship, or to lighten a stranded ship enough to float her to safety.

Cannon were also thrown into rivers such as the Pee Dee to prevent the enemy from capturing or using them.

Many of the cannon that were thrown or lost in our waters have undoubtedly been salvaged but hundreds more must remain waiting for discovery. Some of the cannon will hopefully serve as signposts to guide modern salvors to some of the many, yet undiscovered, shipwrecks.

Another "signpost" of a shipwreck is the ballast, which usually remains long after the hull and other perishable portions of a vessel have disappeared.

Ballast was a necessity on wooden sailing vessels. It allowed the ships to be heavily weighted in their bottoms so they would be less likely to blown on their "beam ends" in a heavy wind. The ballast compensated for the weight of the masts and heavy guns which were above the vessel's water line and would otherwise render the vessel top heavy.

For centuries the ballast of choice was round river rock. It came in convenient sizes and could be had simply for the labor of picking it up. The smooth surface of the rocks added to safety of the vessel. When the ballast shifted in a rough sea, it was less likely to injure the cargo or the vessel.

A pile of round river rock sitting on the bottom in the harbors or along the upper coast of South Carolina usually means that a ship was lost at that spot, as those areas are virtually devoid of any natural rock. Please note that this isn't always the case. Vessels frequently off-loaded ballast in an effort to get off a shoal.

Ballast was also dumped when it was necessary to go up an otherwise too shallow creek or when loading a cargo heavier than that carried on the previous voyage.

By 1734 laws were already being passed to prevent such intentional dumping of ballast, so it means that the practice had to have been common enough prior to that time to have posed a threat

Shipwrecks, Pirates & Privateers:

to the other shipping. The law allowed the ballast to be dumped only in the strip between the low and high tide mark.

Brick, flint, slate, basalt, coral rock, scrap iron, obsolete cannon, lead, sand, and even water were among the materials commonly used as ballast. Marketable cargo was sometimes placed in the bottom of the vessel and referred to as ballast. True ballast, although it might be marketable, was meant for repeated use by the same vessel.

As a vessel went from port to port it slowly acquired a wide assortment of ballast. A vessel might pick up flint in England, basalt in Central America, coral rock in the Bahamas, volcanic rock in the Azores and round river rock (granite cobbles) in New England or Spain. The types of stone or other material used as ballast can help the archeologist speculate on the ports at which a vessel may have stopped.

Artificial or worked materials such as brick, or cut or carved stone, may even help the archeologist in the dating of the wreck. Trash was routinely thrown in the vessel's bilges along with the ballast. The surviving glass and ceramic shards found among the ballast on a wreck, may further help to date and identify the nationality of a ship.

Among the vessels most frequently mentioned as lost are the pilot boats. These are the boats that ferried coast and harbor pilots out to the big ships waiting to cross the treacherous bars that blocked the entrances to most harbors. Theoretically, the pilot would board ship and having intimate and specialized knowledge of the waters would take it safely into the harbor. But the waters were treacherous even for the most knowledgeable pilots and they routinely lost their own boats, the ships they were temporarily in command of, and sometimes their own lives.

Harbor pilots were cursed and praised on a routine basis. One day they would be blamed for the loss of a ship and the next they might be thanked for saving the crew of another unfortunate vessel.

Fishing boats traditionally are of shallower draft than large cargo vessels and they are usually manned by persons familiar with local waters. Therefore, they are less likely to be lost through grounding. But fishing vessels are often the victims of rough weather.

Navigational aids to prevent shipwrecks were immediately recognized as needed along the South Carolina coast. Buoys made of large barrels were quickly anchored in strategic places to mark shoals or channels.

These shards of blue and gray, salt glaze, stoneware mugs and chamber pots, dating from the 18th century, were found by the author while diving in South Carolina's rivers. The "GR" stood for George Rex (King George).
Photo courtesy of the South Carolina Institute of Archaeology & Anthropology.

Shipwrecks, Pirates & Privateers:

A "Notice to Mariners" published in 1822, told of the placement of two spar buoys on the bar at Georgetown, South Carolina.

Around the beginning of the nineteenth century an abandoned windmill (which had lost its wind vanes) on Mill Island, South Carolina, was, on several occasions, mistaken for a lighthouse tower by vessels approaching the coast. Ship captains unwisely counted on the tower to guide them to safety. Instead, it led them to destruction on the treacherous shoals of Cape Romain.

In 1817, Captain Andrews of the ship *Telegraph* mistook the armless windmill for the Charleston Light after he saw a light displayed at or near the wind mill, but whether the light was displayed intentionally to decoy his ship to its doom was not known. Captain Andrews did run his ship aground, but was more fortunate than some of the others. He got off safely.

In 1832, the fine large American ship *Pennsylvania* mistook the Cape Romain Light for the Charleston Light and followed it into the shoals and destruction instead of into a channel and safety.

Ships were sometimes intentionally sunk or run aground during wartime to serve a particular purpose. Vessels were also run aground and used as warehouses or for other temporary purposes.

Vessels were frequently described as abandoned and drifting as derelicts off the coast. Most such reports have been left out of this particular book due to insufficient information and the need to save space. But, as many of those vessels must have eventually gone down off of this coast and may one day be found, it might be best for future books to include them.

Wrecks described in early accounts as in the "Gulf" commonly referred to vessels lost in the "Gulf of Florida" or in the "Gulf Stream". "Gulf of Florida" was the old name for the body of water in the "gulf" formed between Cape Fear, North Carolina, and peninsula Florida, as that entire coastline was once part of Spanish Florida. The Gulf Stream is the major current that flows through that area, but which also extends upwards and across the Atlantic Ocean. Such wrecks are routinely included in this book when there is evidence to indicate that they were, or might have been, lost off the South Carolina coast. The crew of one such ship, bound from Jamaica, which foundered in the "gulph of Florida" in 1757, was reported as having gotten safely to South Carolina.

My estimate of at least one thousand vessels wrecked along the upper coast of South Carolina may seem high at first thought. But, one should consider that this is an estimate of all of the wrecks that took place over a period of some four and a half centuries. That would require an average of fewer than three wrecks a year, yet many storms claimed far more than that in a single day.

Although SCUBA type diving gear was only invented in World War II and did not become widely used in South Carolina until the 1970's, salvage has a long history in this area.

By 1684 laws had already been passed requiring all persons that salvaged wrecks or other things to turn over a set share of "plate, silver, gold or treasure" to the king's agent in Carolina.

In 1716, a royal patent was issued to Captain Archer and Captain Cuthbeard for the recovery of treasure or other wreckage that "they might recover with their new diving machine". Shortly thereafter, they were reported as arrived off the South Carolina coast with their salvage vessels,. The nearby inhabitants were being asked for their "utmost assistance."

In 1735, a chest of newly minted silver coins was saved from a vessel when it burned at sea.

In 1741, the crew of a French sloop saved a quantity of money from their sloop just before it sank off the South Carolina coast. The crew, composed of four Frenchmen, four Englishmen and nine Spaniards, soon had to throw the money overboard to lighten their boat. This apparently caused great aggravation to the Spaniards who would have preferred to have thrown the Englishmen overboard.

Most salvage was more mundane. It consisted of the saving (salvaging) of vessels run ashore by accident or storm.

In fact an extremely high percentage of all of the vessels reported as sunk or driven ashore in rivers and harbors were routinely saved. It was the vessels which were run on the shoals outside of harbors which presented the greatest challenge to the salvors. First of all, such vessels were in a more dangerous position, being subjected to the continual pounding of the surf.

Pounding surf could reduce a ship to pieces in just three or four hours.

Ships not gotten off a shoal in exposed waters in the first few hours, or at least by the next day, were normally lost, whereas a ship stranded within a harbor could be salvaged at leisure.

Time was a critical factor in the outcome of a salvage effort.

Unfortunately, in offshore salvage, such as on Cape Romain, the vessel was frequently destroyed before potential salvors even knew that the wreck existed. Once they did learn of a wreck, distance and bad weather could delay them.

When salvors did manage to get to a stranded ship before it broke up, they grabbed what they could. Normally this was limited to the ship's spars, sails and rigging, which stuck out of the water, and any cargo which may have floated free.

Salvage attempted on a wreck in exposed waters was also far more dangerous than that in a protected harbor.

Wrecks normally occurred in the worst of possible places, i.e. - on the windward side of a shoal and well up in the breakers. That meant that to just get close to the wreck was a risk to your own vessel.

Even if you used a much smaller vessel and managed to get along side of the wreck without going aground yourself, it meant that your boat would be an unstable work platform. You could easily be crushed going back and forth between the two vessels.

In some cases, it was so dangerous that the salvors couldn't even go out to the wreck in an effort to save the people and had to just sit and watch the ship break up.

Once the salvors were on a wreck they faced the chance of the vessel disintegrating beneath them, and throwing them into the sea.

Efforts to salvage a valuable cargo were usually prompted by the promise of a high salvage award. Financial rewards often induced the salvors to take risks to both their lives and their property. The temptation was to keep salvaging a wreck until the last possible minute no matter how bad the weather turned.

The steamer *Planter*, of Civil War fame, was wrecked on Cape Romain in 1876 while attempting save the schooner *Carrie Melvin*.

High on the list of items to be salvaged were cannon and coins, but possibly the first thing to be saved was any liquor that might be aboard the wreck.

The Yankees attempted to salvage the liquor aboard wreck of the blockade running steamer *Dare* at North Inlet on the south end of DeBordieu Island. Their efforts failed when they all got drunk and were captured by local Confederate forces. Naturally the Confederates resumed the salvage. (For more about the *Dare*, please see entry 304 in this book.)

In olden times, brick were apparently not sufficiently valuable to warrant the coast of salvage. Numerous boats with cargoes of brick have been found in South Carolina's rivers. In the 1970's, one such cargo of brick was raised, along with the wrecked vessel, from its resting place in the Black River at Brown's Ferry, near Georgetown. It was estimated to have sunk in the 1740's.

Today, South Carolina has a law claiming ownership of all submerged antiquities which have lain unclaimed on the ocean floor for more than fifty years. The law was passed, at my instigation, shortly after my discovery of five Civil War blockade runners. The law was meant to protect both the rights of the salvor and the state. My company was awarded the first license issued under that law.

Unfortunately, under the law the present licensing authority for the State has "powers of discretion". It can issue or deny salvage licenses to anyone it chooses. A person who happened accidentally or intentionally to find a Spanish galleon or other valuable wreck might be refused a license to salvage. Although not intended by the act, the law gives the licensing authority almost unlimited power. The potential for abuse definitely exists. Licenses could easily be given to those who were friendly with the state licensing people and denied to those who were not. Some salvors feel such abuse has already taken place.

Salvors who are afraid of being cheated of their discoveries, which are often made at great expense and risk, are therefore put in a position of having to keep their discoveries secret to prevent the State from jumping on the band wagon and grabbing their wreck. This is a shame, as many of the wrecks have immense archeological and historical value as well as intrinsic value.

When wrecks are kept secret everyone suffers.

Fortunately, salvors are beginning to fight for their rights in the Federal courts. Although Federal and state statutes currently place jurisdiction over salvage in the hands of the states, the Federal courts have consistently ruled against the states and in favor of the salvors, as the United States Constitution clearly places admiralty matters such as salvage in the exclusive jurisdiction of those Federal courts. The people are protected as the courts have also ruled that the protection of the historical and archeological aspects of ancient wrecks are also a valid consideration in determining custody and salvage awards on a wreck. The court, if it is shown by the State or other interested parties that the wreck is archeologically or historically important, may require that the wreck be worked by people who are qualified under guidelines that the judge sets down.

It is hoped that discoverers will publicize finds and fight for their rights, rather than keep their discoveries secret.

As was said at the beginning of this book, shipwrecks have affected, or are capable of affecting, virtually every aspect of life in South Carolina. This underwater archeologist hopes the reader can now understand why the statement was made.

Shipwrecks are not only interesting, they are an extremely important part of our heritage. They must be protected. But the first step in protecting them is to educate the public as to their archeological, historical and monetary value. Passing restrictive laws, and limiting access to shipwrecks to just state officials is not a realistic way to protect them. Such laws and regulations actually encourage looting.

The public (meaning individuals and private enterprise) needs to educate themselves about all shipwrecks and become actively involved in their discovery, salvage and preservation. And, that is exactly why this book was written.

These crudely cut pieces of silver are actually Spanish pieces-of-eight. Coins like these were used in South Carolina through most of the time period covered in this book. Photo by the author of coins in his private collection.

CHAPTER TWO
Pirates and Privateers

(Part of South Carolina's maritime history includes the stories of the many pirates who called her waters home. Among those were the notorious Edward Low; Edward Teach ("Blackbeard"); Stede Bonnett (the "Gentleman Pirate"); John Rackham ("Calico Jack"); Mary Reade; and Anne Bonney who cursed her husband when he was executed, saying "had he fought like a man, he wouldn't have had to die like a dog." Like Mary Reade, Anne Bonney escaped hanging only by pleading for the life of her unborn child. This chapter tries to dispell the romance surrounding the "Pirate Brotherhood.")

TREASURE
Exciting, but Deadly

Nothing excites the mind like stories of pirate treasure. Accounts of wrecked pirate vessels loaded with pieces of eight and Spanish doubloons have captured people's imaginations for centuries, but few people realize that piracy, once big business, still takes place today. Like in the past, piracy frequently means murder and mayhem.

Outlaws

Pirates are the outlaws of the seas. They are of all races and nationalities.

THROUGH THE CENTURIES
Butchers of the Sea

During the 17th and 18th centuries, the entire American coastline was almost overrun by "blood thirsty" pirates and their almost indistinguishable brothers, the privateers of various countries and their colonies, and the infamous "Guardacosta" (coast guard) of Spain.

In the beginning of the 19th century America fought the Barbary pirates off the coast of Africa. The pirates sponsored by Moslem potentates in Algiers and other coastal countries felt that any Infidels who ventured into their waters were fair game. America, already competing with Great Britain for supremacy in World trade, fought for freedom of the seas as a matter of economic necessity.

19th century, revolutions, sweeping the Caribbean, Central and South America, drove thousands of persons from their homes. After every new revolution, seamen finding themselves without a country turned to piracy. Angered, by the loss of property, friends and family, they robbed and killed not only for survival, but out of revenge for injustices that cut to their souls.

This bare breasted beauty is the notorious female pirate Anne Bonney. She was said to have been from a good South Carolina family, but she had no sympathy for her pirate husband when he was hung, saying "had he fought like a man, he wouldn't have had to die like a dog." 18th century woodcut.

Twentieth century pirates, armed with automatic M-16 assault rifles have high jacked freighters and killed those who resisted.

16TH, 17TH & 18TH CENTURY PIRATES

At one point the pirates grew so numerous that they organized themselves into cooperative ventures, putting forth entire fleets of heavily armed vessels.

Democratic Anarchy

The pirates ruled themselves as a loose democracy. By 1723 they had even codified laws that provided for punishment of their own members who committed certain crimes against the "brotherhood of pirates". A pirate who lost an eye or a limb received a preset amount of money, in sort of an early form of "workmen's compensation". But, their work was theft, murder and mayhem on the high seas.

Pirate Vessels

Pirate vessels ranged in size from small open rowing boats, armed with swivel guns, to three masted, triple decked ships, armed with rows of heavy cannons. Pirate vessels were usually poorly maintained and carried extremely large crews for their size. The pirates were poorly disciplined and their officers, who were often elected for their popularity and not necessarily for their ability, were commonly ill-equipped to command a ship.

Judicious Resistance

Pirates frequently could be driven off by a show of determined armed resistance. During the heyday of piracy virtually all ships were armed and were therefore capable of putting up some resistance. Some merchant vessels carried as many as a dozen cannons. But, if the resistance failed, it often meant death to those who had the "audacity" to put up a defense.

The pirates were mercurial in their attitudes. One day they might look at resistance as an act of bravery. The next they might take resistance as an insult to their authority.

The pirates might hang the captain of a merchant vessel as a coward, if he surrendered without a fight. But, they might just as easily kill him, and everyone else aboard, for fighting back and wounding or killing one of their fellowship.

The wise captain, unless he was sure he could escape or make a successful defense, fired a few token shots and quickly surrendered. The pirates would then board the ship and take whatever appealed to them.

Atrocities

In 1723 the pirate Edward Low slashed and mauled the captain of a vessel. After cutting the unfortunate man's ears off and roasting them, Low forced him to eat them. Other pirates committed far worse atrocities to both men and women.

Females prisoners were frequently raped by the entire crew and then "allowed" to commit suicide. Men were often tortured and castrated.

To elicit secrets, the pirates treated their captives to the "usual compliments" of placing burning "slow matches" (fuses) between their fingers."

Sometimes, pirates would just take a barrel of flour and some wine. But, other times they would take entire cargoes or even the captured vessels themselves.

The pirates did not relish making themselves too unpopular. They knew, that if their crimes were too great, the public would go to the expense of sending out large armed vessels to hunt them down.

Ransom

Not infrequently, the pirates would ransom the vessel (and passengers) back to the captain, or would trade vessels with him.

Pirates routinely stopped and boarded vessels of all nations. They sometimes claimed that they were without adequate provisions to make a safe port and demanded supplies to be turned over to them under the law of the seas that requires all ships to aid others in distress. When they did, the pirates frequently gave receipts, which the ship's owners could supposedly present at a later date for compensation. Such receipts were, in reality, just a ruse to circumvent a provable charge of piracy.

Keeping Secrets

In 1772 the captain of a ship reported seeing several soldiers coats floating in the water off South Carolina. Some of the people on board the ship thought they saw some dead bodies, but whether it was the work of pirates or the result of a storm or accident, their was no way of knowing. The pirates knew that "dead men tell no tales."

PRIVATEERS
Color of Authority

Pirate ships frequently posed as privateers.

Privateers were privately owned vessels which were licensed by a government to commit acts of warfare on enemy vessels, and to seize any vessels which were smuggling or trading with the enemy.

The lure of adventure and good pay led many a young man to risk his life as a privateersman.

In November of 1744, the "South Carolina Gazette" estimated that there would soon be over 113 privateers operating out of the English colonies.

Major Stede Bonnet, a "Gentleman", who had simply tired of a hum drum life that included marriage to a nagging wife, had taken to piracy as a way to spice up his life. Bonnet's short career took him up and down the Carolina coast. Swinging on a gallows was certainly more excitement than he wanted.

Chapter Two: Pirates & Privateers

A privateer's license was officially known as a "Letter of Marque and Reprisal". In practice they were little more than a license to steal.

When the Spanish garrison at St. Augustine, Florida, found its source of supplies greatly curtailed during the "War of Jenkin's Ear" and were on the verge of starving, the Spanish governor sent out privateers for the primary purpose of securing provisions. The Spanish privateers sailed boldly into English waters in search of booty, or more precisely food.

The South Carolina Gazette of December 11, 1762, reported on the exploits of a Spanish privateer that had "the hardiness to infest our coast, even while two of his majesty's ships are out upon a cruize in quest of her." Barely a year later, Don Martín d'Hamassa commanding a poorly armed Spanish privateer brazenly captured and/or burned several ships along the South Carolina coast and even landed and looted some of the coastal plantations.

Prizes & Prize Courts

Privateers operated under more or less a bounty system.

Seized vessels were referred to as "prizes" and were sent into a friendly port to be tried before a government sanctioned "Prize Court."

If the court found in favor of the privateer, the prize would be condemned and sold. The entire crew of the privateer would share in the proceeds resulting from the sale of a condemned prize. The prize court also had the authority to award damages to the owners of the prize if it was found innocent of the charges brought by the privateer.

The English, French and Spanish all had great success with their privateers, and many vessels were captured two or three times.

In 1742, an American privateer captured and carried into Frederica, Georgia, a Spanish sloop with pieces-of-eight and other cargo valued at thirty thousand pounds sterling.

Spanish privateers even took vessels within sight of the Charleston Bar.

The Charleston privateer *Isabella* took a considerable sum of silver from a Spanish flag of truce vessel in 1747. The following year, the Charleston privateer *Cartwright* captured a brigantine with brandy, wine, and bale goods, bound for St. Augustine.

Although privateering was highly profitable to some of the owners and crews of privateers, it discouraged regular trade and ultimately hurt both sides.

The depredations caused by the privateers forced both the English and the Spanish to organize fleets of ships to be convoyed by heavily armed government vessels. Such practice exposed increasingly larger numbers of vessels to loss when storms hit. Fleets in excess of one hundred vessels were not unusual.

Trumped-up Charges

The seizure of vessels was often done on the flimsiest of evidence or reasons. Seizure frequently amounted to little more than legalized piracy.

In 1731 the British Parliament met in a special session to hear the complaints of British sea captains and merchants who had had their ships and cargoes seized by Spanish privateers and "piratical" Spanish "guardacostas." They testified to over a thousand vessels being illegally captured or plundered without "any just Pretense of their having been carrying on a contraband Trade with any of the Spanish Dominions." Despite official complaints on behalf of the English King, Spain still claimed that English ships caught in illicit commerce were lawful prizes. English merchants claimed that Spanish vessels were routinely fitted out to cruise on the "plausible Pretense" of guarding the Spanish dominions frequently "forcibly and arbitrarily" seized English ships. Things had not improved by 1738 when Parliament again met to hear complaints of "unheard of Cruelty and Barbarity" on the part of the Spanish privateers and "guardacostas."

Like the stereotype small town Southern cop (arresting the "Yankee" tourist on a trumped up charge, knowing he will pay a cash "fine" rather than spend the weekend in jail), privateers often stopped innocent merchant vessels. The privateer captain would then claim that the vessel was in violation of some law. He would then tell the merchant captain that he would let him off with a fine. All the merchant captain had to do was sign a statement acknowledging his guilt.

If the merchant captain balked and said that he would rather fight it in court, the privateer captain would simply change tactics. The privateersman would then claim that the prize was unseaworthy or that he couldn't spare the men to send her into port. He would then threaten to sink the prize on the spot. Normally, such a threat was sufficient to coerce the merchant captain into acknowledging his "guilt" and paying the exorbitant fine. He knew it would be awfully hard to prove his innocence with his ship sitting on the bottom.

In many cases English ships and cargoes were carried into Spanish ports and condemned in violation of standing treaties between Spain and England.

By any other Name

Privateers of one country were commonly thought of as pirates by the next country. In 1757, the British government condemned the "Pyratical Behaviour" of some of the privateers sailing out of the British colonies against the Spanish in the West Indies.

In 1757, the governor of Cuba sent out three vessels to search for some English privateers which had committed "outrages" on some Spanish ships.

Possibly worse than either the pirates or the privateers were the "guardacosta" which operated out of Spanish Florida. Much like the United States Coast Guard of today, Spain's "guardacosta" patrolled far and wide in quest of smugglers. Unfortunately, the Spanish "guardacostas" (not unlike many English privateers) didn't play entirely fair.

Guaranteed Guilty

In 1726 the Spanish government took the position that there was no legal way for foreign nationals to get Spanish coinage. Even one "piece-of-eight" (Spanish dollar) aboard a non-Spanish vessel technically meant that the vessel had been engaged in an illegal activity and was subject to seizure. Since Spanish dollars made up a very large portion of the coinage in circulation in British Colonial America, it meant that virtually any vessel was at risk.

The Spanish captains could, in effect, wage an unofficial war, and could be fully as bloodthirsty as the most ruthless of pirates.

When His Majesty's sloop *Spence* captured a Spanish "guardacosta" in 1731 they found the body of a recently murdered Englishman.

Run from the Law

The American colonists naturally viewed both the privateers and the Spanish "guardacosta" as pirates despite the technical differences. As a result, whenever any of these ships (whether pirate, privateer, or "guardacosta") tried to force a merchant ship to stop for inspection, the urge was to resist.

The captain of a well armed merchant ship would often try to put up a fight or make a run for it. Resistance was frequently successful, but other times there was no escape. At those times, the captain, in an effort to save himself and his men from possible torture and/or a long stint rotting in jail, would intentionally run his ship towards the nearest shore. If a captain was lucky he could beach his vessel and escape over the side to land.

When there was time, the captain might order the scuttling and burning of his own ship to deny the attackers a valuable prize. If the vessel wasn't destroyed before they got to it, the attackers would attempt to haul her off. If that failed, the boarding party would try to strip her of any easily portable treasures, food or merchandise.

Hidden Treasures

The stripping of a ship was always done in a hurry, as a beached ship can disintegrate almost instantaneously in a pounding surf. Furthermore, the attackers themselves were vulnerable to attack by larger vessels, which might have heard the earlier cannon fire. The crew of the capturing vessel would try to get the looting over with and clear out. Sometimes the only items saved were the sails and rigging.

The raiders took what easily portable valuables they could find. But frequently the most valuable items were well concealed behind false panels or beneath tons of bulk cargo or ballast and were lost with the ship.

Even when treasure was found on a captured vessel it didn't mean that the pirates took it all. It isn't unusual to find reports of heavy crates of silver and gold being dropped overboard as the pirates tried to pass them from one vessel to another in rough seas. At other times, crates were broken open by pirates who stuffed their clothes with treasure and left the rest.

Today's Treasures

Many interesting, though then inexpensive, items would also be left behind on the wreck. This was true even on vessels which were salvaged at leisure by legitimate salvors.

The captured vessel was then abandoned, scuttled and/or burnt. But, no matter what was done, the remaining artifacts on each wrecked vessel would become an uncataloged collection that would remain on the ocean floor as individual time capsules, each representing a particular period or phase of history.

FATE OF PIRATES

1690's Blind Justice

One piratical vessel in the 1690's was bold enough to anchor off Charleston, South Carolina. Almost within view of the city, it proceeded to capture and rob ships attempting to enter the safety of the harbor. After a few weeks of unchallenged plundering, the freebooters sailed north to Bull's Bay where the ship, loaded to the gunwales with booty, suddenly ended its days of marauding by ingloriously "starting a butt" (bursting a seam), and foundering on the sandy bottom.

The pirates were captured when they sought refuge from the Indians by pretending to be honest shipwrecked sailors.

The local politicians evidently were paid enough to convince themselves that the pirates were really good people at heart, because they merely fined them what were enormous sums of money for the time, and forbade them to leave the city for a period of one year.

1810 Escape

In 1810 a small boat loaded with men tried to secure a pilot to enter the Savannah River. The pilot, seeing their weapons and a large chest in the floor of the open boat, immediately realized that they were pirates and quickly sailed out of their range.

The pirates then rowed on to South Carolina where they scuttled their boat. When it was found, there were cutlasses and coins laying loose in its bottom, but the chest was gone. The pirates had escaped.

1718 Nagged to Death

Piracy did not always go unpunished. In 1718 the famous "Gentleman Pirate", Major Stede Bonnet, was captured with his men and carried to Charleston.

Bonnet and his men were quickly tried and convicted. All but one of them were hung for their crimes.

Bonnet, a "Gentleman", who had simply tired of a hum drum life that included marriage to a nagging wife, had taken to piracy as a way to spice up his life. Obviously, Bonnet got more excitement than he had bargained for and might have been pardoned, except for a series of tactical errors.

Bonnet escaped from Charleston only to be recaptured while dressed as a woman. The brave front he had previously shown, and which had been much admired, quickly crumbled. Bonnet wrote a heart rending plea for mercy crying that if they only cut his arms and legs off that he would spend the remainder of his days in sack cloth and ashes praising the Lord.

Bonnet's ill fated escape and desperately worded plea seemed those of a coward. Bonnet lost the supporters he had, and was hung like the rest of his men.

1726 Hanging the Flag

In 1726 a pirate flag was hoisted up the gallows at Newport, Rhode Island, upon the public hanging of 26 pirates who had previously raided the South Carolina coast. The pirates called their flag "Old Roger" and it was described as a "deep Blew Flagg" and "had pourtraid on the middle of it, an Anatomy (skeleton) with an Hour-glass in one hand and a dart in the Heart with three drops of Blood preceding from it, in the other." "Old Roger" was simply a variation of "Jolly Roger," which is the traditional name given to the better known pirate's flag showing a white skull and cross-bones on a black background. The original "Jolly Roger" had a red background and its name was actually a corruption of the French words "Joli Rouge" or "pretty red."

1788 Execution

Six men convicted of murder and piracy on the high seas were executed opposite Charleston in 1788, and the bodies of two of them were cut down and carried to Morris Island to hang in chains as a warning to all entering the harbor.

1819 Equal Opportunity

In 1819, at least six of the crew of the pirate ship *Louisa* were captured after they scuttled and burned their own ship off South Carolina. The captured men tried to pretend they were from a merchant ship which had supposedly foundered.

Another twenty-four men (including both whites and blacks) were reported at large, but some of them were probably captured as well. The *Louisa*, armed with sixteen guns, had captured a Spanish brig with money and a number of other valuable prizes.

Contemporary accounts are not clear as to just what the crew of the *Louisa's* particular punishment was. But, there is no doubt that justice was both swift and harsh, as, at that date, piracy lacked the aura of romance it enjoys today. Furthermore, the tacit approval by the common man that piracy and smuggling had in the early days, when pirates and smugglers were the only source of many vitally needed goods, was long gone.

RARE BUT DESERVED FINDS

Despite the fact that hundreds of privateers and pirate vessels were lost over the years, relatively few have ever been found.

In virtually all cases, the discoveries that have been made were the result of hard work and quality research.

If you are thinking of going after one, I wish you well. Just remember, do your own research, and until you are finished with your work, keep your theories and discoveries secret unless earlier disclosure is absolutely required by law.

This brass tap (faucet) was designed to be hammered into a keg. The handle is missing. Perhaps the men that consumed the keg's contents had too much to drink and it caused the loss of their vessel. Photo by Charles King.

Pirate Code of Conduct

{Note: The *Boston News-Letter* of August 8, 1723, carried the following list of articles (agreement signed between a captain and his crew) used by the pirate captain, Edward Low, who was one of the pirates that frequented the South Carolina coast.}

"1. The Captain is to have two full Shares; the Master is to have one Share and one Half; the Doctor, Mate, Gunner and Boatswain, one Share and one Quarter."

"2. He that shall be found guilty of taking up any Unlawful Weapon on Board the Privateer or any other prize by us taken, so as to Strike or Abuse one another in any regard, shall suffer what Punishment the Captain and Majority of the Company shall think fit."

"3. He that be found Guilty of Cowardice in the time of Engagement, shall suffer what Punishment the Captain and Majority of the Company shall think fit."

"4. If any Gold, Jewels, Silver, etc. be found on Board of any Prize or Prizes to the value of a Piece of Eight, & the finder do not deliver it to the Quarter Master in the space of 24 hours, shall suffer what Punishment the Captain and Majority of the Company shall think fit."

"5. He that is found guilty of Gaming, or Defrauding one another to the value of a Ryal of Plate (12.5 cents), shall suffer what Punishment the Captain and Majority of the Company shall think fit."

"6. He that shall have the Misfortune to lose a Limb in time of Engagement, shall have the Sum of Six hundred pieces of Eight; and remain aboard as long as he shall think fit."

"7 Good Quarters to be given when Craved."

"8. He that sees a sail first, shall have the best Pistol or Small Arm aboard of her."

"9. He that shall be guilty of Drunkenness in time of Engagement shall suffer what Punishment the Captain and Majority of the Company shall think fit."

"10. No Snapping of Arms in the Hold."

Bronze cannon on an 18th century shipwreck salvaged by the author.

Rare dueling pistol (1842) and map (1855) from the author's private collection.
Photo by Charles King.

These heavily encrusted artifacts (matchlock musket at center, crossbow on right) were recovered from a 17th century pirate wreck discovered by the author. Photo by Darryl Pinck, courtesy of CRIL.

CHAPTER THREE
Pirate Wreck at Cape Romain

(Note: In the late 1970's, I began actively exploring the shallow waters of Cape Romain, South Carolina, in an effort to locate various wrecks I had been researching. The following was originally published in *ShipWrecks™* magazine and deals with one of the more interesting sites that I located. Although I have tentatively identified this ballast pile as the Spanish schooner *Diamante* the overall site is more likely the co-mingled remains of a number of vessels. The article starts off with a letter which I sent to one of my associates. The letter and other data should give you some idea of the problems involved in making a positive identification of a wreck. The designation "Pirate Wreck" is a "code name" I gave to the site for security purposes, and was picked because the *Diamond* appears to have been a pirate vessel. The ballast pile is situated just over three nautical miles off Cape Island at Cape Romain. At the time of this publication I am once again working some of the wrecks I found on the Cape's outer shoal. I am working them under rights recognized in a ruling by the United States District Court.)

BALLAST PILE AT CAPE ROMAIN

Dear Bill:

Please send a copy of this letter to all of the company's crew, shareholders, etc.

Last month, the crew went to a wreck north of Charleston, South Carolina, to check it out. The wreck was the one referred to in the original company prospectus as the "Champagne Wreck". It was called the "Champagne Wreck" in the prospectus because, when I originally found the wreck some years ago, I saw an intact Champagne bottle which was encrusted to the wreck.

I had actually been looking for the Spanish ship "Diamond" when I found the "Champagne Wreck". The "Diamond" was an armed ship lost in 1816. The "Diamond" was definitely carrying some treasure. Contemporary newspaper accounts indicate that the ship may have actually been a pirate vessel.

The artifacts I originally observed on the wreck (the intact Champagne bottle, broken porcelain, etc.), as well as the size and construction of the wrecked vessel, led me to believe that the wreck might have been the ship "America". The "America" was lost in 1788 at approximately the same location as the later wreck of the "Diamond". The "America" was lost while on a voyage from Port L'Orient, France, to Charleston. The

Shipwrecks, Pirates & Privateers:

"America's" cargo would certainly have been valuable and would probably have included such items as porcelain and Champagne. But, our recent investigation proved that the wreck was not the *"America"*. There is no record of the *"America"* having been armed, yet we found a cannon buried in the sand near the wreck site. Furthermore, the cannon is dated 1798, which is a full ten years after the *"America"* was lost.

The artifacts that we have recovered from the wreck include fragments of French Champagne bottles (of a type that could date from as early as 1780 to as late as 1820); fragments of plain white porcelain (which are so heavy that they have almost a military appearance to them); several intact crystal or cut glass decanter tops; two brass syringes; a fancy candle holder which was once silver plated; part of a fancy solid silver serving bowl (broken and sulfided beyond restoration); an intact flintlock pistol (similar to those produced by Simeon North Arms Company under United States government military contracts circa 1783-1823); an intact 4-pounder cannon (weighing 966 pounds, dated 1798, and made on the Clyde River in Scotland); fragments of broken earthenware; part of a sextant; a number of pewter spoons; eight two-part molds (which may have been meant for casting toys or candies); a large brass or bronze hasp (it brings visions of a treasure chest, but was more likely used to lock the ship's gunpowder room); part of a pair of navigational dividers; assorted ship's fittings; etc. The recovered artifacts certainly seem to indicate a very valuable wreck.

Even though we have ruled out the possibility of the wreck being that of the *"America"*, we have been unable to say for sure whether or not it is the wreck of the *"Diamond"*. Research shows that at least one other vessel was lost in the same general area during the approximate era of the wreck. That was the merchant brig *"Consolation"* which was lost in 1804 while traveling from New York to Charleston. It has not yet been determined whether or not the *"Consolation"* was armed. Most ships traveling from New York to Charleston at that time would have carried valuable cargoes of assorted merchandise. There may well have been other vessels lost in this same area during the same general time period.

It should also be remembered that the area in which all three of these wrecks took place is actually quite small. Even if the wreck we have located does not turn out to be the *"Diamond"*, we know that the *"Diamond"* can't be far away. In fact, several years ago, while doing a magnetometer search of an area just a few hundred yards seaward from the *"Pirate Wreck"*, I got readings indicating iron objects buried in the sand. At the time I didn't have the equipment necessary to excavate the site and check out the readings. So, I never learned whether the readings were from cannon or anchors heaved overboard from the "Pirate Wreck" as she was lost, or whether the readings were from an entirely different wreck.

Based on the artifacts seen and recovered to date, I am personally convinced that the ship (regardless of its actual identity) carried an extremely valuable cargo. I definitely feel that we should get back to the wreck as quickly as possible, and that we should make a major salvage effort on the site.

The crew, of course, is hoping that the wreck is that of the "Diamond", and, until we prove otherwise, for good luck, we are calling it the "Pirate Wreck". So remember, the "Pirate Wreck" and the "Champagne Wreck" are simply two different code-names that we are using to refer to the same unidentified wreck.

The vessel names and dates mentioned in this letter should remain confidential.

Sincerely,

E. Lee Spence

WRECK OF THE *DIAMOND*
THE *DIAMOND*, SPANISH SLAVER

The Spanish schooner *Diamante* (or *Diamond*), Captain Christoval Soler, was wrecked near Cape Romain, South Carolina, on August 29, 1816.

She reported herself as bound from Havana, Cuba, to the coast of Africa. The primary purpose for a voyage to Africa at that time would have been to engage in the slave trade. Although the ownership of slaves was still legal in the United States, the importation of new slaves was illegal. Great Britain actually maintained armed cruisers off the coast of Africa in an attempt to stop and capture slavers, who were considered smugglers under British law. By most standards, slavers were the lowest of the smugglers, but were tolerated by Southerners who saw them as a necessary evil. Black men, women and children would have been purchased from slave merchants in Africa and carried to the West Indies to be sold. A large percentage of these blacks would then be illegally transported to the southern United States to be resold.

THE *DIAMOND'S* ARMAMENT

The armament and the large number of men and officers (fifty-one total), reported aboard the *Diamond*, immediately suggests her belligerent and probably illegal character. If she had been an honest merchant ship, it is extremely doubtful that her crew would have exceeded much more than a dozen men. Large numbers of men were only needed on vessels expecting to fight.

A DEMAND FOR HELP

The *Diamond* apparently was truly in distress and could legitimately demand help, but the people from whom she was demanding it weren't qualified to help, and said so. They apparently were not believed, and according to them, were forced to help against their will. Unfortunately for the *Diamond*, the man they pressed into service as a coast pilot couldn't help them. He wasn't a pilot and he mistook the tower of the Cape Romain windmill (which had previously had it's arms blown off in a storm) for the tower of the Charleston light. By the time the mistake was realized, it was too late. The "pilot" ran the schooner aground on the outer shoal of the Cape. Once it became obvious that the *Diamond* would be lost, her crew made plans to board the *Hornet*, with the expressed purpose of dumping overboard the *Hornet's* cargo to make room for the *Diamond's* "valuable" cargo. Such plans may have been made with the consent of the *Hornet's* captain, but such consent was very likely obtained under duress. There was probably a promise that the *Hornet's* captain and owner's would be fairly compensated, but the *Hornet's* captain would have been taking a big risk no matter how legitimate the *Diamond* appeared to be. Either way, the plans were made too late and schooner sank before her cargo could be transferred to the smaller boat. As many as thirty men were drowned or eaten by sharks.

PIRATE OR SLAVER?

The insistence by the heavily manned, armed schooner *Diamond* that the *Hornet* provide the *Diamond* with a pilot was a questionable act to say the least. So the natural question arises as to whether or not the *Diamond* was a pirate, a slaver, or both. Most acts of piracy were, of necessity, subtle, until it became clear to the pirate that he was going to succeed, and that he was going to be able to make a safe escape. Until the successful outcome was clear, most pirates would use a ruse to cover their real intentions. A pirate might use the cover of being a legitimate privateer (in effect a government licensed bounty hunter) or the cover of being a merchant vessel "in distress" to stop and board passing vessels, and/or to seize "needed" foodstuffs and crew. The *Diamond* could have been an outright pirate and may have used the claim of being a slaver simply to win sympathy while operating off South Carolina. When one stops to question why the *Diamond* was in South Carolina waters at all, when she was supposedly bound from Cuba to Africa, it further puts her claim of being a slaver into question.

GUNS AND TREASURE

At least some of the *Diamond's* guns were thrown overboard when she first struck the outer shoal of Cape Romain. The schooner then "drifted in somewhat nearer to the land" where she sank in three fathoms (eighteen feet) of water. It was thought that she lay "some five miles distant" from shore. The *Diamond's* captain attempted to save a "considerable sum of money" from the wreck (but it was later lost an unspecified distance from the wreck). It isn't known if there was additional money left aboard the wreck. But, the original reports make it sound like before abandoning ship the captain had simply taken a pair of pants, tied the legs to make a bag and filled the pants with as many coins as they would hold. It is likely that the captain had only taken part of the money that he had on board. If it had been the entire amount, Captain Soler would have known the exact amount and would have probably mentioned the figure. But, his failure to mention any money left on the wreck itself means nothing, as he could have wanted to keep it quiet, especially if it was stolen loot or if he was hoping to later mount a salvage effort.

IS IT THE *DIAMOND*?

The ballast pile in question lies in approximately eighteen feet of water at half tide and is about five hundred yards inshore of the outer shoal of Cape Romain. The site is just under four miles from the nearest land (Cape Island) and just over five miles from the site of the old windmill on Mill Island. So the physical location of the site matches well with the reported location of the wreck of the *Diamond*, but it could also fit with several other vessels. The nature of artifacts recovered to date indicate a very valuable cargo. Recovered artifacts range from an ornate French clock to a gold chain and a gold thimble. The flintlock pistol, which was recovered from the wreck, appears to be a military style made for shipboard use. Some of the salvaged fragments of porcelain have a heavy almost military appearance. The two cannons, which Shipwrecks, Inc.'s divers recovered, both had the lines usually associated with a much earlier time-period than the 1798 date marked on both guns and are definitely not military issue. The cannon are British not Spanish, raising the possibility that the wreck might be that of the British/American vessel *Brant* (or *Brent*), which was also reported as wrecked on a shoal off Cape Romain. But English cannon were frequently used by the Spanish. Besides the cannons and even the vessel could have been captured booty. A number of toy molds were recovered and they would seem to be out of place on a slaver, but if she was a pirate they could have been part of a captured merchant cargo. None of the trinket type trading goods (such as beads and bracelets) or leg irons normally associated with a slaver have been found on the wreck.

CONSIDER

If the wreck is indeed that of the *Diamond* (and the general date of the artifacts and the location seem to support that theory) then the nature of her cargo, and the lack of artifacts associated with the slave trade, seem to support her being an outright pirate and not a slaver. Remember, the *Diamond* was off the waters of South Carolina when she gave the story of being "bound to the coast of Africa". At that time, slavery was an acceptable institution in South Carolina. By implying that the ship was being used in the slave trade, her intentions would have been acceptable (albeit illegal) to South Carolinians hearing the story, and it would have helped the *Diamond* account for her armament and her large crew, without attracting undue attention.

THE IMPORTANCE

Regardless of her true identity or her real character, the wreck, was a major archeological and historical discovery. Some of the many people who actively assisted E. Lee Spence in the search and recovery phases of this project were: Mark Daugherty; Mick McCoy; Buddy Truett; Kevin Rooney; Carter Glenn; Tom McGarrity; Mark Dyga; Steve Howard; Tony Camillieri; and Russ Wonsock.

ADDITIONAL ON THE *DIAMOND*

The following items were some of the many articles published in local papers immediately after the wreck. Some of the items are repetitive, but together they should give the reader an idea of the difficulty of determining the true facts around a wreck.

Wreck of the <u>Diamond</u>

We have the pleasure of stating to-day the safety of Capt. Soler, of the Spanish schooner <u>Diamond</u> and several others of his crew. Capt. James Hill, arrived here on Saturday, in his wrecking boat, from Cape Romain, and has brought up with him Capt. Soler, and one of the seamen of the <u>Diamond</u>. He informs us, that on Saturday the 31st ult. as he was standing down the coast for the shipwreck, he discovered something at a considerable distance outside him floating upon the water, which at first he supposed to be part of a broken spar; but going to the masthead of his boat, he thought he could discover a person moving upon it, and immediately hauled his wind and stood out for it. After tacking two or three times, he came up with and found it to be a man apparently at his last gasp, floating upon two or three oars lashed together. They took him into their boat, and after administering to him such nourishment as they had, he so far recovered as to inform them that he was the commander of the <u>Diamond</u>, wrecked on Cape Romain, and that he had then been four nights and three days in the water. He also stated, that he had secured a considerable sum of money in his pantaloons, and with them had tied the oars, upon which he was floating, together; in consequence of this information, Capt. H. returned to his little raft, but just as they had got hold of the oars, to save the money for him, the pantaloons sunk to the bottom with the weight of the money, and it was lost. On Sunday morning, 1st inst. while at anchor made Raccoon Keys, Capt. Hill discovered another man wading through the marsh towards him: and on taking him on board, found that he was also one of the crew, who had drifted on shore about 9 o'clock the preceding evening, upon a single oar. He stated that he was upon a raft with six or seven others, that they were attacked by a number of sharks, who cut off several of his companions, when he took to an oar, and fortunately made his way to the shore.

Capt. Hill remained for several days near the wreck, and when he left it, several other wreckers were around it, saving what they could of the cargo, &. - while there, he learnt that a vessel from this port bound to New-York, had fallen in with a raft, having upon it eight of the Spanish seamen; that she took them on board, and proceeded on her voyage; these, with the two brought to town by Capt. H. make the number of thirty who have been saved out of the fifty-one souls on board at the time of the shipwreck.

Capt. Soler has communicated the following statement of the loss of his vessel, for publication: -

Loss of the Spanish Schooner <u>Diamond</u>

Having made, on the 28th August, Cape Romain, being in eleven fathoms water and a schooner in sight, which appeared to us to be a pilot-boat, stood for and spoke her, and inquired for a pilot; they answered, we must send a boat to them, which was immediately done. She returned on board the <u>Diamond</u> with Capt. Gardner, who told us that he was a pilot for all the coast. That there might be no mistake, I asked him again if he was a pilot, to which he replied, yes, yes; if you give me the command, I will carry you into Charleston. The vessel was then put at his command, when he ordered her to be kept away; and continued so until 3 o'clock in the afternoon, at which time we saw something which appeared to be a steeple or tower, Capt. Gardner said he believed it was Charleston Light-House; but I said it could not be - he still insisted upon it. Shoaling our water, however, very fast, he ordered the vessel to be brought to an anchor. He then hoisted the colors and fired a gun.

Shipwrecks, Pirates & Privateers:

Finding himself locked in by the shoals, Captain Gardner sent his small schooner to sound for a passage out over the shoal; she returned and reported, that the tower they had seen was not Charleston Light House. At the same time, the sea began to break very heavy from E.S.E. He ordered the anchor to be weighed; but I told him he had better not get under weigh; to which he replied, that if we did not allow him to get the _Diamond_ under way, he would leave her and go on board his own vessel. Finding my vessel in this disagreeable situation, and knowing that I could not extricate her myself, rather than be left to ourselves, in a place with which we were entirely unacquainted. He was allowed to proceed as he thought proper, he then got her under way, and directly after she struck on the outer bank, and sunk, as has already been stated. Capt. Gardner, on his arrival in Charleston, supposing that I had been drowned alongside the wreck, and probably believing that no one would step forward to contradict his statement has endeavored to exonerate himself from blame in the loss of the _Diamond_, and throw it all upon me - but after drifting at the mercy of the waves for three days and four nights, I was providentially picked up by Capt. James Hill, in his wrecking boat, on the 31st of August, when at the point of death; and I now declare upon my honor, that the statements heretofore given of the causes which led to the loss of my vessel, are not correct.

Christoval Soler
September 8, 1816

More Seamen Saved

Just as we were putting our paper to press, the schooner _Ann_, Capt. White, from Georgetown, S.C. arrived with twelve seamen more of the crew of the schr. _Diamond_, lost on Cape Romain. Capt. W. took them off of the wreck - They state that the Doctor who intended to remain with them, was washed overboard, and was drowned - they speak certainly of twenty-five having perished; among them the Captain. Captain Gardner, with fifteen or sixteen, drifted off on a raft which they had hastily constructed, and it is not known what has been their fate. These poor fellows exhibit a melancholy picture.

Shipwreck

Several vessels arrived here yesterday, gave us information of a vessel being on shore at Cape Romain; but we could gain no certain information on who she was, until last evening, when the schooner _Polly_, capt. Danenport, came in from Edenton, having on board a Spaniard, whom he had picked up at sea about 10 o'clock yesterday morning six or eight miles to the Eastward of Bull's Island, floating upon one of the hatches of a vessel - From this

Spaniard, whose name is Goze Vincente we have obtained the following particulars through the polite assistance of a gentleman speaking the Spanish language, who kindly acted as interpreter - The seaman not speaking a word of English.

It appears from his statement, that the vessel wrecked is called the Diamond, commanded by Capt. Cristobat Soler; that she was fitted out at Havana for a voyage to the Coast of Africa and left that port about the 28th of July, in company with another vessel, having the same destination. - The Diamond had on board forty men before the mast, besides officers, &c. in all about fifty. Soon after sailing parted company with her consort, and about fifteen days since encountered a gale of wind, in which she was dismasted. Having erected jury masts they made for the American coast, and at 8 o'clock on Thursday morning between Georgetown and Cape Romain, they brought too the schr. Hornet, from Philadelphia, for Charleston, the Spanish Captain insisted that the commander of the schooner should send on board a person to take charge of the Diamond, and Captain Edward C. Gardner, of Philadelphia, who was a passenger on board reluctantly agreed to do so. - In the course of the day, the Diamond was brought to anchor some where near Cape Romain Shoals, where she remained until about 4 o'clock in the afternoon, when the Captain and other Officers insisted upon getting the vessel under way, contrary to the advice and opinion of the person they had forced on board as Pilot. At 6 o'clock, she struck upon the Shoals, when her guns and many other things were thrown overboard, her jury mizzen mast cut away, and every expedient resorted to lighten her - she then drifted in somewhat nearer to the land - (now supposed to be some five miles distant) - when she bilged, and was filing fast with water. As the only means remaining to preserve their lives, a raft was hastily constructed, and all the crew embarked upon it, in the hope of reaching land; but they had not drifted far before the raft settled so low in the water, that the sea beat over it, and many were washed off; our informant sustained himself upon it as long as possible, but was at last obliged to swim for his life, when fortunately getting hold of a part of the hatches of the schooner, he got upon it, and was thus providentially preserved from immediate death. He can form no correct opinion, as to what may have been the fate of the remainder of the crew - many were still clinging to the raft when he was washed off and the presumption is but too strong that a large portion of them must have perished. So completely was Vincente overcome with fatigue, that he fell asleep upon the hatch towards morning, and did not awake until after sun-rise, when nothing was to be seen of the wreck or of his wretched fellow sufferers. - Fortunately for him, the wind blew in a parallel direction with the land, to which circumstance he may probably ascribe his escape from a watery grave, as it kept him in the track of vessels running down the coast, and made Captain Davenport the happy instrument of saving the life of a fellow creature.

Further Particulars

Since writing the above, we have conversed with Mr. Juan Achondo, mate of the schooner Diamond, who, with five Spanish seamen, arrived here last evening in the schooner Hornet, from Philadelphia. - He states, that after the Diamond's situation was considered hazardous, he was sent with a boat's crew on board the Hornet, with a view of throwing over a part of her cargo, to make room for goods on board the Spanish schooner - but it coming on to blow, they found it impossible to get along side her; and after making a number of ineffectual attempts, in which the Hornet lost her cables and anchors, they were compelled to give it up; and, while the ill fated Diamond was stranded and dashed to pieces upon the breakers, the small remainder of her crew, who were on board the Hornet, by great exertion only avoided her fate.

Mr. A. thinks the whole crew of the Diamond, with the exception of the man miraculously preserved as above detailed, must have perished; as they ran close in with the beach yesterday morning, without being able to discover a single survivor. Nothing was to be seen but floating fragments of the wreck.

THE SHIPWRECK. - Since our last, we have collected the following additional particulars of the late Shipwreck on Cape Romain.

On Saturday, the coasting schooner Ann arrived here from Georgetown, bringing twelve of the unfortunate seamen, which she took from the fore-mast of the wreck, to which they had been hanging from 9 o'clock on Thursday evening to 2 o'clock on Friday afternoon.

And, last evening, the pilot-boat Hampton, with Mr. WELLSMAN and Mr. PHINNEY, branch-pilots, on board, came in from the Cape, where they had proceeded immediately on hearing of the disaster; and they have brought in with them Capt. Gardner, of Philadelphia, and one black seaman; who it is to be feared, are the last remaining of that ill-fated crew. - Capt. G. who is very much bruised and exhausted, from forty-two hours exposure upon a small raft, most of the time up to his middle in water, informs us, that he was most providentially picked up by the wrecking schooner Polly-Gallup, Mr. Griffen master, about 3 or 4 o'clock on Saturday afternoon; every soul besides himself having previously been washed off and perished, or cut away some portion of the raft, and *in attempting to gain the shore upon it, met a similar fate. Capt. Gardner was afterwards put on board the <u>Hampton</u>, from the wrecker. The black seaman was found by Messrs. WELLSMAN and PHINNEY, stretched upon the sand on the beach at Cape Romain - he was almost gone when they found him, lying flat upon his face. He stated to them, that two others attempted to gain the shore upon the same spar with himself, but both were washed off and drowned. The Spanish Captain, second Mate, and Doctor, were seen to perish by the side of Capt. Gardner; and as the whole beach has now been examined, there can be but faint hopes entertained of any more of the crew being saved. twenty-one have now been rescued and brought to this city; fifty-one was the whole number on board, consequently thirty have been, most probably, lost.*

The hull of the vessel has not gone to pieces, but lays sunk in about three fathoms water; her quarter railing is above water at low tide.

LEGAL NOTICE

"Notice, To all persons who may save any part of the Cargo of the Spanish schooner <u>Diamante</u>, sunk off Cape Romain, with a valuable Cargo, bound to Africa, that they are requested to deliver the same, without delay, at the Custom-House Stores, and give an account thereof to the subscriber, and they shall receive, for their exertions, such salvage as may be legally awarded, and all who neglect this notice will be prosecuted with the utmost rigor of the law.

Charles Mulvey
His Catholic Majesty's Consul
September 2"

References for the schooner Diamond:
The Times, (Charleston, SC), Vol. 33, #5030, Saturday, August 31, 1816, p. 3, c. 1
The Times, (Charleston, SC), Vol. 33, #5030, Saturday, August 31, 1816, p. 3, c. 2
The Times, (Charleston, SC), Vol. 33, #5031, Monday, September 2, 1816, p. 3, c. 4 (advertisement)
The Times, (Charleston, SC), Vol. 33, #5031, Monday, September 2, 1816, p. 3, c. 1
The Times, (Charleston, SC), Vol. 33, #5031, Monday, September 2, 1816, p. 3, c. 3 (legal notice)
"Charleston Courier," (Charleston, SC), #5190, August 31, 1816, p. 2, c. 3)
"Charleston Courier," (Charleston, SC), #5191, September 2, 1816, p. 3, c. 2
"Charleston Courier," (Charleston, SC), #5197, September 9, 1816, p. 2, c. 2

Note: As some cargo was salvaged, it is likely that admiralty court records could shed some additional light on the character of the Diamond. An advertisement by the Spanish consul requesting persons to turn over salvaged material to him also indicates that diplomatic records (consular dispatches) should be reviewed.

Two of the beautiful crystal stoppers salvaged from the pirate wreck at Cape Romain. Photo courtesy of Shipwrecks Inc.

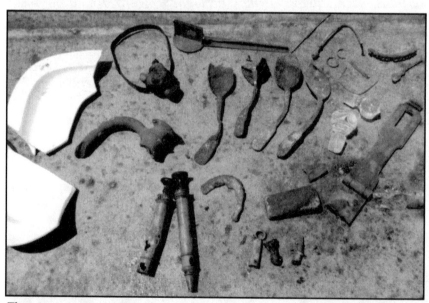

The two syringes may have been used to fight sexually transmitted diseases among the crew. Note the large bronze hasp on the right side of the picture and the mirror arm for a sextant in the top center. Photo courtesy Shipwrecks Inc.

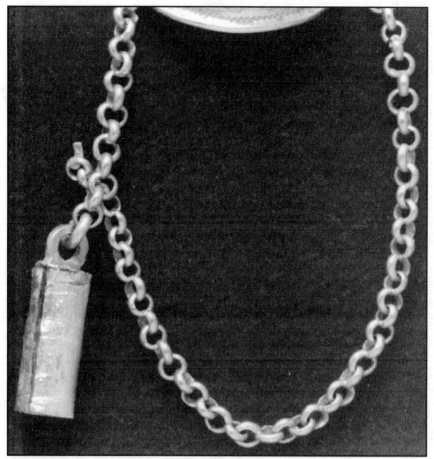

This chain (with barrel type clasp) was one of the first gold artifacts found on the Cape Romain pirate wreck. Photo courtesy of Shipwrecks Inc.

This heavily encrusted flintlock pistol was one of the many weapons salvaged from the pirate wreck at Cape Romain. Photo courtesy of Shipwrecks Inc.

This reproduction pirate ship gives one an idea of the workmanship that went into some of the ships lost on the South Carolina coast. Photo by Pat Spence.

SPENCE'S LIST
of Shipwrecks of the Upper SC Coast

[This list is meant to include all reported shipwrecks between Bulls Island and Little River, including the Bull's Bay, Santee River, Pee Dee River, Black River, Waccamaw River, Winyah Bay, South Island, North Island, DeBordieu Island, Pawley's Island, Myrtle Beach, and Long Bay, South Carolina, from 1521 through the end of 1865, regardless of whether they were later saved or salvaged. Shipwrecks off the Continental Shelf, have not normally been included, unless failure to include them could cause confusion. Most of the following entries refer to single or multiple shipwrecks. A few entries refer to non-shipwreck events which should still be of interest to the reader. References have been listed chronologically by date of publication. The reference section for each entry includes a combination of letters and numbers (called an *SL Code*™) for use in cross referencing. An explanation of *SL Codes*™ may be found in Appendix A of this book. This should not be considered a complete list, and should not be used as the primary basis for any expedition. Remember, by its very nature, all research and data regarding shipwrecks is imprecise, incomplete and unreliable as it is often composed of or effected by numerous assumptions, rumors, legends, deliberate mistatements, historical and scientific inaccuracies and inaccurate interpretations which have or will become a part of such research and data over time.]

1: A Spanish ship (variously identified as a nao or a caravel), Captain Francisco Gordillo, sailing under a license granted by the King of Spain to Don Lucas Vasquez de Ayllon for a voyage of exploration and discovery, was lost in a storm during the summer of 1521 (also shown as lost in 1520). Some historians place the wreck at Cape Romain, South Carolina, while others say it occurred near Cape St. Helena or Hilton Head, South Carolina. The vessel carried a number of Indians who had been illegally captured by the Spanish. The Spanish had planned to sell the Indians into slavery at Santo Domingo. Although a great many Spaniards and Indians were drowned, a number of others were rescued by Captain De Quexos who had been accompanying them in a second vessel. (Note One: Although this was a voyage of exploration, even exploratory ships carried significant amounts of treasure. This was due to the fact that people routinely carried all of their wealth with them in case they didn't return home for years.) (Note Two: When original sources, or sources quoting same, list shipwrecks as having taken place on the coast of Florida during the 16th and 17th centuries, it does not

Shipwrecks, Pirates & Privateers:

necessarily mean that the wreck took place along the peninsula which we know today as the State of Florida. Spanish Florida of the 16th and 17th centuries was far more extensive than today's Florida. It included the areas now known as Georgia and South Carolina. Furthermore, these states lay along the path of one of the major routes followed by the Spanish homeward bound fleets. Together they include as much coastline as the east coast of present day Florida. Although the Florida Keys are a greater natural hazard than anything along the Georgia-South Carolina coast, once past the keys, the ships would actually have been more likely to be lost off Georgia and South Carolina than off the Florida peninsula. There are three major reasons why that would be true. First, the waters off present day Florida were mapped earlier and in greater detail than the waters off Georgia and South Carolina. Charts for the area north of peninsula Florida provided less detail and therefore less safety. Second, the waters off Florida are deeper closer to shore, allowing vessels using the coastline as a navigation aid to operate with a greater margin of safety. A Spanish galleon of 300 tons drew over ten feet and one of 600 tons drew fourteen feet. Much of the waters off Georgia and South Carolina are only 10-15' deep, during low tide, at a distance of a mile from shore. In some spots the water is as shallow as two or three feet even when you are over three miles from shore. The troughs of waves further decreased depths. Deep laden vessels, some running over 1200 tons, would have faced constant danger of "running aground" when still a considerable distance from shore. Shallow waters also make for rougher seas under the same weather conditions. Third, the Spanish vessels returning with their loads of treasure tried to time their departure for home to allow them time to get out of the Caribbean before hurricane season started. The Spaniards were more likely to be off the Georgia or South Carolina coast than the Florida coast, when the first hurricanes of the year hit. The most treacherous place on the entire South Carolina/Georgia coastline is the outer shoal of Cape Romain, which was also the turning point for the Spanish fleets. Each fleet would head up the coast until they saw Cape Romain and then they would turn and run due east until they saw the northern coast of Bermuda.)

References for entry 1 (SL Code™ 1521-8x-US-SC/GA-1:)
Annals of America From the Discovery by Columbus In the Year 1492 to the Year 1826, by Abiel Homes, (Cambridge, 2nd edition, 1829), Volume 1, p. 47
Historical Collections of South Carolina Embracing Many Rare and Valuable Pamphlets and other Documents, Relating to the History of that State, From its First Discovery to its Independence in the Year 1776, compiled by B.R. Carroll, (New York, 1836), Volume 2, p. 393
A Sketch of the History of South Carolina to the Close of the Proprietary Government, 1719, with Appendix Containing Many Valuable Records, by William James Rivers, (Charleston, SC, 1856), p. 16
Glories of the Carolina Coast, by James H. Rice, Jr., (Columbia, SC, 1936), p. 11
The Land Called Chicora, by Paul Quattlebaum, (Gainesville, FL, 1956), p. 13
A History of Georgia from its First Discovery by Europeans to the adoption of the Present Constitution in 1798, by William Bacon Stevens, (Beehive Press, Savannah, GA, 1972), Volume 1, pp. 6-8

2: The Capitana of the fleet of Don Lucas Vasquez de Ayllon was lost at the mouth of the Jordan River (which some believe to have been Winyah Bay) in 1526. Don Lucas Vasquez de Ayllon of Toledo, was a licenciate of the court of Spain, and a member of the Royal Audience of Santo Domingo. In 1524 de Ayllon had fitted out from Hispanola, three ships for the conquest of Chicora (believed to be the present day South Carolina. (Note: Dates given for the loss of this vessel range from 1524 to 1529.) [Special Note on the location of the Jordan River: Diego Gutierrez's map "Americae • • • nova et exactissima descriptio", drawn 1562, shows the "R. Jordan" as a large river between "C. de S. Elena" and "C. de S. Roman". Most historians agree that those two capes are the same ones which are now known as Cape St. Helena, South Carolina, and Cape Romain, South Carolina. As Gutierrez shows no other rivers between those two capes, and, as there are actually several, he may have been trying to indicate the largest of those rivers. The largest "river" in that area is the river formed by the junction of the Ashley and Cooper Rivers at Charleston, South Carolina. The idea that the present day Charleston Harbor is the Rio Jordan of Spanish Florida is further supported by Corneille Wytfliet's map of "Florida et Apalache" of 1597 which shows the "Jordan R". as a large river formed by two major tributaries. Wytfliet also puts the Jordan River between "C. S. Roman" and the "R. S. Helena". In 1562 the French under Captain Jean Ribault left present day Port Royal Harbor, South Carolina, and sailed up the coast in search of the Jordan River. Instead of finding a river with a large, deep harbor like they were looking for, Ribault's men "discovered" a river that they said was to shallow to enter. Ribault named it the French equivalent of the "Shallow River" and sailed on, apparently without ever considering that he may have actually been at the mouth of the Jordan River. The Indians who gave the directions to the Ribault certainly would have known the location of the river that the Spaniards called the Jordan. If the Indians weren't just trying to mislead the French, it may mean that the French had been at the Jordan without realizing it. If you sail fifteen leagues up the coast from St. Helena, you find yourself at the entrance to Charleston Harbor. Charleston Harbor is a large, deep harbor, but in the 1600's entrance to it would have been hampered by the extremely shallow waters of the Charleston Bar. Various historians have identified the Jordan River as being either the Santee or the Winyah rivers in South Carolina, or the Cape Fear River in North Carolina. I am both a historian and a cartographer, and I rule them all out as they all lie north of the present day Cape Romain and all of the contemporary

Spanish maps show the Jordan as south of the cape they knew as Cabo de Santa Romana. Alonso de Chaves the Spanish Royal Cartographer, circa 1536, wrote that the Jordan was four leagues south of Cabo de Santa Romana. That distance matches well with the true north/south distance between Charleston and the present day Cape Romain when figured by latitude. Chaves gave the Jordan's latitude as 33°30' North which would seem to place both the Jordan and Cabo de Stanta Romana north of the present day Cape Romain. But if you use a corrective factor for degrees of latitude to compensate for the fact that the Spaniards believed the earth to be about two percent smaller than its actual size, it puts the location of the Jordan within five miles of the entrance to Charleston. Furthermore, if you don't use the corrective factor and go four leagues up the coast from the latitude Chaves gave for the Jordan, or from any of the rivers variously identified by other modern historians as the Jordan (i.e. the Santee, the Winyah, and the Cape Fear), you would not be on a cape at all. None of those rivers match contemporary Spanish accounts by either latitude or their position relative to any cape by any name. William Hilton and Robert Sandford, two English explorers of the Carolina coast in the 1660's, identified the Jordan as the present day Combahee River, South Carolina, but this, although it would place it between the two capes, would conflict with earlier Spanish accounts and charts.]

References for entry 2 (SL Code™ 1526-12x-US-SC/GA-1):

American Annals, by Abiel Holmes, (1805), Volume 1, pp. 69, 70 and note

A Sketch of the History of South Carolina to the Close of the Proprietary Government, 1719, with Appendix Containing Many Valuable Records, by William James Rivers, (Charleston, SC, 1856), pp. 17, 18, 25

Naufragios de la Armada Española Relacion Historica Formada con Presencia de los Documentos Oficiales Oue Existen en el Archivo del uinisterio de Marina, by Cesareo Fernandez, (Madrid, 1867), p. 10

The Spanish Settlements within the Present limits of the United States, 1513-1561, by Woodbury Lowry, (New York and London, 1901), p. 155, note 2

Genesis of South Carolina 1562-1670, edited by William A. Courtenay, (Columbia, SC, 1907), pp. xxxii, xxxiii

A Land Called Chicora, by Paul Quattlebaum, (Gainesville, Florida, 1956), pp. 20, 21

Hilton Head: A Sea Island Chronicle, by Virginia C. Holmgren, (Hilton Head, SC, 1959), pp. 11, 12, 31

The Southeast in Early Maps, by William P. Cumming, UNC Press, (1962), plates 6, 17, pp. 7, 27, 35, 66, 94, 96

Narratives of Early Carolina, 1650-1708, (John Oldmixon's History, 1708), (New York, 1911, reprinted 1967), edited by Alexander S. Salley, Jr., p. 318

Shipwrecks of the Western Hemisphere: 1492-1825, by Robert F. Marx, (World Publishing Company, New York, 1971), p. 172, #235

A History of Georgia from its First Discovery by Europeans to the adoption of the Present Constitution in 1798, by William Bacon Stevens, (Beehive Press, Savannah, GA, 1972), Volume 1, pp. 6-8

3: An unidentified Spanish galleon was wrecked upon "the coast of Florida" (possibly at Cape Romain) in 1545, with some of its crew slain by the Indians and the remainder enslaved. (Note: When original sources, or sources quoting same, list shipwrecks as having taken place on the coast of Florida during the 16th and 17th centuries, it does not necessarily mean that the wreck took place along the peninsula which we know today as the State of Florida. Spanish Florida of the 16th and 17th centuries was far more extensive than today's Florida. It included the areas now known as Georgia and South Carolina. Furthermore, these states lay along the path of one of the major routes followed by the Spanish homeward bound fleets. Together they include as much coastline as the east coast of present day Florida. Although the Florida Keys are a greater natural hazard than anything along the Georgia-South Carolina coast, once past the keys, the ships would actually have been more likely to be lost off Georgia and South Carolina than off the Florida peninsula. There are three major reasons why that would be true. First, the waters off present day Florida were mapped earlier and in greater detail than the waters off Georgia and South Carolina. Charts for the area north of peninsula Florida provided less detail and therefore less safety. Second, the waters off Florida are deeper closer to shore, allowing vessels using the coastline as a navigational aid to operate with a greater margin of safety. A Spanish galleon of 300 tons drew over ten feet and one of 600 tons drew fourteen feet. Much of the waters off Georgia and South Carolina are only 10-15' deep, during low tide, at a distance of a mile from shore. In some spots the water is as shallow as two or three feet even when you are over three miles from shore. The troughs of waves further decreased depths. Deep laden vessels, some running over 1200 tons, would have faced constant danger of "running aground" when still a considerable distance from shore. Shallow waters also make for rougher seas under the same weather conditions. Third, the Spanish vessels returning with their loads of treasure tried to time their departure for home to allow them time to get out of the Caribbean before hurricane season started. The Spaniards were more likely to be off the South Carolina coast than the Florida coast, when the first hurricanes of the year hit.)

References for entry 3 (SL Code™ 1545-12x-US-SC/GA-1):
The Spanish Settlements Within the Present Limits of the United States, 1513-1561, by Woodbury Lowry, (New York and London, 1911), p. 352
Shipwrecks of the Western Hemisphere: 1492-1825, by Robert F. Marx, (World Publishing Company, New York, 1971), p. 195, #3
Spanish Treasure in Florida Waters: A Billion Dollar Graveyard, by Robert F. Marx, (1979), p. 65, #3

4: Some Spanish ships belonging to Angel de Villafañe and Garcia de Escalante Alvarado were wrecked on the coast of Florida (possibly at Cape Romain) in 1554. (Please see note on the limits of Spanish Florida contained in entry 3 of this book.)

Reference for entry 4 (SL Code™ 1554-12x-US-SC/GA-1):
Naufragios de la Armada Española Relacion Historica Formada con Presencia de los Documentos Oficiales Oue Existen en el Archivo del Ministerio de Marina, by Cesareo Fernandez, (Madrid, 1867), p. 12

5: Several ships of the "Flota de Tierra Firme" (one of the annual Spanish treasure fleets) commanded by Cosme Rodrigues Farfan, which were separated from the rest of the fleet in a storm after entering the Bahama Channel, were wrecked on the coast of Florida on January 22, 1555. (Note on the Bahama Canal or Channel: Ortelius' map "La Florida" of 1584 shows the "Canal de Bahama" as including the body of water off Georgia and parts of South Carolina.) (Please see note on the northern limits of Spanish Florida contained in entry 3 of this book.)

References for entry 5 (SL Code™ 1555-1-US-SC/GA-1):
Naufragios de la Armada Española Relacion Historica Formada con Presencia de los Documentos Oficiales Oue Existen en el Archivo del Ministerio de Marina, by Cesareo Fernandez, (Madrid, 1867), p. 12
Armada Española des de la union de los reinos de Castilla y de Leon, by Cesareo Fernandez Duro, (Madrid, 1895), Volume 1, pp. 215, 445
The Southeast in Early Maps, by William P. Cumming, (UNC Press, 1962), plate 9, pages 95, 116, 117
Spanish Treasure in Florida Waters: A Billion Dollar Graveyard, by Robert F. Marx, (1979), p. 67, #13

6: Three Spanish naos (galleons) under the command of Captain Gonzalo de Carbajal, were lost on the coast of Spanish Florida (possibly at Cape Romain) in 1556, while bound from Porto Rico to Spain. Two of the naos were reported with the same name, *Sancta Salbador*, and both of 120 tons. They were captained by Guillen de Lugo and Martin de Artaleco. The name, tonnage and captain of the third nao were not stated. (Please see entry 3 of this book for note on wrecks listed in original sources as occurring in "Florida", but which may actually lie off the South Carolina or Georgia coast.)

References for entry 6 (SL Code™ 1556-12x-US-SC/GA-1):
Archivo General de las Indias, Seville, Seccion de Contratacion, legajo 2898, folio 197 vto.
Shipwrecks of the Western Hemisphere: 1492-1825, by Robert F. Marx, (World Publishing Company, New York, 1971), p. 196, #10
Spanish Treasure in Florida Waters: A Billion Dollar Graveyard, by Robert F. Marx, (1979), #15, pp. 67, 68

7: In 1561 Angel de Villafañe, who had been one of the original "Conquistadors" with Cortez in the conquest of Mexico, was sent by the governor of New Spain to St. Helena (South Carolina) to look for castaways from a Spanish treasure fleet captained by Farfan and shipwrecked near St. Helena in December, 1560. Villafañe must have received additional information as he left the St. Helena area and searched in the vicinity of Cape Romain for the wrecks. Woodbury Lowry, in his book on Spanish settlements, gives the date of Farfan's fleet being lost on the Atlantic coast as in 1554 and states that there were fifteen vessels in the fleet.

References for entry 7 (SL Code™ 1560-12-US-SC/GA-1):
Carta que escrivio Franco Duarte a S.M. desde la Playa de Zahara con Fecha de Enero de 1555
North America 1500-1560, by Buckingham Smith, pp. 331, 332
The Spanish Settlements Within the Present Limits of the United States 1513-1561, by Woodbury Lowry, (New York, 1911), p. 353 and note
Hilton Head, A Sea Island Chronicle, by Virginia C. Holmgren,

8: While searching the coast from St. Helena (South Carolina) northwards, for a safe port in which to anchor, the fleet of Angel de Villafañe, was struck by a hurricane which lasted an entire night and another day until noon. Two frigates were lost during the hurricane with pilots Juan de Puerta and Heran Perez and 22 soldiers and mariners. On June 8, 1561, one of Villafañe's vessels lost her anchors in the shallows of Cape Romain.

Sunken Treasures of the Upper SC Coast, 1521-1865

References for entry 8 (SL Code™ 1561-6-US-SC/GA-1):
The Spanish Settlements Within the Present Limits of the United States 1513-1561, by Woodbury Lowry, (New York, 1911), p. 353-375

9: The 250 ton, Spanish galleon *La Madalena*, Captain Cristobel Rodriquez, was cast on a shoal (possibly Cape Romain) during a storm in 1563 with an almost total loss of life. Sixteen people out of about three hundred survived by taking to the galleon's small boat. She carried fifty tons of silver in bars and coins; 170 boxes of silver plates, candle sticks, etc; and over a half ton of gold in jewelry and small ingots. She was armed with 28 bronze guns. which today would be extremely valuable works of art due to the beautiful ornate workmanship that was common at that time. A salvage vessel was sent up from Havana six months after loss, but it found no trace of the wreck and her location remains unknown. (Note: Some sources classify her as a Florida wreck, but for the reasons stated in the note for entry 3 of this book, this rich galleon may actually lie off South Carolina or Georgia, and in particular on Cape Romain.)

References for entry 9 (SL Code™ 1563-12x-US-SC/GA-1):
Archivo General de las Indias, Seville, Seccion de Contracion, legajo 2899
Spanish Treasure in Florida Waters: A Billion Dollar Graveyard, Robert F. Marx, (1979), pp. 68, 69. #17

10: A 250 ton Spanish merchantman (owned or part of a fleet commanded by Pedro Menendez) was sunk in 1567 on the coast of Spanish Florida (possibly at Cape Romain).John Potter's *The Treasure Diver's Guide*, says she sank at the entrance of the "New Bahama Channel" off Florida. Potter also states that this "nao" went down in deep water and was lost with all of her cargo and many lives. (See entry 3 of this book for note on why this vessel might actually lie off of South Carolina or Georgia.) [See note for entry 5 of this book, for information on the location of the Bahama Channel.]

References for entry 10 (SL Code™ 1567-12x-US-SC/GA-1):
The Treasure Diver's Guide, John S. Potter, Jr., Revised Edition, (1972), p. 263
Spanish Treasure in Florida Waters: A Billion Dollar Graveyard, Robert F. Marx, (1979), p. 69, #20

11: Two treasure galleons were wrecked in the waters of Spanish Florida in a storm in 1571. They may have actually been lost in the waters along South Carolina or Georgia (possibly at Cape Romain). One was the *San Ignacio*, 300 tons, Captain Juan de Canovas, with 22 iron cannon. The other was the *Santa Maria de la Limpia Concepcion* of 340 tons. Together, the two galleons carried over 2,500,000 pesos in gold and silver. Both galleons suffered almost total loss of life and when salvors reached the area months after the storm all they "found were wooden fragments of one or both wrecks" washed up on shore. (See note for entry 3 of this book.)

References for entry 11 (SL Code™ 1571-12x-US-SC/GA-1):
Archivo General de las Indias, Seville, Seccion de Contracion, legajo 2901
Spanish Treasure in Florida Waters: A Billion Dollar Graveyard, Robert F. Marx, (1979), p. 70, #24

Brass spikes recovered from various 18th & 19th century shipwrecks. The ruler is in inches. Photo by Charles King.

12: According to the "Georgia Historical Quarterly" by the year 1579 French corsairs had established strongholds along the swampy coasts of Spanish Florida (i.e. present day Florida, Georgia and South Carolina), made allies of the Indians through trade and periodically attacked the Spanish gallons "following the usual route to Spain". But by 1581 it was said that the Indians were again in league with the Spaniards and depredations by the French corsairs had been checked.

References for entry 12 (SL Code™ 1579x-12x-US-SC/GA-1):
"Georgia Historical Quarterly", Volume 15, 1931, pp. 308, 309

13: English accounts of Spanish shipping for the year 1591 showed that no less than 29 Spanish vessels were lost "many off the coast of Florida". There is no record of any registered treasure on these vessels, but the possibility that significant amounts of private or smuggled treasure may have been lost with them should not be ruled out. {Please see note in entry 3 of this book for an explanation of why the possibility that one or more of these wrecks may have occurred off South Carolina and/or Georgia (and in particular at Cape Romain) should be considered.}

Reference for entry 13 (SL Code™ 1591-12x-US-SC/GA-1):
Spanish Treasure in Florida Waters: A Billion Dollar Graveyard, by Robert F. Marx, (Boston, 1979), pp. 73, 74, #36

14: Mr. Westlead; four Negroes; and John Bampfield, the "Provost Marshal", were drowned by the oversetting of their canoe while crossing a creek near Cape Romain, South Carolina, on July 24, 1732.

Reference for entry 14 (SL Code™ 1732-7-US-SC/GA-1):
"South Carolina Gazette", (Charleston, SC), #29, July 15, 1732, to August 5, 1732, p. 4, c. 1

15: The "South Carolina Gazette" of February 3, 1732, (old calendar) reported that the sloop *Triumph*, Captain Richard Cupit, bound from Jamaica to New York, was lost on the Raccoon Keys, near Cape Romain, South Carolina, and one man drowned."

References for entry 15 (SL Code™ 1733-2-US-SC/GA-1):
"South Carolina Gazette", (Charleston, SC), #55, January 27, 1732, to February 3, 1732, (old calendar), p. 3, c. 1

16: The pink *Jesus-Maria-Joseph*, Captain Thomas Carr, of Teneriffe, bound from Havana for Santa Cruz, with a cargo of sugar, tobacco, hides and "some money", was burned at sea on September 18, 1735. Her last known position was latitude 33°06' North (which is the latitude of Cape Romain or more precisely Murphy Island, South Carolina). The pink's carpenter and one man were lost. The remainder of the crew were saved by Captain John Smart of the ship *Ogle*, bound from Antigua to Boston. Nothing else was saved except one chest of silver containing $28,076 in new milled money. She had been insured in London and was 150 tons "burthen", 52 men (crew and passengers) and 12 guns. Her first mate was Christobal Debera. Josinto Hernandes Medina was her boatswain and her gunner was Joseph Antonio Caparo. The Court of Vice Admiralty in Boston awarded Captain Smart and his ship's owners $2,240 for "the Trouble and Risque", they went to in saving the people and the money. (Note: The term pink just means it was a sharp sterned vessel, probably having a false overhang with considerable sheer.)

References for entry 16 (SL Code™ 1735-9-US-SC/GA-1):
"South Carolina Gazette", (Charleston, SC), #93, November 1-8, 1735, p. 2, c. 1, 2
"South Carolina Gazette", (Charleston, SC), #97, November 22, 1735, to December 6, 1735, p. 2, c. 1
"American Weekly Mercury", (Philadelphia, PA), #823, October 2-9, 1735
"American Weekly Mercury", (Philadelphia, PA), #826, October 23-30, 1735
Calendar of State Papers, America and the West Indies, 1735-1736, pp. 98, 99, #152

17: A wreck filled with stacks of brick was discovered by Mike Freeman of Oxen Hill, Maryland, during a side-scan sonar search of the Black River. The wreck was located at Brown's Ferry near Georgetown, South Carolina. The wreck was incorrectly thought to be a nineteenth century barge and was largely ignored until 1975 when Hampton Shuping, a diver from North Myrtle Beach recovered some artifacts, including the only Davis Quadrant ever recovered from a wreck. Further investigation showed the wreck to be a double ended, two masted, sailing vessel. [Note: The wreck has since been raised by the South Carolina Underwater Archeological research Council (SCUWARC) and the Institute of Archeology and Anthropology at the University of South Carolina. It has been tentatively identified as dating prior to 1740 and probably around 1735. Over 10,000 bricks were recovered from the wreck along with numerous other artifacts. The wreck has been called the "most important single nautical discovery in the United States to date" by J. Richard Steffy of the Institute of Nautical Archeology at Texas A & M University. Although I was co-founder of SCUWARC, and campaigned for the funds for this project even before Hampton Shupen's involvement, and even though I personally loaned a large amount of equipment for the salvage effort, due to petty politics within the Institute, I was never credited for my role in this project. Furthermore, my equipment was never returned.]

References for entry 17 (SL Code™ 1735x-12x-US-SC/GA-1):
Early Man, Volume 3, #4, (article "Hard Times in the Black River" by Derek V. Goodwin), pp. 4-9
Personal knowledge of Edward Lee Spence

18: A large ship was reported ashore on Cape Romain Shoals, South Carolina, during the second week in February, 1741.

Reference for entry 18 (SL Code™ 1741-2-US-SC/GA-1):
"South Carolina Gazette", (Charleston, SC), #365, February 12-19, 1741, p. 2, c. 2

19: *Lloyd's List* of April 21, 1741, reported the vessel *Woolford*, Captain Kenlock, which sailed with *H.M.S. Norwich*, from Jamaica for London, as lost on the "Coast of Carolina". An advertisement in the "South Carolina Gazette" of March 5, 1741, read: "Whereas the good Ship the *Woolford*, John Kinloch commander, was unluckily stranded on Cape Romain Shoals, (South Carolina), the said Commander is apprehensive that since he was obliged to leave her, to apply for Assistance from Charlestown, she is beat to Pieces by the Violence of the Weather. This is to forewarn all persons whosoever, not to harbor or conceal any Part of the said Ship's Cargo. Some Part thereof having already been seized in Charlestown by the said Commander, for which the Venders and Purloiners are at present under Prosecution in the Court of Vice Admiralty; all Persons who receive any of the said Goods, are desired to inform the Officers of His Majesty's Customs of the same, (who are in that case appointed,) or Mr. William Wallace Merchant, otherwise they may expect the like Prosecution from John Kinloch". (Note: Robert Marx's *Shipwrecks of the Western Hemisphere* lists the *Woolford* as wrecked at Cape Hatteras, North Carolina.)

References for entry 19 (SL Code™ 1741-3-US-SC/GA-1):
"South Carolina Gazette", (Charleston, SC), #367, February 26, 1741, to March 5, 1741, p. 3, c. 1 (advertisement)
"Daily Advertiser", (London, England), #3198, April 21, 1741, p. 1, c. 1
Lloyd's List, (London, England), #588, April 21, 1741, p. 2, c. 2
Shipwrecks of the Western Hemisphere: 1492-1825, by Robert F. Marx, (World Publishing Company, New York, 1971), p. 172, #242

20: A ship bound from Winyah, South Carolina, to London, England, with a cargo of rice, was driven ashore on September 6, 1741, off Santee River, South Carolina, and was "stove to pieces and her cargo entirely lost."

References for entry 20 (SL Code™ 1741-9-US-SC/GA-1):
"South Carolina Gazette", (Charleston, SC), #394, September 5-12, 1741, p. 2, c. 1
"South Carolina Gazette", (Charleston, SC), #395, September 12-19, 1741, p. 2, c. 1

21: A vessel, only described as a snow, was driven on shore three miles within Winyah Bar, South Carolina, during the second week of September, 1741. (Note: A snow was similar to a brigantine.)

Reference for entry 21 (SL Code™ 1741-9-US-SC/GA-3):
"South Carolina Gazette", (Charleston, SC), #394, September 5-12, 1741, p. 2, c. 1

22: On October 16, 1741 an unidentified brigantine was driven ashore on the shoals of Cape Romain, South Carolina.

Reference for entry 22 (SL Code™ 1741-10-US-SC/GA-1):
"South Carolina Gazette", (Charleston, SC), #401, October 24-31, 1741, p. 2, c. 1

23: The ship *Queen of Carolina*, Captain Abraham Snelling, bound from Boston to Charleston, was driven ashore and bilged near the shoals of Cape Romain, South Carolina, on April 14, 1742. She was consigned to Mr. William Yeomens. Part of the cargo was owned by Thomas Hutchinson and company of Boston, who had a package of ribbons, which were saved from the wreck. A package of garden seeds sent to Mrs. Robert Pringle by Sarah Comrin (wife of Captain John Comrin of Boston) was "all Damnified by the Ships being Run a Ground & Lost."

References for entry 23 (SL Code™ 1742-4-US-SC/GA-1):
"South Carolina Gazette", (Charleston, SC), #421, April 10-17, 1742, p. 2, c. 1; p. 3, c. 1 (advertisement)
"South Carolina Gazette", (Charleston, SC), #422, April 17-24, 1742, p. 2, c. 1; p. 3, c. 1 (advertisement)
"South Carolina Gazette - Postscript", (Charleston, SC), #423, May 1, 1742, p. 1, c. 1
Letterbook of Robert Pringle, pp. 6, 273, 389, 392, 721

24: The snow *George*, Captain Alexander Raitt, bound from Boston to North Carolina, ran aground on a shoal at Cape Romain, South Carolina, in January of 1744. She lay there for several days before she got off safely through the efforts of Captain Thomas Frankland of *H.M.S. Rose*, and Captain Henry Ward of *H.M.S. Tartar*. It was said that the *George* was the first vessel that ever got off the Cape after having been ashore. (Note One: *Lloyd's List* of February 28, 1744, had reported her as ashore "on the coast of Carolina" and said she was expected to be lost.) (Note Two: Robert Marx's *Shipwrecks of the Western Hemisphere* gives the year of loss as 1743 and places the wreck at Oregon Inlet, North Carolina.)

References for entry 24 (SL Code™ 1744-1-US-SC/GA-1):
"South Carolina Gazette", (Charleston, SC), #512, January 16, 1744, p. 3, c. 1
"South Carolina Gazette", (Charleston, SC), #513, January 23, 1744, p. 2, c. 2
Lloyd's List, (London, England), #863, February 28, 1743 (old calendar), p. 2, c. 2
Shipwrecks of the Western Hemisphere: 1492-1825, by Robert F. Marx, (World Publishing Company, New York, 1971), p. 172, #243
Letterbook of Robert Pringle, p. 643

25: *Lloyd's List* of April 13, 1744, reported the vessel *Anne and Sarah*, Captain Gregory, from Pool, as lost on the bar at Winyah, South Carolina.

Reference for entry 25 (SL Code™ 1744-3x-US-SC/GA-1):
Lloyd's List, (London, England), #876, April 13, 1744, p. 2, c. 2

26: The ship *Hare*, Captain William Smith, bound from South Carolina for London, was reported in *Lloyd's List* of June 22, 1744, as "lost coming out". (Note: *Lloyd's List* did not state from which port in South Carolina she was "coming out", but since the "South Carolina Gazette" of February 13, 1744, showed the *Hare* as "Cleared for departure to Winyah", South Carolina, she may have made it there and actually been lost while coming out of Georgetown, South Carolina.)

References for entry 26 (SL Code™ 1744-5x-US-SC/GA-1):
"South Carolina Gazette", (Charleston, SC), #514, January 30, 1744, p. 2, c. 2
"South Carolina Gazette", (Charleston, SC), #516, February 13, 1744, p. 2, c. 2
Lloyd's List, (London, England), #896, June 22, 1744, p. 2, c. 2

27: The sloop *Black Joak*, Captain Marsh, of and from Cape Fear, North Carolina, bound for Charleston, South Carolina, was chased ashore in Poole's Inlet, near Winyah, South Carolina, by a privateer sloop, and plundered of some things on August 18, 1745. Captain Marsh and his people escaped ashore. (Note: A sloop by the same name was reported cleared for departure at Charleston on December

2, 1745, but, as that sloop's captain was Benjamin Lightbourn, it was not necessarily the same vessel.)

References for entry 27 (SL Code™ 1745-8-US-SC/GA-1):
"South Carolina Gazette", (Charleston, SC), #595, August 19, 1745, p. 2, c. 3
"South Carolina Gazette", (Charleston, SC), #610, December 2, 1745, p. 2, c. 1

28: A small ship was cast away on Cape Romain Shoals, South Carolina, on March 6, 1746. The ship had been on a voyage from Providence for Charleston, South Carolina, when she had been captured on February 9, 1746, off Stono, South Carolina, by a Spanish privateer. She was subsequently recaptured by the American privateer *Mercury*, Captain Lampree, and was being sent to Charleston when she was lost.

Reference for entry 28 (SL Code™ 1746-3-US-SC/GA-1):
"South Carolina Gazette", (Charleston, SC), #624, March 10, 1746, p. 2, c. 2

29: Captain Saltus' sloop, bound from Bermuda for Georgia, was cast away on the shoals of Cape Romain, South Carolina, on June 3, 1749, but her cargo was saved. (This may have been the sloop *Nassau*, Captain Samuel Saltus, reported cleared from Charleston, South Carolina, to Bermuda, on May 11, 1747.)

Reference for entry 29 (SL Code™ 1749-6-US-SC/GA-1):
"South Carolina Gazette", (Charleston, SC), #682, May 4-11, 1747, p. 3, c. 1
"South Carolina Gazette", (Charleston, SC), #787, May 29, 1749, to June 5, 1749, p. 2, c. 1

30: *Lloyd's List* of June 4, 1751, reported the vessel *Martha*, Captain Patrick Shea, bound from the Canary Islands for Carolina, as lost on the "Roman Sand on the Coast of Carolina" (Note One: The report obviously referred to the shoals of Cape Romain, South Carolina). (Note Two: Robert Marx's *Shipwrecks of the Western Hemisphere*, shows the *Martha* as a "Scottish merchantman" and her crew as saved.)

References for entry 30 (SL Code™ 1751-5x-US-SC/GA-1):
Lloyd's List, (London, England), #1621, June 4, 1751, p. 2, c. 3
Shipwrecks of the Western Hemisphere: 1492-1825, by Robert F. Marx, (World Publishing Company, New York, 1971), p. 180, #301

31: The large brigantine *William*, Captain Thomas Duckworth, belonging to London and Bermuda and bound from Providence for Charleston, with a cargo of mahogany planks, etc., struck on Cape Romain, South Carolina, on February 24, 1754, and went down in four hours. She was beat to pieces and her cargo entirely lost.

Reference for entry 31 (SL Code™ 1754-2-US-SC/GA-1):
"South Carolina Gazette", (Charleston, SC), #1029, February 26, 1754, to March 5, 1754, p. 2, c. 3, p. 3, c. 1

32: In May of 1754 a forty foot long whale was stranded near Cape Romain, South Carolina. The whale was said to be on a small island owned by Daniel Horry.

Reference for entry 32 (SL Code™ 1754-5-US-SC/GA-1):
"South Carolina Gazette", (Charleston, SC), #1042, June 4, 1754

33: The sloop *Polly*, Captain Alexander Innes, bound from St. Kitts to Charleston, with over 70 hhds. of rum, went ashore on Cape Romain, South Carolina, on January 1, 1755. She was beat to pieces.

Reference for entry 33 (SL Code™ 1755-1-US-SC/GA-1):
"South Carolina Gazette", (Charleston, SC), #1072, January 9-16, 1755, p. 2

34: A Cape Fear pilot boat, bound to Charleston with several passengers, was lost on Cape Romain, South Carolina, on January 27, 1757. Some of the bodies were found nearby.

References for entry 34 (SL Code™ 1757-1-US-SC/GA-1):
"South Carolina Gazette", (Charleston, SC), #1182, February 10, 1757, p. 2, c. 1
"New York Mercury", (New York, NY), #239, March 7, 1757, p. 2, c. 2

35: The snow *Peggy*, Captain Colin Buchannan, of and from Glasgow for Charleston, went ashore on Cape Romain, South Carolina, on February 12, 1757. Her cargo was mainly consigned to John Jamieson of Charleston and was valued at 2000 Pounds Sterling. The *Peggy* and most of her cargo were expected to be lost. The crew and passengers were reported safe. (An advertisement in the "South Carolina Gazette" of January 6, 1757, showed John Jamieson as importing such goods as cloths, clothing, hats, stockings, spices, shot, bar lead, frying pans, powder flasks, gun flints, watch chains, ink stands, etc.)

References for entry 35 (SL Code™ 1757-2-US-SC/GA-3):
"South Carolina Gazette", (Charleston, SC), #1177, January 6, 1757, p. 3, c. 1(advertisement)
"South Carolina Gazette", (Charleston, SC), #1183, February 17, 1757, p. 2, c. 1
"South Carolina Gazette", (Charleston, SC), #1184, February 24, 1757, p. 1, c. 2, p. 2, c. 2

36: The wreck of a large schooner was spotted in latitude 33°30' North, longitude 59° (79°?) West, in November of 1757. She had lost her masts and her bowsprit and was described as newly sheathed; her upper streak was yellow, with a rise aft, which took in her main mast and pump. She had a sea-horse figurehead. Her hatches were open and she appeared stripped so the crew was "probably saved". She was believed to have been bound for Surranam (sic) and commanded by Captain John Lovell of Boston. (Note: 33°30' is the latitude of Huntington Beach, South Carolina.)

Reference for entry 35 (SL Code™ 1757-11-US-SC/GA-1):
"Boston Newsletter", (Boston, Mass.), #2893, December 15, 1757, p. 1, c. 2 (dateline: Portsmouth, N.H., December 4, 1757)

37: The "South Carolina Gazette" of January 26, 1758, reported that "no part of the cargo of the ship *Peggy*" cast away on Cape Romain, South Carolina, was expected to be saved. It did not give any other information. (This may have been the vessel *Peggy*, Captain Abercrombe, bound from Philadelphia for South Carolina, which was reported in *Lloyd's List* of April 4, 1758, as "lost near North Carolina.")

References for entry 37 (SL Code™ 1758-1-US-SC/GA-1):
"South Carolina Gazette", (Charleston, SC), January 19-26, 1758, p. 2, c. 1
Lloyd's List, (London, England), #2320, April 4, 1758, p. 2, c. 2

Sunken Treasures of the Upper SC Coast, 1521-1865

"Daily Advertiser", (London, England), #8497, April 5, 1758, p. 1, c. 1

38: The "South Carolina Gazette" of January 26, 1758, reported that a "snow or brigantine" from Dartmouth, bound for Cape Fear, was cast away on Cape Romain, South Carolina, on January 21, 1758. (Note: Since this report appeared in the same paper that reported the loss of the ship *Peggy* it appears as though two separate vessels were lost. But, that is not necessarily the case. See the previous entry.)

Reference for entry 38 (SL Code™ 1758-1-US-SC/GA-2):
"South Carolina Gazette", (Charleston, SC), January 19-26, 1758, p. 2, c. 1

39: The "South Carolina Gazette" of February 17, 1759, reported "Last Week a loaded coasting Schooner from Santee, belonging to Col. Horry, went ashore upon the Raccoon Keys, (Cape Romain, South Carolina), in a Fog and was lost."

Reference for entry 39 (SL Code™ 1759-2-US-SC/GA-1):
"South Carolina Gazette", (Charleston, SC), #1271, February, 1-17, 1759, p. 1, c. 3

40: The ship *Judith*, Captain Arno, of and for Falmouth, bound from Cape Fear, with about two hundred barrels of pitch, tar, etc., went ashore on Cape Romain, South Carolina, on October 25, 1759, and was entirely lost. The crew saved themselves in the ship's boat and underwent "great hardships" before getting to Charleston. Three of the crew died on a small island near the Cape. Robert Marx's *Shipwrecks of the Western Hemisphere* shows her as an English merchantman. Both Marx and *Lloyd's List* of February 1, 1760, show the captain's name as Martin.

References for entry 40 (SL Code™ 1759-10-US-SC/GA-1):
"South Carolina Weekly Gazette", (Charleston, SC), #5, October 24-31, 1759, p. 3, c. 1
"South Carolina Gazette", (Charleston, SC), #1316, November 3-10, 1759, p. 3, c. 1
Lloyd's List, (London, England), #2510, February 1, 1760, p. 2, c. 3
Shipwrecks of the Western Hemisphere: 1492-1825, by Robert F. Marx, (World Publishing Company, New York, 1971), p. 180, #305

41: The "South Carolina Weekly Gazette" of October 31, 1759, reported a ship "thought to be from Jamaica" as aground on Cape Romain, South Carolina.

Reference for entry 41 (SL Code™ 1759-10-US-SC/GA-2):
"South Carolina Weekly Gazette", (Charleston, SC), #50, October 24-31, 1759, p. 3, c. 1

42: A tender belonging to the privateer *Eagle*, Captain Dibdin, of London, was lost on the shoals of Cape Romain, South Carolina, on November 8, 1762, but all the crew were saved.

Reference for entry 42 (SL Code™ 1762-11-US-SC/GA-1):
"South Carolina Gazette", (Charleston, SC), #1479, November 13-20, 1762, p. 3, c. 1

43: A sloop bound from Havana, which was temporarily in English hands, to Georgia, was chased ashore at the mouth of the Santee River, South Carolina, on November 18, 1762, by the Spanish privateer schooner *St. Joseph*, of St. Augustine, Florida. The privateer mounted four 3-pounders.

References for entry 43 (SL Code™ 1762-11-US-SC/GA-2):

Shipwrecks, Pirates & Privateers:

"South Carolina Gazette", (Charleston, SC), #1480, November 20-27, 1762, p. 2, c. 3
Trade and Privateering in Spanish Florida 1732-1763, by Joyce Elizabeth Harmon, (St. Augustine Historical Society, Paramount Press, Jacksonville, FL, 1969), p. 74

44: A boat belonging to a party of Spaniards that landed on North Island, South Carolina, was stove in while landing on that island on December 5, 1762. Before leaving the island, the privateersmen looted the home of Mr. Dubourdieu (the coast pilot) and stole a large new longboat belonging to the *Elizabeth and Mary*. (Note: The Spaniards were described as from a "French" privateer sloop, out of St. Augustine.)

References for entry 44 (SL Code™ 1762-12-US-SC/GA-3):
"South Carolina Gazette", (Charleston, SC), #1482, December 4-11, 1762, p. 3, c. 2
Trade and Privateering in Spanish Florida 1732-1763, by Joyce Elizabeth Harmon, (St. Augustine Historical Society, Paramount Press, Jacksonville, FL, 1969), p. 71

45: The schooner *General Wolf*, which had been captured on December 10, 1762, by the Spanish privateer *Sancta Maria*, and converted to a "consort", chased a schooner from Antiqua ashore on the south end of North Island, South Carolina, on December 11, 1762.

Reference for entry 45 (SL Code™ 1762-12-US-SC/GA-4):
"South Carolina Gazette", (Charleston, SC), #1485, December 25, 1762, to January 1, 1763, p. 2, c. 3

46: The Spanish privateer *Sancta Maria*, Captain Don Martin d'Hamassa, drove a schooner ashore near Winyah, South Carolina, on December 13, 1762. The schooner was also described as ashore near Georgetown.

References for entry 46 (SL Code™ 1762-12-US-SC/GA-5):
"South Carolina Gazette", (Charleston, SC), #1483, December 11-18, 1762, p. 2, c. 3
"South Carolina Gazette", (Charleston, SC), #1485, December 25, 1762, to January 1, 1763, p. 2, c. 3

47: His British Majesty's snow *L'Epreuve*, Captain Peter Blake, returned to Charleston on December 19, 1762, after she had "scoured the coast from Winyah to Port Royal," South Carolina, in an unsuccessful search for Spanish privateers. She reported seeing a schooner ashore. (Note: This appears to have been in addition to the schooner mentioned in the previous entry.)

References for entry 47 (SL Code™ 1762-12-US-SC/GA-6):
"South Carolina Gazette", (Charleston, SC), #1484, December 18-25, 1762, p. 2, c. 3
Trade and Privateering in Spanish Florida 1732-1763, by Joyce Elizabeth Harmon, (St. Augustine Historical Society, Paramount Press, Jacksonville, FL, 1969), pp. 71, 72

48: The "South Carolina Gazette" of September 7, 1765, reported that the ship *Friends Goodwill*, Captain John Briggs (or Biggs), had been driven ashore on an oyster bank in the gale of September 3, 1765. (Note: She had been bound from Georgetown, South Carolina, to London, England, and had lain for some time wind bound, near North Island, South Carolina, so the grounding probably took place in that vicinity.) It was thought that she had received no damage and was expected off. She did get off, but when she came into Charleston on October 2, 1765, it was reported that she had lost her rudder and received other damage. The ship *Friends Goodwill* was built in Great Britain in 1758 and drew 6' of water. She was owned by Workington.

References for entry 48 (SL Code™ 1765-9-US-SC/GA-1):
"South Carolina Gazette", (Charleston, SC), #1600, August 31, 1765, to September 1, 1765, p. 1, c. 1
"South Carolina Gazette", (Charleston, SC), #1604, September 28, 1765, to October 5, 1765, p. 2, c. 3
Lloyds' Register of Shipping, (London, England, 1764), entry for *Friends Goodwill*, John Briggs

49: The schooner *Good Intent*, Captain William Blyth, bound from Winyah (Georgetown, South Carolina) to Charleston, struck and lost her rudder while attempting to come in at the Middle or Swash Bar, Charleston Bar, South Carolina, on February 2, 1767. Soon after striking, the sea stove in her dead lights, so that the water came in at the cabin windows, filled her, and as she got over the bar, she fell on her broadside and sank in the channel. Her crew barely escaped with their lives. "Some days after" the schooner was found and towed to Sullivan's Island where she sank again. She was entirely lost except for a small amount of her indigo and rum. The schooner and her cargo were valued at a total of over 4000 pounds sterling. Her cargo consisted of 20 hogsheads of rum, 200 barrels of pork, 20,000 pounds of indigo contained in 50 casks, 100 bushels of hemp and other articles. The principal owners of the indigo were given as Messrs. Brewton & Smith; Claudius Pegues; Philip Pledger; Anthony Pawley; George Hicks; Benjamin Rogers; Thomas Bingham; Samuel Butler; Abel Wiles; and David Evans. The schooner was described as "a coaster".

References for entry 49 (SL Code™ 1767-2-US-SC/GA-1):
"South Carolina Gazette", (Charleston, SC), #1643, February 2-9, 1767, p. 3, c. 1
"South Carolina Gazette and Country Journal", (Charleston, SC), #61, February 10, 1767, p. 2, c. 1
"South Carolina and American General Gazette", (Charleston, SC), #430, January 30, 1767, to February 6, 1767, p. 2 (26), c.4

50: A sloop, Captain Mustard, bound from Boston to Georgetown, South Carolina, was lost on Cape Romain, South Carolina, in April, 1769.

Reference for entry 50 (SL Code™ 1769-4-US-SC/GA-2):
"South Carolina and American General Gazette", (Charleston, SC), #547, April 24, 1769, to May 1, 1769, p. 2 (34), c. 2

51: The vessel *Prosperous*, Captain Henry Thompson, of and from Bristol for Charleston, South Carolina, got ashore on Cape Romain Shoals, South Carolina, on May 30, 1769. The *Prosperous* was got off with the assistance of Captain Waldron's pilot boat and three schooners. Her crew was made up of the captain, nine men and two lads. She was afterwards reported as safely arrived at Charleston.

References for entry 51 (SL Code™ 1769-5-US-SC/GA-2):
"South Carolina Gazette", (Charleston, SC), #1758, June 1, 1769, p. 3, c. 2
"South Carolina Gazette", (Charleston, SC), #1759, June 8, 1769, p. 3, c. 2
Lloyd's List, (London, England), #3496, July 25, 1769, p. 2, c. 3

52: The schooner *Liberty*, Captain Benjamin Peabody, of and for New London from Jamaica, was driven ashore and was entirely lost with her cargo on September 5, 1772, between North Santee Inlet and Murphy's Island, South Carolina. Forty casks of oil and 300 pounds sterling in cash were reported lost. (Note: One report said she went ashore in Sewee Bay. Sewee Bay was the old name for the entirety of Bulls Bay, South Carolina, but now represents just an off shoot or sub bay of it.)

References for entry 52 (SL Code™ 1772-9-US-SC/GA-1):
"South Carolina Gazette", (Charleston, SC), #1914, September 10, 1772, p. 3, c. 1
"South Carolina Gazette", (Charleston, SC), #1915, September 17, 1772, p. 3, c. 1
"South Carolina Gazette and Country Journal", (Charleston, SC), #354, September 8, 1772, p. 3, c. 1
"South Carolina Gazette and Country Journal", (Charleston, SC), #356, September 22, 1772, p. 3, c. 1

53: A French sloop, with a cargo of "12,000 lb. of gunpowder, etc". got ashore on Cape Romain Shoals, South Carolina, in the third week of November, 1776, and was entirely lost. The crew was saved.

Reference for entry 53 (SL Code™ 1776-11-US-SC/GA-1):
"Virginia Gazette", (Williamsburg, VA), #1327, January 10, 1777, p. 3, c. 1, (dateline: "Charlestown, SC, Nov. 21")

54: The sloop *Nancy*, Captain Baker Gibbs, which had been bound from Pensacola to Jamaica, laden with lumber, when it was captured on May 3, 1777, by the South Carolina privateer sloop *Rutledge*, Captain Jacob Milligan, of Charleston, was run ashore and deserted at Cape Romain, South Carolina, but was afterwards reported as safely arrived at Charleston.

References for entry 54 (SL Code™ 1777-6x-US-SC/GA-1):
Naval Documents of the American Revolution (1777), edited by William J. Morgan, (Washington, DC, 1980), Volume 8, pp. 998, 1033
Charleston's Maritime Heritage 1670-1865, by P.C. Coker III, (CokerCraft Press, Charleston, SC, 1987), p. 89

55: The "South Carolina and American General Gazette" of January 1, 1778, reported an unidentified ship ashore at Cape Romain, South Carolina.

Reference for entry 55 (SL Code™ 1777-12-US-SC/GA-1):
"South Carolina and American General Gazette", (Charleston, SC), #991, January 1, 1778, p. 3, c. 2

56: A snow, loaded with provisions and bound from Cork to Barbadoes (sic), "recently" taken as a prize by the South Carolina brig *Notre Dame*, was lost on the Georgetown Bar, South Carolina, in May of 1778.

Reference for entry 56 (SL Code™ 1778-5-US-SC/GA-1):
"South Carolina and American General Gazette", (Charleston, SC), #1011, May 28, 1778, p. 3, c. 1

57: Prevost and Wilder's book *Pawley's Island, A Living Legend* told of a Mr. Neufville of Charleston who was the sole survivor of a ship wrecked in 1778 on the "seashore of Waccamaw" (probably Pawley's Island, South Carolina) and who made his way to the home of Captain William Allston, where he was greeted by his former fiancee (Rachel Moore Allston) who fainted at the sight of him. It seems Rachel had thought him dead for the past several years and had married Captain Allston. Upon seeing him, Rachel thought he had come back from the dead for her.)

References for entry 57 (SL Code™ 1778-8-US-SC/GA-20):
Pawley's Island, A Living Legend, by Charlotte Kaminski Prevost and Effie Leland Wilder, (Columbia, SC 1972), p. 41
Life and Letters of Washington Allston, by Jared B. Flagg, (1892), New York, pp. 2-4

58: On March 7, 1779, several British privateers drove a schooner from New England ashore on the "reef off Santee", South Carolina.

Reference for entry 58 (SL Code™ 1779-3-US-SC/GA-1):
"Gazette of the State of South Carolina", (Charleston, SC), #2130, March 31, 1779, p. 2, c. 1

59: A ship from Boston (referred to as "the old *Live Oak*"), Captain Chapman, was driven ashore on the reef at South Santee, South Carolina, by some British privateers on March 9, 1779. (Note: This may have been the ship *Live Oak*, built on James Island, South Carolina, in 1749. The 1749 *Live Oak* was one hundred and twenty-five tons. *Lloyd's Register of Shipping for Underwriters for 1778* shows a (different?) ship called the *Live Oak*, Captain Thomas Fortune, as built in Carolina in 1751, and does not list it in the register of the following year. That *Live Oak* was shown as one hundred and sixty tons and drew fourteen feet of water. It had been refitted in 1772 and had a new deck put on in 1773. The vessel was classed as E-1 for insurance purposes and was shown as trading out of Boston.)

References for entry 59 (SL Code™ 1779-3-US-SC/GA-2):
"Gazette of the State of South Carolina", (Charleston, SC), #2130, March 31, 1779, p. 2, c. 1
"Ship Register, Port of Charleston, South Carolina", Volume 1, pp. 65, 66
Lloyd's Register of Shipping for Underwriters for 1778, (London, 1778), L-171

60: The brig *Peace and Harmony,* Captain Rogers, was driven ashore near Winyah, South Carolina, on March 28, 1779, and burned by the privateer *Vengenance* (sic) of New York, Captain Dean. A small sloop was in company with the privateer. (Note: This may have been the brig *Peace and Harmony,* Captain G. Kennedy, listed in *Lloyd's Register of Shipping for Underwriters for 1778*. Captain Kennedy's brig was built in Boston in 1775, was classed A-1 for insurance purposes, was single decked, eighty tons, and drew nine of water.)

References for entry 60 (SL Code™ 1779-3-US-SC/GA-5):
Lloyd's Register of Shipping for Underwriters for 1776, (London, 1778), P-56
Lloyd's Register of Shipping for Underwriters for 1778, (London, 1778), P-49
"Gazette of the State of South Carolina," (Charleston, SC), #2131, April 7, 1779, p. 2, c. 2

61: The "South Carolina Weekly Gazette", of October 31, 1780, reported that a ship was aground on Cape Romain, South Carolina. The ship was believed to have been from Jamaica.

Reference for entry 61 (SL Code™ 1780-10-US-SC/GA-2):
"South Carolina Weekly Gazette", (Charleston, SC), October 24, 1780

62: General William Moultrie in his *Memoirs of the American Revolution* recorded that on May 18, 1781, Lord Cornwallis began his march for Huger's Bridge, Huger, South Carolina, with about two thousand five hundred men and five field pieces. From Huger they marched to Leneau's Ferry, Santee River, South Carolina, where they found that the Americans had destroyed most of the boats.

Reference for entry 62 (SL Code™ 1781-5-US-SC/GA-3):
Memoirs of the American Revolution so far as it Related to the States of North and South Carolina, and Georgia, by William Moultrie, (Arno Press, 1968), Volume 2, p. 203

63: The privateer schooner *Peggy*, Captain Mansen, of Charleston, South Carolina, chased a sloop ashore near the Winyah Bar, at Georgetown, South Carolina. The sloop bilged and her cargo was lost except for a small quantity of indigo and a few other articles which were saved.

Reference for entry 63 (SL Code™ 1781-7-US-SC/GA-3):
"Royal Gazette", (Charleston, SC), #43, July 28, 1781, p. 3, c. 2

64: In a letter from "R. Lushington" to "Wakefield", dated at Georgetown, South Carolina, on September 7, 1782, Lushington wrote: "I am sorry to inform you of an unlucky circumstance which happened to one of our prizes, a sailor went to get some Rum for a Keg with a Candle, he put it to close; the Rum catched, the Keg bursted and the Vessel was on fire in a few moments: the sailor and one Negro burnt". Lushington went on to say that the sugar and rum aboard the prize had been lost, but he failed to make it clear whether or not the vessel itself was lost. The accident apparently took place at Georgetown, South Carolina.

Reference for entry 64 (SL Code™ 1782-9-US-SC/GA-2):
"Royal Gazette", (Charleston, SC), #154, September 21-28, 1782, p. 3, c. 2

65: *New-Lloyd's List* of March 18, 1785, reported the vessel *Two Friends* Captain M'Allester, as having gone ashore at Georgetown, South Carolina and as having afterwards got off, unloaded and refitted. (Note: Customs house records show that on a previous voyage the brigantine *Two Friends*, Captain A. McAllister, had carried rum, lime, and slaves, from St. Kitts to Charleston.)

References for entry 65 (SL Code™ 1785-2x-US-SC/GA-1):
New-Lloyd's List, (London, England), #1656, March 18, 1785, p. 1, c. 3
South Carolina Archives Microcopy #6, ("Duties on Trade at Charleston, 1784-1789"), Volume B, p. 104, #336; p. 105, #343

66: The ship *Fanny*, Captain Burnham, bound from New London to Charleston, struck on the Cape Romain shoals, South Carolina, in May of 1785, which "obliged the Captain" to run her ashore near Five Fathom Hole to save the lives of those on board. She had been out ten days and had cattle aboard. It was thought that she would be entirely lost.

References for entry 66 (SL Code™ 1785-5-US-SC/GA-3):
"South Carolina Gazette and Public Advertiser", (Charleston, SC), #186, June 1, 1785

Sunken Treasures of the Upper SC Coast, 1521-1865

"State Gazette of South Carolina", #2303, June 2, 1785

67: The London papers, "Daily Universal Register" of June 6, 1785, and the *New-Lloyd's List* of June 7, 1785, both reported the vessel *Dispatch*, Captain Shields, bound from South Carolina to London, as totally lost near Georgetown, South Carolina, with all of her cargo. (Note: Robert Marx's *Shipwrecks of the Western Hemisphere* shows the *Dispatch* as an English merchantman and as "lost at Georgetown harbor", South Carolina.)

References for entry 67 (SL Code™ 1785-5-US-SC/GA-2):
New-Lloyd's List, (London, England), #1679, June 7, 1785, p. 1, c. 3
"Daily Universal Register", (London, England), #138, June 6, 1785, p. 3, c. 4
Shipwrecks of the Western Hemisphere: 1492-1825, by Robert F. Marx, (World Publishing Company, New York, 1971), p. 182, #317

68: A schooner, Captain Smith, bound to Charleston, with a cargo of shingles and lightwood posts, was lost off Georgetown, South Carolina, on November 11, 1785.

Reference for entry 68 (SL Code™ 1785-11-US-SC/GA-1):
"South Carolina Gazette and Public Advertiser", (Charleston, SC), #251, November 12, 1785

69: The American built ship *America*, Captain O. Goodwin, of Boston, bound to Charleston, South Carolina, from Port L'Orient, France, was cast away on Cape Romain, South Carolina, on December 13, 1788. A sloop saved the crew but the vessel and cargo were lost. She was sheathed with copper in 1783 and was classed E-1 (meaning she could carry dry cargo in safety) by Lloyd's when surveyed at Liverpool in 1787. She was described as a regular trader between Liverpool and Boston in *Lloyd's Register of Shipping*. The *America* was 160 tons and drew 11 feet when loaded. (Note: Port L'Orient is located on the west coast of France and was the trans-shipping port of the French East India Company. It was from Port L'Orient that France shipped the "treasures" of the Orient. Those treasures would have included porcelains, silks, tea, jewelry, spices, etc.) (See also chapter 3 in this book.)

References for entry 69 (SL Code™ 1788-12-US-SC/GA-1):
"Georgia Gazette", (Savannah, GA), #310, January 1, 1789, p. 2, c. 3
"Herald of Freedom", (Boston, MA), #34, January 9, 1789, p. 139, c. 3
"Massachusetts Centinel", (Boston, MA), #34, January 10, 1789, p. 137, c. 2
Lloyd's Register of Shipping for Underwriters for 1787, (London, 1787), A-192
Lloyd's Register of Shipping for Underwriters for 1787, (London, 1787), A-229

70: The vessel *Speedwell*, Captain Kerr, bound from Wilmington to London, was shown in *Lloyd's List* of December 24, 1790, as "ashore off Georgetown", South Carolina, and that a "great part" of the cargo was landed.

Reference for entry 70 (SL Code™ 1790-11x-US-SC/GA-1):
Lloyd's List, (London, England), #2258, December 24, 1790, p. 1, c. 3

71: A schooner commanded by Captain Matthews, bound from Georgetown to Charleston, with 117 barrels and 40 half barrels of rice, 9 barrels of pork, etc., struck on the Georgetown Bar, South

Carolina, on January 22, 1791, and bilged. The passengers and crew were reported safe, but the cargo was lost.

Reference for entry 71 (SL Code™ 1791-1-US-SC/GA-1):
"State Gazette of South Carolina", (Charleston, SC), #3947, February 7, 1791

72: The American ship *Termagant*, Captain J. McGrude (or M'Gruder), bound from London, was burnt at Georgetown, South Carolina, on April 29, 1791. The *Termagant*, was built in Virginia in 1786, single deck with beams, pine sides, 250 tons, and 13' draft. She was sheathed in 1787, and was classed A-1 by Lloyd's. She was owned by S. Bourke.

References for entry 72 (SL Code™ 1791-4-US-SC/GA-1):
Lloyd's List, (London, England), #2306, June 10, 1791, p. 1, c. 3
The Times, (London, England), #2046, June 10, 1791, p. 2, c. 3
Lloyd's Register of Shipping for Underwriters for 1790, (London, 1790), T-19
Lloyd's Register of Shipping for Underwriters for 1791, (London, 1791), T-21

73: The schooner *Governor Hamilton*, belonging to Bermuda, with a cargo of corn, was run aground on the Georgetown Bar, South Carolina, on June 5, 1791. The accident was caused by the neglect of the pilot and the vessel and cargo were entirely lost.

References for entry 73 (SL Code™ 1791-6-US-SC/GA-2):
"The South Carolina Independent Gazette and Georgetown Chronicle", (Georgetown, SC), #11, June 11, 1791
"Georgia Gazette", (Savannah, GA), #439, June 23, 1791

74: The brig *Patsy Wentworth*, Captain Cooper, of and for Norfolk from Lisbon, with a cargo of salt and wine, was cast away on North Island, South Carolina, near the entrance to Georgetown Harbor, South Carolina, on January 7, 1797.

Reference for entry 74 (SL Code™ 1797-1-US-SC/GA-1):
"City Gazette and Daily Advertiser", (Charleston, SC), #2949, January 12, 1797, p. 2, c. 2

75: The sloop *Seaflower,* Captain Busden, bound from Jamaica to Charleston, was lost on Georgetown Bar, South Carolina, on August 16, 1799. The sloop and the whole of her cargo were lost except for one hogshead of rum. (Note: Robert Marx's *Shipwrecks of the Western Hemisphere* gives her captain's name as Williams.)

References for entry 75 (SL Code™ 1799-8-US-SC/GA-1):
"Georgia Gazette", (Savannah, GA), #827, August 29, 1799, p. 2, c. 3
Lloyd's List, (London, England), #4008, October 22, 1799, p. 1, c. 3
The Times, (London, England), #4620, October 23, 1799, p. 3, c. 3
Shipwrecks of the Western Hemisphere: 1492-1825, by Robert F. Marx, (World Publishing Company, New York, 1971), p. 182, #323

76: "The Times" of Charleston, South Carolina, reported that a ship loaded with dry goods and salt, and bound from Liverpool to Wilmington, North Carolina, was wrecked "on Long Bay" on December 24, 1800, but failed to say whether in the North Carolina or South Carolina part of the bay.

Reference for entry 76 (SL Code™ 1800-12-US-SC/GA-1):
"The Times," (Charleston, SC), Volume 1, #71, December 17, 1800, p. 3, c. 2

77: Captain Adams of the brig *Dispatch* bound from Boston, reported seeing a wreck in latitude 33°21' North, longitude 74° West

(which is off DeBordieu Island, South Carolina), on April 20, 1801. The next day the *Dispatch* picked up a bag of upland cotton.
Reference for entry 77 (SL Code™ 1801-4-US-SC/GA-2):
"The Times", (Charleston, SC), Volume 2, #179, May 4, 1801, p. 3, c. 1

78: A boat overturned between North Island and South Island, near Georgetown, South Carolina, on September 9, 1801, drowning Mr. Samuel Dubois and Mr. Nathaniel Vail. Mr. Vail was buried in the Baptist burial ground.
Reference for entry 78 (SL Code™ 1801-9-US-SC/GA-1):
"The Times", (Charleston, SC), Volume 2, #296, September 19, 1801, p. 3, c. 2

79: The schooner *Beginning*, commanded and partly owned by Mr. Samuel Holmes, and bound from Philadelphia, was driven on the point of North Island near Georgetown, South Carolina, on September 14, 1801. Her cargo was expected to be saved. She was three days from Delaware. (Note: This may have been the schooner *Beginning*, of Bridgetown, New Jersey, which was issued a temporary register at Philadelphia, Pennsylvania, on August 31, 1801. That schooner was built at Cape May, New Jersey, in 1796. She was 61 76/95 tons.)
References for entry 79 (SL Code™ 1801-9-US-SC/GA-2):
"The Times", (Charleston, SC), Volume 2, #296, September 19, 1801, p. 3, c. 2
Ship Registers of the Port of Philadelphia, Pennsylvania Historical Survey, W.P.A., (Philadelphia, 1942), Volume 1, p. 90, #577

80: The brig *Peggy*, Captain William S. Brown, Jr., bound from New York, was cast away off Georgetown, South Carolina, about December 27, 1801. Part of her cargo was saved, but the vessel was lost. (Note: This may have been the brig *Peggy*, Captain W. Brown. listed in *Lloyd's Register of Shipping for Underwriters for 1800*. That brig was built in Yarmouth in 1798, was 103 tons, drew 10' and had a single deck with beams. It was owned by the captain and others, and had been classed A-1 in 1798 for insurance purposes.
References for entry 80 (SL Code™ 1801-12-US-SC/GA-1):
Lloyd's Register of Shipping for Underwriters for 1800, (London, 1799), p, 78
"The Times", (Charleston, SC), Volume 3, #382, December 30, 1801, p. 3, c. 3

81: A brig laden with coffee was cast away at Little River, South Carolina, shortly before October 18, 1802.
Reference for entry 81 (SL Code 1802-10-US-SC/GA-1):
"The Times," (Charleston, SC), #634, October 23, 1802, p. 3, c. 3, (date-line: Raleigh, October 18, 1802)

82: The schooner *William* of Boston, Captain A. Fernald, bound from Trinidad to Wilmington, North Carolina, with a cargo of sugar, sprang a leak in a heavy gale off Charleston, South Carolina, on January 4, 1803, and was run ashore by her crew to save their lives. Her position was given as in Long Bay, near Little River, South Carolina, and as thirty miles south of the Cape Fear, North Carolina, lighthouse. The schooner was full of water when they reached shore. One of the crew died from exposure. The vessel went to pieces and the cargo was lost. Part of her sails and rigging were saved. She was owned by Mr. Jonathan Merry of Boston.

References for entry 82 (SL Code 1803-1-US-SC/GA-1):
"The Times," (Charleston, SC), #717, January 31, 1803, p. 3, c. 2
"Charleston Courier," (Charleston, SC), #19, January 31, 1803, p. 3, c. 2

83: The American ship *Roxa*, Captain A. Rickers (or Ricker), bound from Nantes to Wilmington, North Carolina, and out 56 days, foundered at sea in latitude 33°30' North, longitude 76° West (which is off Murrel's Inlet, South Carolina), sometime in late January, 1803. The *Roxa* was 220 tons, drew 14' of water, and had been built at Philadelphia. She was single decked with beams. She was built of live oak and cedar and had been sheathed. She was classed E-1 for insurance purposes and was owned by R. Adam. Damages had been repaired in 1801.

References for entry 83 (SL Code™ 1803-1-US-SC/GA-5):
"The Times", (Charleston, SC), #745, March 4, 1803, p. 3, c. 2, (dateline: Wilmington, February 4, 1803)
Lloyd's Register for Shipping for Underwriters for 1803, (London, 1803), R-348

84: Captain Atkins of the schooner *Sally*, arrived at Charleston, South Carolina, about December 31, 1803, reported seeing the wreck of a vessel in latitude 33°41' N. (which would be off Myrtle Beach, South Carolina). The bows of the wreck "were painted in streaks of red, yellow and black; she was to appearance almost new, of about sixty tons; the bitts of the windlass and the forescuttle were painted red; the leads in her hawse-holes were quite new, and very little worn, she appeared as if she had run on some shoal, and was entirely split in two parts, the quarter deck and stern were entirely gone". Captain Atkins went on to say that she probably had not been wrecked for long as the paint still appeared quite fresh.

Reference for entry 84 (SL Code™ 1803-12-US-SC/GA-2):
"Charleston Courier", (Charleston, SC), Volume 2, #1, January 2, 1804, p. 3, c. 2

85: The schooner *Favorite*, Captain Culley, bound from Baltimore to Charleston, with a cargo of corn, was upset, and immediately went down off Cape Romain, South Carolina, during the hurricane of September 8, 1804. "There were on board at the time, capt. Culley, his mate, and three seamen - Mr. and Mrs. Groves, and a Mr. Stewart, passengers, and a Negro fellow said to be the property of Mr. Wescott. Mr. Groves, and a seaman by the name of Wallace, caught hold of a hen-coop, the other persons on board, it is believed, went down with the vessel. Wallace kept his hold on the hen-coop about four hours, when exhausted, he fell off and was drowned. Mr. Groves was then left alone, and remained in this situation" for 22 hours when he was "fortunately picked up by capt. Smith, of the *Venus*, from New York."

Reference for entry 85 (SL Code™ 1804-9-US-SC/GA-22):
"Charleston Courier", (Charleston, SC), Volume 2, #218, September 13, 1804, p. 3, c. 2

*The two pewter spoons, the silver fork and the corner of a brass picture frame
were all found on the same dive, but span a time period of over 200 years.*

86: The schooner *Iona* (or *Ino*), Captain George Bunker, of Baltimore, bound from Kingston to Baltimore, was driven ashore on the beach at Cape Romain, South Carolina, "near Mr. Bowman's Windmill", during the hurricane of September 9, 1804. The crew were saved. The packet brig *Consolation* wrecked about four miles from the *Iona* on the same day. Two other vessels wrecked within sight of the *Iona*, but Captain Bunker was unable to learn their names. (Note One: Please see the next entry for further information on the brig *Consolation*.) (Note Two: The wind mill was located on present day Mill Island inside of Cape Bay.)

References for entry 86 (SL Code™ 1804-9-US-SC/GA-23):
"Charleston Courier", (Charleston, SC), Volume 2, #219, September 14, 1804, p. 3, c. 2, 3
"Charleston Courier", (Charleston, SC), Volume 2, #229, September 26, 1804, p. 3, c. 2
"Columbian Museum and Savannah Advertiser", (Savannah, GA), #890, September 19, 1804, p. 3, c. 4

87: The packet brig *Consolation*, Captain Webb, bound from New York to Charleston, went ashore four miles to the southward of the wind mill on Cape Romain, South Carolina, in the hurricane of September 7-9, 1804. The *Consolation's* position was also described as four miles from the schooner *Ino*. (Note One: This may have been the brig *Consolation*, 120 tons, built in 1803 at Saybrook, Connecticut, which was issued a certificate of enrollment at New York, New York, on December 8, 1803.) (Note Two: Please see the previous entry for information of the *Ino*.)

References for entry 87 (SL Code™ 1804-9-US-SC/GA-24):
"Charleston Courier", (Charleston, SC), Volume 2, #219, September 14, 1804, p. 3, c. 2, 3
"Charleston Courier", (Charleston, SC), Volume 2, #229, September 26, 1804, p. 3, c. 2
"Columbian Museum and Savannah Advertiser", (Savannah, GA), #890, September 19, 1804, p. 3, c. 4
American Flag Merchant Vessels that received Certificates of Enrollment or Registry at the Port of New York, 1789-1867, National Archives "Special List #22", (Washington, DC, 1968), Volume 1, p. 148

88: The schooner *Perseverance*, owned by Thomas Shubrick, and bound from Georgetown to Charleston, was blown ashore on South Island, South Carolina, near Georgetown. The vessel was entirely lost, but the people were saved.

Reference for entry 88 (SL Code™ 1804-9-US-SC/GA-27):
"City Gazette", (Charleston, SC), #5297, September 15, 1804, p. 2, c. 3

89: The "Charleston Courier" of September 26, 1804, reported that the works of a new vessel, "supposed to be a schooner", had been driven ashore on the beach at Little Murphy Island, six miles from Cape Romain, South Carolina. It apparently came ashore immediately after the hurricane of September 7-9, 1804.

Reference for entry 89 (SL Code™ 1804-9-US-SC/GA-31):
"Charleston Courier", (Charleston, SC), Volume 2, #229, September 26, 1804, p. 3, c. 2

90: The "Charleston Courier" of September 26, 1804, reported that a sign painted "*Liberty*, of Richmond, I. Smith, master;" had been driven ashore on the beach at Little Murphy Island, six miles from Cape Romain, South Carolina. It apparently came ashore immediately after the hurricane of September 7-9, 1804.

Reference for entry 90 (SL Code™ 1804-9-US-SC/GA-32):

Sunken Treasures of the Upper SC Coast, 1521-1865

"Charleston Courier", (Charleston, SC), Volume 2, #229, September 26, 1804, p. 3, c. 2

91: The "Charleston Courier" of September 26, 1804, reported that a small female figure-head with a book under one arm and a bunch of roses in the other had been driven ashore on the beach at Little Murphy Island, six miles from Cape Romain, South Carolina. It apparently came ashore immediately after the hurricane of September 7-9, 1804.

Reference for entry 91 (SL Code™ 1804-9-US-SC/GA-33):
"Charleston Courier", (Charleston, SC), Volume 2, #229, September 26, 1804, p. 3, c. 2

92: The "Charleston Courier" of September 26, 1804, reported that a stern marked *"Lydia*, of Newport had been driven ashore on the beach at Little Murphy Island, six miles from Cape Romain, South Carolina. It apparently came ashore immediately after the hurricane of September 7-9, 1804.

Reference for entry 92 (SL Code™ 1804-9-US-SC/GA-34):
"Charleston Courier", (Charleston, SC), Volume 2, #229, September 26, 1804, p. 3, c. 2

93: The "Charleston Courier" of September 26, 1804, reported that part of the hull of a very old vessel had been driven ashore on the beach at Little Murphy Island, six miles from Cape Romain, South Carolina. It apparently came ashore immediately after the hurricane of September 7-9, 1804.

Reference for entry 93 (SL Code™ 1804-9-US-SC/GA-35):
"Charleston Courier", (Charleston, SC), Volume 2, #229, September 26, 1804, p. 3, c. 2

94: The "Charleston Courier" of September 15, 1804, reported the following. "Two Negroes, attempting to cross Sampit river (South Carolina) in a canoe, were overset, and fortunately saved themselves by swimming. Two others, in a similar attempt, were drowned."

Reference for entry 94 (SL Code™ 1804-9-US-SC/GA-82):
"Charleston Courier," (Charleston, SC), #220, September 15, 1804, p. 2, c. 4

95: The "Charleston Courier" of November 24, 1804, reported that Captain Clark, of the sloop *Polly*, fell in with a wreck "gone to pieces" in latitude 33° North (which is the latitude of Cape Romain), on November 21, 1804. Captain Clark thought her to be one of two schooners he had seen in a gale the day before. There were boxes, casks of tallow, etc. floating around the wreck.

Reference for entry 95 (SL Code™ 1804-11-US-SC/GA-1):
"Charleston Courier", (Charleston, SC), Volume 2, #280, November 24, 1804, p. 3, c. 2

96: Captain Beckwith, of the sloop *Caroline*, reported that on November 22, 1804, he saw the deck of a vessel, "almost new, and lately painted red", on shore on Cape Romain, South Carolina, near where the brig *Consolation* was stranded. From the appearance of the hatchways, he thought it must have belonged to a vessel of "considerable burdon". (Note: The *Consolation*, reported in an earlier entry, was wrecked in the hurricane of September 7-9, 1804, and was said to have been four miles southward of the wind mill at Cape Romain.)

References for entry 96 (SL Code™ 1804-11-US-SC/GA-2):
"Charleston Courier", (Charleston, SC), Volume 2, #279, November 23, 1804, p. 3, c. 2
"Columbian Museum and Savannah Advertiser", #890, September 19, 1804, p. 3, c. 4

97: The "Charleston Courier" of November 26, 1804, reported that Captain Blythwood of the *Experiment*, from Amsterdam, fell in with a wreck, and about 150 empty Havana sugar boxes, in sixteen fathoms of water in latitude 33°26' North (which would place it off Pawley's Island, South Carolina). The boxes were marked R.C.H. and were branded M.J.V.

Reference for entry 97 (SL Code™ 1804-11-US-SC/GA-3):
"Charleston Courier", (Charleston, SC), Volume 2, #281, November 26, 1804, p. 3, c. 2

98: The "Charleston Courier" of November 26, 1804, reported that Captain Lewin of the brig *Betsy & Polly*, fell in with the wreck of a large vessel in latitude 33°30' North, 77°50' West (which would place it off Huntington Beach, South Carolina). The vessel was believed to be from Havana and had gone to pieces. A number of sugar boxes, etc. were reported floating around the wreck.

Reference for entry 98 (SL Code™ 1804-11-US-SC/GA-4):
"Charleston Courier", (Charleston, SC), Volume 2, #281, November 26, 1804, p. 3, c. 2

99: Captain Sturges of the sloop *Akerly* met with the wreck of a brig in latitude 33°50' North (which would have placed it off North Myrtle Beach, South Carolina) on February 1, 1805. The next day Captain Sturges was forced to throw half of his cargo of flour, bread and porter overboard to save his own vessel.

Reference for entry 99 (SL Code™ 1805-2-US-SC/GA-1):
"Charleston Courier", (Charleston, SC), Volume 3, #32, February 7, 1805, p. 3, c. 2

100: The "Charleston Courier" of February 19, 1805, reported that a schooner from New York was ashore near Georgetown, South Carolina.

Reference for entry 100 (SL Code™ 1805-2-US-SC/GA-1):
"Charleston Courier", (Charleston, SC), Volume 3, #42, February 19, 1805, p. 3, c. 1

101: The "Charleston Courier" of February 23, 1805, reported that Captain Hildreth saw a large new ship on shore between Cape Romain and Bull's Island, South Carolina, on February 22, 1805.

Reference for entry 101 (SL Code™ 1805-2-US-SC/GA-1):
"Charleston Courier", (Charleston, SC), Volume 3, #46, February 23, 1805, p. 3, c. 1

102: The schooner *Patience*, Captain Blunt, bound from Norfolk to Charleston, went ashore on North Island near Georgetown, South Carolina, on May 25, 1805, in a severe gale from the eastward. The vessel and cargo were entirely lost and the crew barely escaped with their lives.

Reference for entry 102 (SL Code™ 1805-5-US-SC/GA-1):
"Charleston Courier", (Charleston, SC), Volume 3, #128, May 31, 1805, p. 3, c. 3

103: The "Charleston Courier" of May 31, 1805, reported a schooner on shore near the same place as the schooner *Patience*. (Note: The schooner *Patience* was reported ashore on North Island, South Carolina, in the previous entry.)

Reference for entry 103 (SL Code™ 1805-5-US-SC/GA-2):
"Charleston Courier", (Charleston, SC), Volume 3, #128, May 31, 1805, p. 3, c. 3

104: The ship *Jenny*, Captain Jones, bound for Bordeaux to Charleston, with wine and goods, got ashore near the Georgetown Bar, South Carolina, on January 14, 1806, but was got off the next day. (Note: The first report, which appeared in the "Charleston Courier" of January 17, 1806, identified her simply as a "Guineaman.")

References for entry 104 (SL Code™ 1806-1-US-SC/GA-1):
"Charleston Courier", (Charleston, SC), Volume 4, #934, January 17, 1806, p. 3, c. 2
"Charleston Courier", (Charleston, SC), Volume 4, #935, January 18, 1806, p. 3, c. 2
"Charleston Courier", (Charleston, SC), Volume 4, #936, January 20, 1806, p. 3, c. 2

105: The schooner *Experiment*, Captain Merryhew, bound from Gonaives, loaded with coffee and cotton, was cast away on Waccamaw Beach, near Georgetown, South Carolina, on March 16, 1806.

References for entry 105 (SL Code™ 1806-3-US-SC/GA-2):
"Charleston Courier", (Charleston, SC), Volume 4, #989, March 22, 1806, p. 3, c. 2
"Charleston Courier", (Charleston, SC), Volume 4, #992, March 26, 1806, p. 3, c. 1

106: The "Charleston Courier" of April 21, 1806, reported an unidentified brig ashore at Cape Romain, South Carolina.

Reference for entry 106 (SL Code™ 1806-4-US-SC/GA-1):
"Charleston Courier", (Charleston, SC), Volume 4, #1013, April 21, 1806, p. 3, c. 2

107: The "Charleston Courier" of September 4 and 5, 1806, reported that the brig *Lucinda*, Captain Shove, of Newport, R, went ashore in the breakers between Great and Little Murfee (sic) Islands near Cape Romain, South Carolina, on August 27, 1806. The *Lucinda* was bound from Jamaica to Wilmington in ballast with specie. The vessel was lost, but the specie was saved. The *Lucinda* had two decks, two masts, and no figurehead. She measured 69'6" in length 22'7" in breadth; 11'3.5" in depth of hold; 150 30/95 tons; and drew 11' of water. She was built in 1794 at Rochester, Massachusetts, and was owned by Fish and Company. The *Lucinda* was registered at New York on January 28, 1804. She was enrolled and licensed for the coast trade at Newport, Rhode Island, on May 2, 1805, and was registered at Newport on October 10, 1805. Her October 10, 1805, register gave her owners as Robert Stevens and Jonathan Bowen (merchants) of Newport; Joseph Shove; Edward Shove and Josiah Paddock (merchants) of Freetown, Massachusetts; and her master as Joseph Shaw. That register was surrendered on October 7, 1806, with the notation "vessel lost".

Shipwrecks, Pirates & Privateers:

Lloyd's Register of Shipping for Ship Owners for 1806 showed the captain as J. Crandon.

References for entry 107 (SL Code™ 1806-8-US-SC/GA-5):
"Charleston Courier", (Charleston, SC), Volume 4, #1129, September 4, 1806, p. 3, c. 2
"Charleston Courier", (Charleston, SC), Volume 4, #1130, September 5, 1806, p. 3, c. 3
Lloyd's Register of Shipping for Ship Owners for 1806, (London), L-254
Ship's Documents of Newport, Rhode Island, 1790-1939, (W.P.A., 1941), Volume 1, p. 385

108: A large ship (variously identified as the *Sally*, Captain Willis, from Baltimore, and as the *Two Friends*, Captain Livingston, from London) went ashore on the north side of Cape Romain, South Carolina, on November 18, 1806. If was indeed the *Two Friends* it must have gotten off, as a *Two Friends*, Captain Livingston, is shown in *Lloyd's Register of Shipping for Ship Owners for 1812*, as surveyed at Leith as E-1 in 1807.

References for entry 108 (SL Code™ 1806-11-US-SC/GA-1):
"Charleston Courier", (Charleston, SC), Volume 4, #1194, November 21, 1806, p. 3, c. 2
"Charleston Courier", (Charleston, SC), Volume 4, #1195, November 22, 1806, p. 3, c. 1
Lloyd's Register of Shipping for Ship Owners for 1812, (London, England), T-563

109: Captain Reynolds of the brig *Trio* reported seeing a hemaphrodite brig ashore on Cape Romain, South Carolina, on December 26, 1806.

Reference for entry 109 (SL Code™ 1806-12-US-SC/GA-1):
"Charleston Courier", (Charleston, SC), Volume 4, #1225, December 29, 1806, p. 3, c. 2

110: The sloop *John*, Captain Pearce, bound from Little River to Charleston, was lost on Cape Romain Shoals, South Carolina, on August 4, 1807. She carried a cargo of tar and live oak. Forty-six barrels of tar were saved. The captain and crew were saved by Captain Clark of the sloop *Revival*.

Reference for entry 110 (SL Code™ 1807-8-US-SC/GA-1):
"Charleston Courier", (Charleston, SC), Volume 5, #1415, August 11, 1807, p. 3, c. 2

111: The schooner *Clotilda*, Captain Godwin (or Goodwin), bound from Charleston, South Carolina, to Richmond, foundered off Cape Romain, South Carolina, on January 19, 1808. The captain and crew were picked up the following day by the schooner *Wolf*.

References for entry 111 (SL Code™ 1808-1-US-SC/GA-2):
"Charleston Courier", (Charleston, SC), #1568, February 10, 1808, p. 3, c. 1
"Republican and Savannah Evening Ledger", (Savannah, GA), #609, February 13, 1808, p. 3, c. 3, 4

112: The sloop *Hibernia*, Captain Donnelly, of Albany, was wrecked on February 28, 1809, on the South Breakers at the entrance of Santee River, South Carolina. The vessel and cargo were lost, but the crew was saved. (Note: This may have been the sloop *Hibernia*, 98 tons, built in 1794 at Albany, New York, which was issued a certificate of enrollment at New York, New York, on July 17, 1798.)

Reference for entry 112 (SL Code™ 1809--2-US-SC/GA-2):
"Charleston Courier", (Charleston, SC), #1901, March 9, 1809, p. 3, c. 2
American Flag Merchant Vessels that received Certificates of Enrollment or Registry at the Port of New York, 1789-1867, National Archives "Special List #22", (Washington, DC, 1968), Volume 1, p. 321

113: The brig *Venus*, Captain Dinsmore, which had her rudder carried away and was much damaged in her stern while bound from New York to New Orleans, with sugar, etc., was believed to have foundered in latitude 33°31' North, longitude 78°53' West (which would have placed her in about 5 fathoms of water just below and 7 miles east of Murrels Inlet, South Carolina), during March of 1809.

References for entry 113 (SL Code™ 1809-3-US-SC/GA-1):
"Charleston Courier", (Charleston, SC), #1920, March 31, 1809, p. 3, c. 2
"Charleston Courier", (Charleston, SC), #1923, April 5, 1809, p. 3, c. 2

114: Captain Armstrong of the schooner *Lydia* saw a light ship on shore near Georgetown Bar, South Carolina, on April 14, 1809.

Reference for entry 114 (SL Code™ 1809-4-US-SC/GA-1):
"Charleston Courier", (Charleston, SC), #1932, April 15, 1809, p. 3, c. 2

115: The schooner *Industry*, Captain J. Findley, loaded with rice and cotton, and bound from Charleston to New York, was stranded on May 9, 1809, in Long Bay to the southward of Murray's (sic) Inlet, South Carolina.

Reference for entry 115 (SL Code™ 1809-5-US-SC/GA-1):
"Charleston Courier", (Charleston, SC), #1961, May 19, 1809, p. 3, c. 2

116: The sloop *Revival*, Captain Carter, bound from Charleston to Santee, was lost on Cape Romain, South Carolina, on May 22, 1809. Captain Carter and his crew were carried to Charleston in the pilot boat *William*.

Reference for entry 116 (SL Code™ 1809-5-US-SC/GA-2):
"Charleston Courier", (Charleston, SC), Volume 7, #1968, May 27, 1809, p. 3, c. 2

117: Captain Snow of the sloop *Sally* reported seeing a sloop on fire off Georgetown, South Carolina, on January 2, 1811. He described her as a small sloop with a figurehead. The "Charleston Courier" of January 4, 1811, mentioned that a sloop fitting that description was expected from Boston with a cargo of lime and speculated that it may have been her.

Reference for entry 117 (SL Code™ 1811-1-US-SC/GA-1):
"Charleston Courier", (Charleston, SC), #2470, January 4, 1811, p. 3, c. 3

118: The schooner *Lucy*, Captain Mubson Bennett, of New York, bound from Boston to St. Jago de Cuba, with 26 tons of stone ballast; 12,000 feet of lumber; some cases of furniture; a few boxes of candies; and about 70 cases and trunks "said to contain dry goods to the value of 20,000 dollars", sprang a leak and was abandoned and sunk in latitude 33°38' North (which is due east of the mouth of the Santee River), on July 6, 1811. The captain and crew were taken off by the schooner *Industry*, of Plymouth. The ship was owned by Augustus Massel, a Frenchman, belonging to Philadelphia. The "Charleston Courier" of October 14, 1811, carried a detailed account of the entire affair which they attributed to fraud committed by the captain and owners for the insurance which was carried in Boston, Philadelphia, and Norfolk.

Reference for entry 118 (SL Code™ 1811-7-US-SC/GA-1):
"Charleston Courier", (Charleston, SC), #2710, October 14, 1811, p. 3, c. 3

119: Captain Lehue of the schooner *Brothers* saw a vessel ashore on the Middle Ground of Georgetown Bar, South Carolina, on November 4, 1811. The vessel had only one mast standing. He thought she was a brig and said she had yellow sides and a high quarter deck. She was later reported to have gotten off safely and was identified as the brig *Amazon*.

References for entry 119 (SL Code™ 1811-11-US-SC/GA-1):
"Charleston Courier", (Charleston, SC), #2729, November 5, 1811, p. 3, c. 2
"Charleston Courier", (Charleston, SC), #2732, November 8, 1811, p. 3, c. 4

120: The Charleston "Times" of April 20, 1813, mentioned that Charles Pinckney, Esq., had lost 100 barrels of rice in Captain Brown's coaster, which was lost while bound from Georgetown, South Carolina, to Charleston, in 1812.

Reference for entry 120 (SL Code™ 1812-4-US-SC/GA-1):
"The Times", (Charleston, SC), #4001, April 20, 1813, p. 2, c. 2

121: A large schooner was seen on shore at Cape Romain, South Carolina, on June 20, 1812.

Reference for entry 121 (SL Code™ 1812-6-US-SC/GA-2):
"Charleston Courier," (Charleston, SC), #3001, June 23, 1812, p. 3, c. 3

122: The schooner *Judgment*, Captain Hand, was seen on shore at Cape Romain, South Carolina, on June 21, 1812. It was not expected to get off.

Reference for entry 122 (SL Code™ 1812-6-US-SC/GA-3):
"Charleston Courier", (Charleston, SC), #3002, June 23, 1812, p. 3, c. 2

123: The wreck of the brig *Matthew*, Captain Lee, was reported totally destroyed in Long Bay, South Carolina, on June 24, 1812, when she was pounded by a heavy surf. (Note: According to the report she had actually been wrecked on March 15, 1812).

Reference for entry 123 (SL Code™ 1812-6-US-SC/GA-4):
"Charleston Courier," (Charleston, SC), #3003, June 24, 1812, p. 1, c. 4

124: A canal boat, having upon deck seventy-four bales of cotton, owned by Mr. Joel Adams, took fire in the Santee River, South Carolina, on January 4, 1813, and fifty bales of cotton were destroyed before the fire could be put out. It was said to have been the second such fire within a few weeks.

Reference for entry 124 (SL Code™ 1813-1-US-SC/GA-1):
"Charleston Courier", (Charleston, SC), Vol. 11, #4070, January 12, 1813, p. 3, c. 1

125: On December 30, 1812, Theodosia Burr Alston, beautiful 29 year old daughter of Aaron Burr (former vice president of the United States), and wife of Joseph Alston (then governor of South Carolina), boarded the schooner *Patriot*, Captain Overstocks, bound from Georgetown, South Carolina, for New York. The actual fate of the schooner, Theodosia and her fellow passengers is not known, and it is included in this work because of its Georgetown connection. A South Carolina legend has it, that the schooner was taken by pirates and that Theodosia, who refused the advances of the pirate captain, was made to walk the plank before it was scuttled. However, North Carolina folklore says that the schooner (described as an ex-pilot boat and ex-privateer) drifted ashore two miles below Nags Head, North Carolina, in January of 1813, with no one aboard. Supposedly, all sails were set, the rudder lashed, and the craft in good condition but entirely deserted. In the cabin were several fancy silk dresses, a vase of beautiful waxed flowers, and an oil portrait of a young woman. Some believe the subject was Theodosia. In 1833, the Mobile *Register* reported that a man "residing in one of the interior counties of this State" made a deathbed confession that he had participated in the capture of the *Patriot*, the murder of all those on board, and the scuttling of the vessel "for the sake of her plate and effects". On March 22, 1842, an article was published in the *Charleston Courier* which told of three sailors, one in Maine, one in Mobile, and one at Matagorda, who had, in separate confessions on their respective deathbeds, stated that they had been part of the *Patriot's* crew. They each confessed that they had participated in a mutiny and piracy which resulted in the murder of Theodosia and the other passengers. They had stolen the *Patriot's* cargo and a "large amount of money and plate". (Note One: James Rogers in his book *Theodosia and other Pee Dee Sketches* wrote that the *Patriot* had previously been a privateer, but that her privateer crew had been discharged, her guns hidden under her deck, and the spoils she had captured concealed beneath the hatches. Rogers went on to write that some believed her guns had shifted causing her to lay on her side and sink. However, the idea that her guns would have been removed or stowed away doesn't seem to make since, as the entire United States Atlantic coast was embroiled in the War of 1812. Any armament the *Patriot* may have carried would have been mounted and ready to use for her defense against the British.) (Note Two: This entry also appears under *SL Code™* 1813-1-US-NC-5 in the North Carolina segment of *Spence's List™*.)

References for entry 125 (SL Code™ 1813-1-US-SC/GAx-1):
"Charleston Courier", (Charleston, SC), #12037, March, 22, 1842, p. 2, c. 4
Dictionary of American Biography, edited by Johnson and Malone, (New York, 1930), Volume 2, p. 323
Graveyard of the Atlantic: Shipwrecks of the North Carolina Coast, by David Stick, (UNC Press, Chapel Hill, NC, 1952, pp. 5-7, 244
Theodosia and Other Pee Dee Sketches, by James A. Rogers, pp. 3-5
Shipwrecks of the Western Hemisphere: 1492-1825, by Robert F. Marx, (World Publishing Company, New York, 1971), p. 177, #283
Pawley's Island, A Living Legend, by Prevost and Wilder, (Columbia, SC, 1972), pp. 43-46
Shipwrecks on the Chesapeake: Maritime Disasters on Chesapeake Bay and its Tributaries, 1608-1978, by Donald G. Shomette, (Tidewater Publishers, Centreville, Maryland, 1982), p. 248

Shipwrecks, Pirates & Privateers:

Shipwrecks of South Carolina and Georgia, 1520-1865, by E. Lee Spence, (Sullivan's Island, SC, 1984), Volume 1, pp. 25, 365, 366, entry 1813-A

126: The schooner *Boston*, Captain Reed, bound from Kennebuck to Charleston, with a cargo of lumber, went ashore on Cape Romain, South Carolina, on February 5, 1813, and got off with the loss of her rudder. She afterwards drifted upon the Georgetown Bar, South Carolina, where it was considered doubtful that she or her cargo could be saved.

Reference for entry 126 (SL Code™ 1813-2-US-SC/GA-1):
"Charleston Courier", (Charleston, SC), #4094, February 10, 1813, p. 3, c. 2

127: The brig *Tartar*, a prize to the American privateer ship *General Armstrong*, was chased ashore on the shoals of North Island near Georgetown, South Carolina, by a British brig of war in April, 1813, and by April 16 it had already gone to pieces. The *Tartar* had been taken by the *General Armstrong* (of New York, 18 guns, 115 men, 270 tons, Captain Guy R. Champlin), while on a voyage from St. Barts and carried a cargo of 160 hogsheads of rum. Some of that cargo reportedly drifted ashore where it was saved. The rest was taken from the wreck by the *Orion*, Captain Weaver.

References for entry 127 (SL Code™ 1813-4-US-SC/GA-2):
"Charleston Courier", (Charleston, SC), #5061, April 19, 1813, p. 3, c. 2
"Charleston Courier", (Charleston, SC), #5064, April 23, 1813, p. 3, c. 3
"The Times", (Charleston, SC), Volume 25, #4001, April 20, 1813, p. 3, c. 2
"The Times", (Charleston, SC), Volume 25, #4003, April 22, 1813, p. 3, c. 3
The Weekly Register, edited by H. Niles, (1813), Volume 4, p. 133, c. 2; p. 151, c. 2; p. 152, c. 1
"Petition of Frederick Jenkins to James Monroe", dated New York, January 22, 1813, contained in "Letters from Collectors of Customs", (bound manuscript), NARS, RG 45, entry 388
A full and correct account of the chief naval occurrences of the late war between Great Britain and the United States of America • • •, by William James, (London, 1817), pp. 484, 485

128: The "Charleston Courier" of May 17, 1813, reported that a "large smoke" had been seen off Cape Romain, South Carolina, and that it was believed to have been from a vessel burning.

Reference for entry 128 (SL Code™ 1813-5-US-SC/GA-4):
"Charleston Courier", (Charleston, SC), ##5085, May 17, 1813, p. 3, c. 3

129: A schooner was reported on shore ten or twelve miles from the Georgetown, South Carolina, light on May 28, 1813. The schooner had her foremast cut away.

Reference for entry 129 (SL Code™ 1813-5-US-SC/GA-6):
"Charleston Courier", (Charleston, SC), #4195, May 29, 1813, p. 3, c. 3

130: Two schooners were driven ashore at Georgetown, South Carolina, during the hurricane of August 30, 1813, and it was expected that there would be some difficulty in getting them off.

Reference for entry 130 (SL Code™ 1813-8-US-SC/GA-35):
"Charleston Courier", (Charleston, SC), #4275, September 2, 1813, p. 3, c. 1

131: A sloop was driven ashore at Georgetown, South Carolina, during the hurricane of August 30, 1813, and it was expected that there would be some difficulty in getting it off.

Reference for entry 131 (SL Code™ 1813-8-US-SC/GA-36):
"Charleston Courier", (Charleston, SC), #4275, September 2, 1813, p. 3, c. 1

132: The hull of a brig was driven ashore at Georgetown, South Carolina, during the hurricane of August 30, 1813, and it was expected that there would be some difficulty in getting it off.

Reference for entry 132 (SL Code™ 1813-8-US-SC/GA-37):
"Charleston Courier", (Charleston, SC), #4275, September 2, 1813, p. 3, c. 1

133: An armed barge commanded by Captain Lord, which lay between North and South Islands, near Georgetown, South Carolina, was driven ashore on South Island, South Carolina, during the hurricane of August 30, 1813. It was thought that she would be got off.

Reference for entry 133 (SL Code™ 1813-8-US-SC/GA-38):
"City Gazette and Commercial Daily Advertiser", (Charleston, SC), #10777, September 2, 1813, p. 3, c. 1

134: The schooner *Inca*, Captain Griggs, from La Teste, France, was chased ashore on November 2, 1813, by the British brigs of war *Dotterell* and *Recruit*. The *Inca's* position was described as on Raccoon Key near the Wind Mill on Cape Romain, South Carolina. She carried a cargo of about 80 bales of silks, muslins, etc.; over 100 casks and several boxes of wine; 17 pipes of brandy; and a quantity of oil, cream of tartar, virdigris, etc. The most valuable part of her cargo was taken out of her by the British who captured 22 men and scuttled her. The schooner was armed with six guns and manned by 32 men.

References for entry 134 (SL Code™ 1813-11-US-SC/GA-2):
"Charleston Courier", (Charleston, SC), #4329, November 5, 1813, p. 3, c. 1
"Charleston Courier", (Charleston, SC), #4330, November 6, 1813, p. 3, c. 2
"Charleston Courier", (Charleston, SC), #4331, November 8, 1813, p. 3, c. 2
"Charleston Courier", (Charleston, SC), #4332, November 9, 1813, p. 3, c. 2
"Charleston Courier", (Charleston, SC), #4333, November 10, 1813, p. 3, c. 1
"Charleston Courier", (Charleston, SC), #4336, November 13, 1813, p. 3, c. 2
"Charleston Courier", (Charleston, SC), #4337, November 15, 1813, p. 3, c. 2
"Charleston Courier", (Charleston, SC), #4339, November 17, 1813, p. 3, c. 2

135: The three masted schooner *Ploughboy*, Captain Benjamin, bound from Georgetown with a valuable cargo, was reported ashore inside of Cape Romain, South Carolina, on November 29, 1813. (Note: She may have been got off as a similarly described vessel arrived a Charleston a few days later.)

References for entry 135 (SL Code™ 1813-11-US-SC/GA-6):
"Charleston Courier", (Charleston, SC), #4351, December 1, 1813, p. 3, c. 3
"Charleston Courier", (Charleston, SC), #4353, December 3, 1813, p. 3, c. 2

136: Captain Pattridge of the schooner *Mohawk* saw a small schooner ashore at the point of North Island, South Carolina, around December 22, 1813. Captain Pattridge believed the schooner to be from North Carolina.

Reference for entry 136 (SL Code™ 1813-12-US-SC/GA-2):
"Charleston Courier," (Charleston, SC), #4370, December 23, 1813, p. 3, c. 2

137: The schooner *Hazard*, Captain Heywood, bound from Elizabeth City, North Carolina, to Charleston, South Carolina, with flour and tobacco, was run ashore on a reef at North Inlet, near the

Georgetown, South Carolina, light-house on December 21 (or 23), 1813. The vessel and most of her cargo were expected to be lost. She was also mentioned as being one day out of Wilmington, North Carolina.

References for entry 137 (SL Code™ 1813-12-US-SC/GA-3):
"Charleston Courier", (Charleston, SC), #4373, December 28, 1813, p. 3, c. 3
"Charleston Courier", (Charleston, SC), #4380, January 6, 1814, p. 3, c. 1

138: The "Charleston Courier" of January 24, 1814, reported that a British schooner went ashore on the beach near the Georgetown Bar, South Carolina, on January 23, 1814. The paper said the schooner was lost through the treachery of one of the pilots. It also said that the schooner had been bound from Surinam, with a cargo of coffee, sugar and rum, when she had been taken as a prize by the privateer *Caroline* of Baltimore. (Note: This may have been the schooner *Jasper* mentioned in Niles' *Weekly Register*. The *Jasper* was reported as having been taken as a prize by the *Caroline* of Baltimore, while bound on a voyage from Surinam with coffee, sugar and rum, and as having been sent into Georgetown, South Carolina. *The Weekly Register* stated that the *Jasper* "would have been wrecked and lost on the bar, but for the meritorious exertions of Lieut. Mork of the U.S. Navy.").

References for entry 138 (SL Code™ 1814-1-US-SC/GA-1):
"Charleston Courier", (Charleston, SC), #4395, January 24, 1814, p. 3, c. 1
"Charleston Courier", (Charleston, SC), #4396, January 25, 1814, p. 3, c. 2
The Weekly Register, edited by H. Niles, (1813-1814), Volume 5, p. 414, c. 1, #765

139: The schooner *Friends*, Captain Danby, bound from Charleston to Elizabeth City, North Carolina, with cotton and molasses, was chased into Morrels (sic) Inlet, near Georgetown, South Carolina, by a British brig on May 28, 1814, and burnt. Her crew made it safely to shore.

References for entry 139 (SL Code™ 1814-5-US-SC/GA-2):
"Charleston Courier", (Charleston, SC), #4506, June 3, 1814, p. 3, c. 1
"Charleston Courier", (Charleston, SC), #4511, June 9, 1814, p. 3, c. 2

140: The "Charleston Courier" of November 5, 1814, reported "another prize on shore at Debordeau's Island, North Inlet (South Carolina)" which was said "to be loaded with oil." Subsequently she was identified as the British brig *Roper* which had been captured by the privateer *Pulaski* of Baltimore, while on a voyage from Malta to London with a cargo of sweet oil. Her cargo was expected to be mostly saved.

References for entry 140 (SL Code™ 1814-11-US-SC/GA-2):
"Charleston Courier," (Charleston, SC), November 5, 1814, p. 2, c. 2
"Charleston Courier," (Charleston, SC), November 7, 1814, p. 2, c. 2

141: A small vessel was captured and burnt by the British in Alligator Creek near Cape Romain, South Carolina, on January 6, 1815.

Reference for entry 141 (SL Code™ 1815-1-US-SC/GA-1):
"Charleston Courier", (Charleston, SC), February 10, 1815, p. 2, c. 1

142: The "Charleston Courier" of January 20, 1815, reported a schooner bound from Wilmington, North Carolina, to Georgetown, South Carolina, as ashore on Debordeau's (sic) Island, near Georgetown, South Carolina.

Reference for entry 142 (SL Code™ 1815-1-US-SC/GA-6):
"Charleston Courier", (Charleston, SC), January 20, 1815, p. 2, c. 2

143: Several coasting vessels were reported as captured and burned by some British barges in the mouth of the Santee River, South Carolina, during the first week in February, 1815.

References for entry 143 (SL Code™ 1815-2-US-SC/GA-1):
"Charleston Courier", (Charleston, SC), February 6, 1815, p. 2, c. 3
"Charleston Courier", (Charleston, SC), February 7, 1815, p. 2, c. 1

144: The "Charleston Courier" of February 10, 1815, reported that two vessels had been burnt by the British on February 7, 1815. (Note: Although the location was not mentioned in the paper, it most likely was in the immediate vicinity of Cape Romain, South Carolina.)

Reference for entry 144 (SL Code™ 1815-2-US-SC/GA-2):
"Charleston Courier", (Charleston, SC), February 10, 1815, p. 2, c. 1

145: The schooner *Brant* (or *Brent*), which had been captured by the British frigate *Severn*, 50 guns, on her passage from Wilmington, North Carolina, to Charleston, South Carolina, and had been manned as a tender to *H.M.S. Severn*, was run aground on a shoal near Cape Romain, South Carolina, where she was recaptured by the Americans under Commodore Dent on February 11, 1815. Unfortunately, she went to pieces in a gale that same night before she could be got off. Two midshipmen and thirteen men were captured by the Americans who had sailed in a flotilla of galleys and barges from Charleston on February 10, 1815.

References for entry 145 (SL Code™ 1815-2-US-SC/GA-3):
"Charleston Courier", (Charleston, SC), February 16, 1815, p. 2, c. 1
"Charleston Courier", (Charleston, SC), February 17, 1815, p. 2, c. 2
The Weekly Register, edited by H. Niles, Volume 8, (1815), p. 13 (shown as p. 429), c. 2
Ships of the Royal Navy: An Historical Index, by J.J. Colledge, (New York, 1969), Volume 1, p. 502

146: The schooner *Favorite*, Captain Baker, of and from Boston, bound to Charleston, South Carolina, was driven ashore on Cape Romain, South Carolina, in an easterly gale and bilged on April 9, 1815. Her crew and part of her cargo were saved.

References for entry 146 (SL Code™ 1815-4-US-SC/GA-1):
"Charleston Courier", (Charleston, SC), Volume 13, #4767, April 15, 1815, p. 2, c. 2
"Charleston Courier", (Charleston, SC), Volume 13, #4778, April 28, 1815, p. 2, c. 3

147: Captain Tarbox of the schooner *David Porter* reported seeing a schooner ashore on the Santee Breakers (South Carolina) on April 12, 1815.

Reference for entry 147 (SL Code™ 1815-4-US-SC/GA-4):
"Charleston Courier", (Charleston, SC), #4768, April 17, 1815, p. 2, c. 2

148: The schooner *Planter's Friend*, Captain Howren, in working down the "Georgetown River", South Carolina, accidentally ran afoul of the schooner *Nonsuch* on May 15, 1815, and caused the *Nonsuch* to fill and sink. The *Nonsuch* carried a cargo of rough rice. The crew took to their boat and landed at Cat Island, South Carolina.

Reference for entry 148 (SL Code™ 1815-5-US-SC/GA-1):
"Charleston Courier", (Charleston, SC), #4793, May 16, 1815, p. 2, c. 4

149: The British brig *Spring*, Captain Job Colcock Smith, bound from Liverpool (or London) to Wilmington, North Carolina, was totally lost on the Raccoon Keys, near Cape Romain, South Carolina, on August 31, 1815. The crew reached Charleston having saved nothing but their clothing. The *Spring* carried a valuable cargo of salt, crates, hardware, porter, bale goods, etc. She was 138 (or 145) tons and drew 12'. She was built in Stockton in 1801. The *Spring* was single decked with beams, was sheathed with copper over boards, and was part copper bolted. She was classed E-1 by "Lloyd's" and was owned by S. Holland. The brig had undergone major repairs, and had a new main deck put on in 1813. The *Spring* was armed with four 6-pounder cannons and two 9-pounder carronades.

References for entry 149 (SL Code™ 1815-8-US-SC/GA-1):
"Charleston Courier", (Charleston, SC), #4883, September 1, 1815, p. 3, c. 3
"Charleston Courier", (Charleston, SC), #4885, September 4, 1815, p. 3, c. 2
"City Gazette and Commercial Daily Advertiser", (Charleston, SC), #11384, September 4, 1815, p. 2, c. 3
"The Times", (London, England), #9657, October 20, 1815, p. 3, c. 5
Lloyd's List, (London, England), #5015, October 20, 1815, p. 1, c. 3
Lloyd's Register of Shipping for Ship Owners for 1815, (London, England), S-747
Lloyd's Register of Shipping for Underwriters for 1815, (London, England), S-747
Shipwrecks of the Western Hemisphere 1492-1825, by Robert F. Marx, (World Publishing Company, New York, 1971), p. 183, entry #334

150: The American brig *Sterling*, of Rhode Island, Captain George Laughton, 75 days from Liverpool, bound to Savannah, Georgia, with dry goods, 8000 bushels of salt, iron, crockery, etc., was run ashore about four miles to the northward of Murrell's Inlet, South Carolina, on October 31, 1815. Her location was also given as "on Waccamaw". The brig and her cargo of salt were lost, but the remainder of her cargo was expected to be saved.

References for entry 150 (SL Code™ 1815-10-US-SC/GA-1):
"Charleston Courier", (Charleston, SC), #4938, November 6, 1815, p. 2, c. 3, 4
"City Gazette and Commercial Daily Advertiser", (Charleston, SC), #11440, November 8, 1815, p. 3, c. 1

151: The American ship *Alexander*, Captain S. (or J.) Hunter, bound from Wilmington to Antiqua, with a cargo of rice, naval stores and ranging timber, ran ashore near North Inlet, South Carolina, sixteen miles from Georgetown, South Carolina, on November 12, 1815. She had 9' of water in her hold when she went ashore. The *Alexander* had been built in 1800, had been put in good repair in 1811, and was classed E-1 by Lloyd's in 1814. She was single decked with beams and was armed with two 6-pounder carronades. She was 189 tons and drew 12' of water. She was owned by Goodwin.

References for entry 151 (SL Code™ 1815-11-US-SC/GA-2):
"Charleston Courier", (Charleston, SC), #4947, November 17, 1815, p. 2, c. 3
Lloyd's Register of Shipping for Ship Owners for 1815, (London, England), A-481
Lloyd's Register of Shipping for Underwriters for 1815, (London, England), A-450

152: An unidentified ship was seen ashore on Cape Romain, South Carolina, on December 7, 1815.

Reference for entry 152 (SL Code™ 1815-12-US-SC/GA-2):
"City Gazette and Commercial Daily Advertiser", (Charleston, SC), #11466, December 9, 1815, p. 2, c. 3

153: The small schooner *Elizabeth*, Captain Mansard, bound from Elizabeth City, North Carolina, with a cargo of staves, peas and tow cloth, was driven ashore at Cape Romain, South Carolina, during the blow of December 29, 1815.

References for entry 153 (SL Code™ 1815-12-US-SC/GA-9):
"Charleston Courier", (Charleston, SC), #4984, January 1, 1816, p. 2, c. 3
"Charleston Courier", (Charleston, SC), #4985, January 3, 1816, p. 2, c. 2

154: A "new ship" was reported ashore on Cape Romain, South Carolina, on January 16, 1816, but the editor of the "Charleston Courier" of January 17, 1816, was unable to trace the report and doubted its accuracy.

Reference for entry 154 (SL Code™ 1816-1-US-SC/GA-2):
"Charleston Courier", (Charleston, SC), #4997, January 17, 1816, p. 2, c. 2

155: A sloop, bound from Georgetown to Charleston, South Carolina, was reported ashore near Georgetown, South Carolina, on January 25, 1816, by Captain Terry of the schooner *Resolution*.

Reference for entry 155 (SL Code™ 1816-1-US-SC/GA-5):
"Charleston Courier", (Charleston, SC), #5005, January 26, 1816, p. 2, c. 4

156: The schooner *John Gallup*, Captain Auten, and the schooner *Little John*, Captain Chaires, arrived in Charleston on February 5, 1816, with the sails, rigging, etc., saved from the wreck of the schooner *Young Sea Horse*, of New York, Captain Reeves. Captain Reeves' schooner was cast away on Cape Romain, South Carolina, in a dead calm on January 30, 1816, while on her passage from Charleston to Georgetown. The *Young Sea Horse*, 75 tons, was built in 1805 at Killingsworth, Connecticut. She was issued a certificate of registry at New York on April 5, 1808.

References for entry 156 (SL Code™ 1816-1-US-SC/GA-6):
"Charleston Courier", (Charleston, SC), #5015, February 7, 1816, p. 2, c. 3
American Flag Merchant Vessels that received Certificates of Enrollment or Registry at the Port of New York, 1789-1867, National Archives "Special List #22", (Washington, DC, 1968), Volume 2, p. 746

157: Captain Lahue of the schooner *Patsey*, reported seeing the upper deck and hatchway of a brig or a ship a little to the southward of Cape Romain, South Carolina, during the second week of February, 1816.

Reference for entry 157 (SL Code™ 1816-2-US-SC/GA-2):
"Charleston Courier", (Charleston, SC), #5023, February 16, 1816, p. 2, c. 3

Shipwrecks, Pirates & Privateers:

158: The brig *Almira*, of Duxbury, Massachusetts, Captain Delano, 110 days from Cadiz via Martinique, with a cargo of salt, raisins and wine, was stranded on the Georgetown, South Carolina, bar on March 1, 1816, and was expected to be lost, but was afterwards got off by throwing two thousand bushels of salt overboard.

References for entry 158 (SL Code™ 1816-3-US-SC/GA-1):
"Charleston Courier", (Charleston, SC), #5037, March 4, 1816, p. 2, c. 2
"Charleston Courier", (Charleston, SC), #5039, March 6, 1816, p. 2, c. 3

159: Captain Lahue of the schooner *Two Brothers* saw a brig ashore near the Georgetown, South Carolina, light-house on March 12, 1816. She was believed to in-bound.

Reference for entry 159 (SL Code™ 1816-3-US-SC/GA-9):
"Charleston Courier", (Charleston, SC), #5044, March 12, 1816, p. 2, c. 2

160: The brig *Post Von Rigs* (or *Post Von Riga*), Captain Crosby, sixty days from Belfast, bound to Charleston, with an assorted cargo of dry goods, glassware, etc., went ashore on the shoals of Cape Romain, South Carolina, on March 21, 1816. At one point the waves were breaking entirely over her, but she got off by throwing overboard part of her cargo of slate and potatoes. The brig was two hundred tons and drew thirteen feet of water.

References for entry 160 (SL Code™ 1816-3-US-SC/GA-11):
"Charleston Courier", (Charleston, SC), #5053, March 22, 1816, p. 2, c. 3
"Charleston Courier", (Charleston, SC), #5054, March 23, 1816, p. 2, c. 3

161: Captain Wiggins of the sloop *Decatur*, reported a coasting schooner ashore on Cape Romain, South Carolina, on April 2, 1816. The coasting schooner had run ashore in a fog and Captain Wiggins doubted that she would be got off.

Reference for entry 161 (SL Code™ 1816-4-US-SC/GA-2):
"Charleston Courier", (Charleston, SC), #5063, April 3, 1816, p. 2, c. 3

162: Captain Lahue of the schooner *Two Brothers*, saw a sloop ashore on the outer shoal of the South Breaker of Cape Romain, South Carolina, on April 2, 1816.

Reference for entry 162 (SL Code™ 1816-4-US-SC/GA-3):
"Charleston Courier", (Charleston, SC), #5064, April 4, 1816, p. 2, c. 3

163: Captain Gray of the schooner *Balyporeen*, saw a sloop on shore to the westward of Cape Romain, South Carolina, on April 2, 1816.

Reference for entry 163 (SL Code™ 1816-4-US-SC/GA-4):
"Charleston Courier", (Charleston, SC), #5067, April 8, 1816, p. 2, c. 3

164: The British brig *Sunbury*, Captain Cray, bound from Georgetown to Liverpool, with a cargo of naval stores, etc., got ashore on Georgetown Bar, South Carolina, on April 3, 1816, but was afterwards got off.

References for entry 164 (SL Code™ 1816-4-US-SC/GA-5):
"Charleston Courier", (Charleston, SC), #5065, April 5, 1816, p. 2, c. 3
"Charleston Courier", (Charleston, SC), #5067, April 8, 1816, p. 2, c. 3

165: Captain Cook of the schooner *Lana-Maria*, saw a large ship ashore on the north side of Cape Romain, South Carolina, on July 19, 1816. It may have been the ship *Tronhiem*, Captain Richelieu, which went ashore in that area on the 18th but afterwards was got off safely.

References for entry 165 (SL Code™ 1816-7-US-SC/GA-1):
"Charleston Courier", (Charleston, SC), #5154, July 20, 1816, p. 2, c. 4
"Charleston Courier", (Charleston, SC), #5155, July 22, 1816, p. 2, c. 4

166: The Spanish schooner *Diamante* (or *Diamond*), Captain Cristobat Soler, fitted out at Havana for a voyage to the coast of Africa, was wrecked on the outer shoal of Cape Romain, South Carolina, on August 30, 1816, with the loss of twenty lives. She was sunk in three fathoms of water, five miles from land. Her guns were thrown overboard when she first ran aground. Captain Soler saved himself on a raft, but a considerable amount of money, which he had taken from the wreck was lost when his raft washed out to sea and sank. The *Diamante* had left Havana about July 28, 1816, with a crew of fifty, including officers. (Note: In 1978, E. Lee Spence discovered a wreck, just inside of the outer shoal of Cape Romain, which Spence tentatively identified as that of the *Diamante*. Spence is currently working an area around this wreck under an order from the United States Federal District Court at Charleston, South Carolina.) (Note Two: Please see Chapter Three of this book for extensive additional information on this shipwreck.)

References for entry 166 (SL Code™ 1816-8-US-SC/GA-2):
"Charleston Courier", (Charleston, SC), #5190, August 31, 1816, p. 2, c. 3; p. 3, c. 1
"Charleston Courier", (Charleston, SC), #5191, September 2, 1816, p. 3, c. 2
"Charleston Courier", (Charleston, SC), #5197, September 9, 1816, p. 2, c. 2
"The Times", (Charleston, SC), Vol. 33, #5030, Saturday, August 31, 1816, p. 3, c. 1, . 2
"The Times", (Charleston, SC), Vol. 33, #5031, Monday, September 2, 1816, p. 3, c. 1, c. 3 (legal notice), c. 4 (advertisement)
Civil Action Cases #2:88-0154-1J and #2:88-0237-1J, (United States District Court for the District of South Carolina, Charleston Division, in Admiralty)
ShipWrecks™ (magazine, Shipwreck Press, Inc. 1990), "How To Protect Your Wreck Through Secrecy" by E. Lee Spence, Vol. 1, #2, pp. 38, 39
ShipWrecks™ (magazine, Shipwreck Press, Inc. 1990), "Pirate Wreck (Shipwrecked at Cape Romain)" by E. Lee Spence, Vol. 1, #2, pp. 59-66
Treasure Diver (magazine, Jess Publishing, 1990), "Piracy at Cape Romain", by E. Lee Spence, Vol. 2, #2, pp. 34-39, 72-73

167: Mr. Samuel Gillespie's flat, bound from Chatham, Georgia, with 1200 bushels of corn, was driven ashore near the fort at Georgetown, South Carolina, on September 19, 1816, and was expected to be a total loss.

Reference for entry 167 (SL Code™ 1816-9-US-SC/GA-2):
"Charleston Courier", (Charleston, SC), #5215, September 30, 1816, p. 2, c. 5

168: The ship *Telegraph*, Captain Fanning, passed a brig off Cape Romain, South Carolina, on January 1, 1816, which appeared to be ashore. This may have been the same brig reported by Captain Weeks of the schooner *Eliza*, as being ashore on the same date with American colors flying and "in a bad situation". That brig was later

Shipwrecks, Pirates & Privateers:

identified as the brig *Hope*, Captain Andrews, which arrived safely at Charleston, South Carolina, on January 3, 1817. Captain Andrews had mistaken the windmill on Mill Island near Cape Romain for the light-house at Charleston. He reported a light displayed at or near the windmill, but whether the light was displayed intentionally to decoy ships to their doom was not stated.

References for entry 168 (SL Code™ 1817-1-US-SC/GA-1):
"Charleston Courier", (Charleston, SC), #5294, January 3, 1817, p. 2, c. 3
"Charleston Courier", (Charleston, SC), #5295, January 4, 1817, p. 2, c. 5

169: The "Charleston Courier" reported that the British brig *Nancy*, of Liverpool, Captain James Livingston, fourteen days from Barbadoes (sic) to Georgetown, South Carolina, in ballast and specie, struck and went to pieces in attempting to go into Georgetown on March 12, 1817. The Captain, the 2nd mate, a seaman, and the cook, were the only persons to reach shore after being in the water for five hours. They saved themselves by swimming from buoy to buoy. The remainder of the crew, fourteen in number, drowned. The captain died two hours after reaching shore. William Thomas - the seaman, and George Rogers the cook, were taken to the Marine Hospital in a deplorable state. The 2nd mate's name was given as Nathaniel Ashton. (Note: Despite the seeming wealth of details provided by the "Charleston Courier" the report was questioned by the editor and later attributed by him to be pure fabrication.)

References for entry 169 (SL Code™ 1817-3-US-SC/GA-2):
"Charleston Courier", (Charleston, SC), #5357, March 18, 1817, p. 2, c. 3
"Charleston Courier", (Charleston, SC), #5358, March 19, 1817, p. 2, c. 3
"Charleston Courier", (Charleston, SC), #5360, March 21, 1817, p. 2, c. 3

170: The sloop *William*, Captain Jenkins, bound from Charleston, South Carolina, to Santee, South Carolina, got ashore on the bar of Cape Romain, South Carolina, bilged and filled in late January or early February, 1818. Being light, the *William* did not sink. She was got off and was towed into the Santee River by the sloop *Rambler*, Captain Burges.

Reference for entry 170 (SL Code™ 1818-2-US-SC/GA-1):
"Charleston Courier", (Charleston, SC), #5637, February 9, 1818, p. 2, c. 4

171: Captain Jones of the ship *Bramin* passed the wreck of a ship off Cape Romain, South Carolina, on March 15, 1820. From the dimensions of her deck, hatchway, and breadth of beam, Captain Jones estimated her at 300 tons. The wreck was covered with large barnacles and long grass. From all appearances she had been wrecked at least five or six months earlier.

References for entry 171 (SL Code™ 1820-3-US-SC/GA-3):
"Charleston Courier", (Charleston, SC), #6285, March 20, 1820, p. 2, c. 4
"Charleston Courier", (Charleston, SC), #6286, March 21, 1820, p. 2, c. 4
"Columbia Museum and Savannah Daily Gazette", (Savannah, GA), Volume 4, #38, p. 3, c. 1

172: The French brig *Venus*, Captain Deslandes, bound from Le Havre, France, mistook the windmill on Cape Romain, South Carolina, for the light-house at Charleston, South Carolina, and struck on Cape Romain on March 18, 1820. She was got off with the loss of two anchors.

Reference for entry 172 (SL Code™ 1820-3-US-SC/GA-4):
"Columbian Museum and Savannah Daily Gazette", (Savannah, GA), Volume 4, #38, March 22, 1820, p. 2, c. 4; p. 3, c. 1

173: Captain Wood of the sloop *Windham*, saw a black brig, with yellow sides and one tier of ports, and a Danish jack flying, ashore off the north end of Cape Romain, South Carolina, on March 19, 1820.

Reference for entry 173 (SL Code™ 1820-3-US-SC/GA-5):
"Charleston Courier", (Charleston, SC), #6285, March 20, 1820, p. 2, c. 4

174: Captain Childs of the sloop *Little Sarah* saw the wreck of a sharp built vessel, believed to be a brig of less than one hundred tons burden, with both masts gone, ashore upon the shoals of Cape Romain, South Carolina, on September 25, 1820. Several boats were seen about the wreck, apparently engaged in taking things to shore. The people were later reported camped on the beach.

References for entry 174 (SL Code™ 1820-9-US-SC/GA-1):
"Charleston Courier", (Charleston, SC), #6448, September 27, 1820, p. 2, c. 5
"Charleston Courier", (Charleston, SC), #6449, September 28, 1820, p. 2, c. 4
"Charleston Courier", (Charleston, SC), #6450, September 29, 1820, p. 2, c. 4

175: The sloop *Young Romp*, Captain Hobart, bound from Georgetown, South Carolina, with a cargo of rough rice, in coming in on November 16, 1820, missed stays and went ashore on the Middle Ground of Charleston Bar, South Carolina. After beating over the shoal, the sloop drifted on Cumming's Point on Morris Island, South Carolina, where she bilged and sank. Both the vessel and her cargo were lost. The sloop's rigging and spars were saved. (Note One: The cargo belonged to Colonel John A. Alston of Georgetown, South Carolina, which is why this vessel has been included in this list.) (Note Two: This may have been the sloop *Young Romp*, 63 tons, built in 1815 at Southold, New York, which was issued a certificate of enrollment at New York, New York, on October 3, 1815.) (Note Three: Despite the report that the sloop was lost, the "Charleston Courier" of December 25, 1820, shows Captain Hobart as sailing between Georgetown and Charleston a sloop by the name of *Young Romp*. Whether this means the sloop was saved or that Captain Hobart simply acquired another sloop and used his former sloop's name, like a trade-mark, has not been determined.)

References for entry 175 (SL Code™ 1820-11-US-SC/GA-1):
"Charleston Courier", (Charleston, SC), #6492, November 18, 1820, p. 2, c. 4
"Charleston Courier", (Charleston, SC), #6528, December 25, 1820, p. 2, c. 4
American Flag Merchant Vessels that received Certificates of Enrollment or Registry at the Port of New York, 1789-1867, National Archives "Special List #22", (Washington, DC, 1968), Volume 2, p. 746

176: The schooner *Monroe*, Captain Springer, of Trenton, Maine, was upset off South Island Point, South Carolina, within the Georgetown Bar, on February 13, 1821. The crew was carried to Georgetown, South Carolina, by the schooner *Jane-Maria*, Captain Williams.

Reference for entry 176 (SL Code™ 1821-2-US-SC/GA-3):
"Charleston Courier", (Charleston, SC), #6569, February 19, 1821, p. 2, c. 5

177: Wiggin's boat, bound from Marion, South Carolina, to Georgetown, South Carolina, with 120 bales of cotton, was sunk in a heavy blow "some distance" from Georgetown on February 20, 1822. Less than a week later she was raised and her cargo saved.

Reference for entry 177 (SL Code™ 1822-2-US-SC/GA-1):
"The Charleston Mercury and Morning Advertiser", (Charleston, SC), Volume 1, #50, February 28, 1822, p. 3, c. 1

178: On March 15, 1822, the sloop *William & Ann*, Captain Sears, with a cargo of corn and bacon, having left Norfolk, Virginia, on March 8 and having sprung a leak in a gale on March 14, was "obliged to" run ashore at Cape Romain, South Carolina, not being able to keep free with both pumps and the crew worn out with fatigue. The sloop grounded within two miles of shore and the crew saved themselves with difficulty in their boat. They were picked up the next day by Captain Miller in the schooner *Gleaner*.

Reference for entry 178 (SL Code™ 1822-3-US-SC/GA-8):
"The Charleston Mercury and Morning Advertiser", (Charleston, SC), Volume 1, #69, March 22, 1822, p. 3, c. 2

179: The *Rice Bird*, Captain Tarbox, with oats, etc., which went ashore on South Island Beach, near Georgetown, South Carolina, during the first week of April, 1822, was afterwards reported off without any damage.

Reference for entry 179 (SL Code™ 1822-4-US-SC/GA-1):
"The Charleston Mercury and Morning Advertiser", (Charleston, SC), Volume 1, #86, April 12, 1822, p. 3, c. 1

180: A "Notice to Mariners" published in the "Charleston Mercury and Morning Advertiser" of April 29, 1822, told of the placement of two spar buoys on the bar at Georgetown, South Carolina. The first was "on the point of the South Breaker, in ten feet at low water and bearing from the lighthouse South 1/2 East". The second was "placed on the point of the North Breaker, in nine feet at low water, and bearing from the latter buoy Northwest by North 1/2 North."

Reference for entry 180 (SL Code™ 1822-4-US-SC/GA-5):
"The Charleston Mercury and Morning Advertiser", (Charleston, SC), Volume 1, #100, April 29, 1822, p. 3, c. 2

181: The schooner *Little Jack*, Captain Thomas Davis, which was up Waccamaw River, South Carolina, taking on a load of rice, was driven on shore and bilged during the hurricane of September 28, 1822. She was afterwards raised.

References for entry 181 (SL Code™ 1822-9-US-SC/GA-23):
"The Charleston Mercury and Morning Advertiser", (Charleston, SC), #242, October 12, 1822, p. 2, c. 1, 2
"The Charleston Mercury and Morning Advertiser", (Charleston, SC), Volume 1, #252, October 24, 1822, p. 3, c. 2

182: The patroon of Mr. Deas' schooner boarded a wreck off Cape Romain, South Carolina, on September 29, 1822, cut a hole in her bottom, and entered her cabin and took therefrom some papers and books. The vessel was loaded with sugar and molasses. This may have been the same wreck, spotted in 23 fathoms of water off Cape Romain on October 2, 1822, by the brig *Homer*. That vessel was described as "apparently a schooner" painted green from the "deck to the saddle ••• Some Havana sugar boxes (Marked J.P.) were floating near the wreck".

Reference for entry 182 (SL Code™ 1822-9-US-SC/GA-29):
"The Charleston Mercury and Morning Advertiser", (Charleston, SC), Volume 1, #235, October 4, 1822, p. 3, c. 2

183: The schooner *Hazard*, Captain John Maderson, from Boston, half full of water and in distress, was unable to get a pilot to take her into Georgetown, South Carolina, for safety, and her captain was faced with the unpleasant choice of going down or running ashore. He chose the latter and ran the schooner ashore on North Inlet Bar, South Carolina, on January 6, 1823. The people were saved, but both the vessel and cargo were expected to be lost.

Reference for entry 183 (SL Code™ 1823-1-US-SC/GA-1):
"Charleston Mercury and Morning Advertiser", (Charleston, S.C), #316, January 10, 1823, p. 3, c. 1

184: The schooner *Fame*, Captain Brown, bound from Charleston to Santee, South Carolina, was lost on Cape Romain, South Carolina, on February 19, 1823. Her captain and crew were saved. Her spars, sails and rigging were salvaged and carried to Charleston by the schooner *Exchange*. The vessel was entirely lost.

Reference for entry 184 (SL Code™ 1823-2-US-SC/GA-6):
"Charleston Mercury and Morning Advertiser", (Charleston, S.C), #355, February 26, 1823, p. 3, c. 1

185: The sloop *Eagle*, bound from Wilmington to Charleston, got aground on Georgetown Bar, South Carolina, on March 18, 1823, and was compelled to throw her deck load of cotton and tar overboard, before she could be got off. She was taken to Georgetown the next day, half full of water.

Reference for entry 185 (SL Code™ 1823-3-US-SC/GA-1):
"Charleston Mercury and Morning Advertiser", (Charleston, S.C), #375, March 21, 1823, p. 3, c. 2

186: The schooner *Mulberry*, Captain Patterson, was wrecked on February 19, 1824, near North Inlet, South Carolina. She was bound from Charleston to Norfolk in ballast and had been in a gale for eight days when she went ashore. No lives were lost and everything was saved "excepting a sum of money, which was capsized in the small boat."

Reference for entry 186 (SL Code™ 1824-2-US-SC/GA-2):
"Charleston Mercury and Morning Advertiser", (Charleston, SC), Volume 3, #665, March 1, 1824, p. 2, c. 5

187: The schooner *Live Oak*, Captain Brown, bound from Santee, went ashore on the point of Cape Romain Shoals, South Carolina, at high tide on March 1, 1824, and was expected to be lost.

Reference for entry 187 (SL Code™ 1824-3-US-SC/GA-1):
"Charleston Mercury and Morning Advertiser", (Charleston, SC), Volume 3, #667, March 3, 1824, p. 2, c. 6

188: "Several parts of a large schooner, a binnacle and side steps newly painted green, fore top mast, railings, buoy and several spars" were reported ashore on the beach at North Island, South Carolina, on September 28, 1824. It was thought that they came from a schooner lost in the hurricane of September 15, 1824.

References for entry 188 (SL Code™ 1824-9-US-SC/GA-25):
"Charleston Courier", (Charleston, SC), #7683, September 30, 1824, p. 2, c. 6
"Charleston Mercury and Morning Advertiser", (Charleston, SC), Volume 3, #846, September 30, 1824, p. 3, c. 1

189: A tow boat, being towed from Cheraw, South Carolina, to Georgetown, South Carolina, with a load of cotton, by the steamboat *Columbia*, Captain Clark, was run upon a snag about five miles below Godfrey's Ferry, South Carolina, on January 10, 1825, and sank in three or four minutes. About 100 bales of cotton were badly damaged.

References for entry 189 (SL Code™ 1825-1-US-SC/GA-2):
"Charleston Mercury and Morning Advertiser", (Charleston, SC), #936, January 17, 1825, p. 2, c. 4
"Charleston Courier", (Charleston, SC), #7774, January 17, 1825, p. 2, c. 4

190: The brig *Clarissa Ann*, Captain Owens, 21 days from Bath, with fish and lumber, struck on Cape Romain, South Carolina, in a thick fog on January 11, 1825, and remained for twelve hours. She got off after throwing a great part of her cargo overboard. (Note: This may have been the brig *Clarissa Ann*, 197 tons, built in 1811 at Bowdoinham, Maine, which was issued a certificate of registry at New York, New York, on December 26, 1822.)

References for entry 190 (SL Code™ 1825-1-US-SC/GA-3):
"Charleston Courier", (Charleston, SC), #7774, January 17, 1825, p. 2, c. 3
"Charleston Mercury", (Charleston, SC), #936, January 17, 1825, p. 2, c. 3
American Flag Merchant Vessels that received Certificates of Enrollment or Registry at the Port of New York, 1789-1867, National Archives "Special List #22", (Washington, DC, 1968), Volume 1, p. 134

191: The Charleston, South Carolina, papers of January 13, 1825, stated that Commander Rogers of the United States ship *North Carolina* saw a large "bright sided" brig ashore on Cape Romain, South Carolina, on January 11, 1825. They stated that at the same time he passed a quantity of lumber and spars adrift. (Note: Checking the log of the United States ship *North Carolina*, Commander John Rogers, for the period December 11, 1824, through January 13, 1825, I was unable to find anything to support the report contained in the Charleston papers. Her log is unclear, but does not seem to indicate that she came within even fifty miles of Cape Romain or Charleston, at any time during the period checked, so how the report originated is not known.)

Sunken Treasures of the Upper SC Coast, 1521-1865

References for entry 191 (SL Code™ 1825-1-US-SC/GA-4):
"Charleston Mercury and Morning Advertiser", (Charleston, SC), #933, January 13, 1825, p. 2, c. 5
"Charleston Courier", (Charleston, SC), #7771, January 13, 1825, p. 2, c. 6
"Log of the United States Ship *North Carolina*", December 11, 1824, to January 13, 1825, NARS

192: Captain Harvey of the steamboat *South Carolina*, which arrived at Charleston from Granby (Columbia, South Carolina), on January 14, 1825, reported a brig ashore on Cape Romain, South Carolina. Her name was not known, and Captain Harvey believed that her crew had abandoned her.

Reference for entry 192 (SL Code™ 1825-1-US-SC/GA-5):
"Charleston Mercury and Morning Advertiser", (Charleston, SC), #935, January 15, 1825, p. 2, c. 6

193: Captain Chase of the schooner *Superb Hope*, of Edenton, North Carolina, saw a large topsail schooner ashore on Cape Romain, South Carolina, on February 9, 1825. He stood in for her, but finding the water to shoal, stood off again. After dark he saw her hoist a lantern.

References for entry 193 (SL Code™ 1825-1-US-SC/GA-7):
"Charleston Mercury and Morning Advertiser", (Charleston, SC), #958, February 11, 1825, p. 2, c. 5
"Charleston Courier", (Charleston, SC), #7796, February 11, 1825, p. 2, c. 6

194: The sloop *Pandora*, of Shrewsbury, Captain Wood, bound from Norfolk, Virginia, for Charleston, South Carolina, was abandoned at sea on December 28 (or 29), 1826, in a sinking condition in latitude 33°15' North, longitude 77°10' West. All hands were saved and were carried to New York in the brig *Pheasant*. They saved nothing but the clothes they wore. Her position was also reported as latitude 32°40' North, longitude 78°35' West. She was described as a very handsome sloop, with a high quarter-deck, a billet head, yellow sides and a green bottom. (Note: 33°15' is the latitude of North Island, South Carolina.)

References for entry 194 (SL Code™ 1826-12-US-SC/GA-1):
"Charleston Mercury", (Charleston, SC), #1552, January 10, 1827, p. 2, c. 6
"Charleston Mercury", (Charleston, SC), #1557, January 16, 1827, p. 2, c. 5

195: A small canoe was upset in Winyah Bay, South Carolina, during a thunderstorm and a gale on April 21, 1827. Both of the people in the canoe succeeded in reaching shore.

Reference for entry 195 (SL Code™ 1827-4-US-SC/GA-1):
"Charleston Mercury", (Charleston, SC), #1642, April 27, 1827, p. 3, c. 1

196: The ferry boat at Black River near Georgetown, South Carolina, was upset in a hurricane on August 26, 1827, drowning three slaves owned by Mr. Trapiee.

Reference for entry 196 (SL Code™ 1827-8-US-SC/GA-1):
"Charleston Courier", (Charleston, SC), #8554, August 30, 1827, p. 2, c. 4

197: The schooner *Rice Plant*, Captain Corson, drug her anchors in the gale of August 23, 1829, and drifted on to the Goose Bank at Georgetown, South Carolina. She was also described as having been driven high and dry on South Island, South Carolina. She was got off and taken to the old shipyard at Georgetown for repairs. The

Rice Plant had been loaded and was "waiting for wind" when the storm hit, but she definitely got more wind than she wanted.

References for entry 197 (SL Code™ 1829-8-US-SC/GA-2):
"Charleston Mercury", (Charleston, SC), #2255, August 27, 1829, p. 2, c. 2
"Charleston Mercury", (Charleston, SC), #2258, August 31, 1829, p. 2, c. 6
"Charleston Courier", (Charleston, SC), #9164, August 31, 1829, p. 3, c. 2

198: Captain Atwood of the brig *Sea Island*, bound from Boston to Savannah, saw a schooner painted all black, lying on her beam ends in latitude 33°30' North, longitude 76° West, on November 28, 1829. The schooner's sails and spars were lying alongside. A dead man was seen lashed to one of the "stancheons" (sic) on the starboard side. Captain Atwood was unable to board her as she was "scudding". (Note: 33°30' is the latitude of Huntington Beach, South Carolina.)

Reference for entry 198 (SL Code™ 1829-11-US-SC/GA-3):
"Charleston Mercury", (Charleston, SC), #2338, December 7, 1829, p. 3, c. 2

199: The ship *Trescott*, Captain Bishop, met with the wreck of a schooner in latitude 33°30' North, longitude 70°30' West, on December 31, 1829. The schooner was "on her beam ends, her masts were standing, and the sails attached, all of which were hoisted up; she had a green boot top and a black bottom, and appeared to have been not long in that situation". (Note: 33°30' is the latitude of Huntington Beach, South Carolina.)

Reference for entry 199 (SL Code™ 1829-12-US-SC/GA-3):
"Charleston Mercury", (Charleston, SC), #2365, January 12, 1830, p. 2, c. 5

200: The schooner *George Washington*, Captain Pugh, bound from North Carolina to Charleston, in attempting to make a harbor in the South Santee River, South Carolina, on January 10, 1830, ran ashore on the breakers. She was got off with the assistance of several other vessels.

Reference for entry 200 (SL Code™ 1830-1-US-SC/GA-1):
"Charleston Mercury", (Charleston, SC), #2365, January 12, 1830, p. 2, c. 4

201: The schooner *Milo*, Captain Clark, bound from Georgetown, South Carolina, to Charleston, South Carolina, with staves and lightwood posts, consigned to W. Jones and S. Mowry and Company, ran ashore on the North Breaker of the Georgetown Bar on January 21, 1830. The *Milo* was forced to throw over part of her deck load to get off.

Reference for entry 201 (SL Code™ 1830-1-US-SC/GA-2):
"Charleston Mercury", (Charleston, SC), #2376, January 25, 1830, p. 2, c. 6

202: A flat at Vance's Ferry on the Santee River, South Carolina, carrying the stage from Camden, South Carolina, for Charleston, South Carolina, was swept from its course and overset on February 10, 1831. The stage, horses, and mails were lost. The passengers were saved, although one lady was badly hurt.

Reference for entry 202 (SL Code™ 1831-2-US-SC/GA-1):
"Charleston Courier", (Charleston, SC), #9525, February 12, 1831, p. 2, c. 2

203: The Union Line schooner *Nile*, Captain Brown, passed a ship's long boat with a varnished bottom, and several spars adrift forty miles east of Georgetown, South Carolina, on February 26, 1831.

Reference for entry 203 (SL Code™ 1831-2-US-SC/GA-2):
"Charleston Courier", (Charleston, SC), #9538, February 28, 1831, p. 2, c. 6

204: The schooner *Ortolan*, Captain Cogdell, bound from Charleston to Georgetown, South Carolina, went ashore on the breakers near South Island, South Carolina, on May 5, 1832. The principal part of the *Ortolan's* cargo of corn and hardware was expected to be lost. It was thought that she might be got off as she had not bilged by May 7, 1832.

Reference for entry 204 (SL Code™ 1832-5-US-SC/GA-1):
"Charleston Courier", (Charleston, SC), #9904, May 9, 1832, p. 2, c. 4

205: The ship *Coriolanus*, Captain Waterman, bound from Boston, Massachusetts, mistook the Cape Romain, South Carolina, light-house, for the Charleston, South Carolina, light-house and struck and grounded on November 23, 1832. She was got off the same day with the loss of her small bower anchor, her stream anchor and cable, her kedge anchor and hawser, and her stern boat.

Reference for entry 205 (SL Code™ 1832-11-US-SC/GA-2):
"Charleston Mercury", (Charleston, SC), #31832, November 26, 1832, p. 3, c. 1

206: The fine large American ship *Pennsylvania*, Captain Patterson, bound from La Havre, France, to Pennsylvania, went ashore on the outer shoal of Cape Romain, South Carolina, on December 2, 1832. Captain Patterson had mistaken the Cape Romain light for the Charleston light. A short time afterwards her crew cut away her mizzenmast and a few hours later the mainmast. A strong gale was reported blowing from the north east. The ship was later reported bilged and totally lost with her cargo. The *Pennsylvania* was described as having painted ports. She carried about 105 crew and passengers (Swiss emigrants). Captain Jones of the schooner David R. Williams lost his boat and best bower anchor in attempting to "rescue the unfortunate sufferers". A 65 year old lady died of exposure and fatigue. The ship carried a cargo of wine, porcelain, fruit, etc., consigned to G.Y. Davis and others. The wreck later drifted to within one mile of South Santee Bar and was in 24' of water. She was reported as floating on her beam ends but anchored. The smack *Intrepid*, Captain Hill, salvaged ninety fathoms of chain cable and an anchor of 15-50ths, but could find nothing else worth saving and supposed that her cargo and baggage had washed out. The smack *John Drake*, Captain Racket, reported the *Pennsylvania* as ashore on a shoal about three miles north of Cape Romain and one mile from shore. Captain Racket salvaged ninety fathoms of chain cable and two anchors weighing 1550 pounds and 6-50ths.

References for entry 206 (SL Code™ 1832-12-US-SC/GA-1):
"Charleston Mercury", (Charleston, SC), #31838, December 3, 1832, p. 2, c. 1
"Charleston Mercury", (Charleston, SC), #31839, December 4, 1832, p. 2, c. 2
"Charleston Mercury", (Charleston, SC), #31841, December 6, 1832, p. 2, c. 3
"Charleston Mercury", (Charleston, SC), #31842, December 7, 1832, p. 2, c. 2
"Charleston Mercury", (Charleston, SC), #31845, December 11, 1832, p. 2, c. 6
"Charleston Mercury", (Charleston, SC), #31847, December 13, 1832, p. 2, c. 2
"Charleston Mercury", (Charleston, SC), #31849, December 15, 1832, p. 2, c. 5
"Charleston Mercury", (Charleston, SC), #31850, December 17, 1832, p. 3, c. 1, 2, 3

207: The schooner *Maria* was driven into Mr. Hume's rice field on Santee River, South Carolina, during the hurricane of September 4, 1834.

Reference for entry 207 (SL Code™ 1834-9-US-SC/GA-1):
"Charleston Courier", (Charleston, SC), #10706, September 8, 1834, p. 2, c. 2

208: The sloop *Exchange*, Captain Runciman, was wrecked at Georgetown, South Carolina, during the hurricane of September 4, 1834. She was empty and her location was given as in Dr. M.C. Myer's field and within 150 yards of the house. (Note: See also previous entry.)

References for entry 208 (SL Code™ 1834-9-US-SC/GA-3):
"Charleston Courier", (Charleston, SC), #10706, September 8, 1834, p. 2, c. 2
"Southern Patriot", (Charleston, SC), #5183, September 6, 1834, p. 2, c. 5
"Southern Patriot", (Charleston, SC), #5184, September 8, 1834, p. 2, c. 5

209: The schooner *John Stoney*, Captain Lehue, with 3400 bushels of rough rice, went ashore at Mayrant's on the south west side of Winyah Bay, near Georgetown, South Carolina, in the hurricane of September 4, 1834. The schooner's location was also described as "at Dover". She was expected to be lost.

References for entry 209 (SL Code™ 1834-9-US-SC/GA-4):
"Charleston Courier", (Charleston, SC), #10706, September 8, 1834, p. 2, c. 2
"Southern Patriot", (Charleston, SC), #5183, September 6, 1834, p. 2, c. 5
"Southern Patriot", (Charleston, SC), #5184, September 8, 1834, p. 2, c. 5

210: The brig *Francis Ann*, from New York, was reported ashore on Cat Island, South Carolina, near Georgetown after the hurricane of September 4, 1834. (Note: This may have been the brig *Francis Ann*, 184 tons, built in 1811 at Bucksport, Maine, which was issued a certificate of registry at New York, New York, on August 22, 1818. That *Francis Ann* is also shown as built at Hartford in 1831 and as drawing 10' of water. She had "chenamed" felt on her bottom and a locust top. She was "well found" and was classed A-1 1/2 for insurance purposes. She had two chains. That *Francis Ann* was described as a "half model" brig. Her captains had been Morseley, Baker & Pearce and she had been owned in Hartford by Pease.)

References for entry 210 (SL Code™ 1834-9-US-SC/GA-5):
"Charleston Courier", (Charleston, SC), #10706, September 8, 1834, p. 2, c. 2
"Southern Patriot", (Charleston, SC), #5183, September 6, 1834, p. 2, c. 5
"Southern Patriot", (Charleston, SC), #5184, September 8, 1834, p. 2, c. 5
"Hull Register and Survey Record, 1831-1832", (bound manuscript, survey data, Atlantic Mutual Insurance Company of New York, Marine Library), entry for *Francis Ann*

American Flag Merchant Vessels that received Certificates of Enrollment or Registry at the Port of New York, 1789-1867, National Archives "Special List #22", (Washington, DC, 1968), Volume 1, p. 252

211: The fourteen month old schooner *Comet*, from New York, with about forty hogsheads of sugar and coffee, was sunk at the wharf at Georgetown, South Carolina, during the hurricane of September 4, 1834.

References for entry 211 (SL Code™ 1834-9-US-SC/GA-6):
"Charleston Courier", (Charleston, SC), #10706, September 8, 1834, p. 2, c. 2
"Southern Patriot", (Charleston, SC), #5183, September 6, 1834, p. 2, c. 5
"Southern Patriot", (Charleston, SC), #5184, September 8, 1834, p. 2, c. 5

212: The sidewheel steamer *Walter Raleigh* was burnt at Georgetown, South Carolina, on August 5, 1835. No lives were lost. She was built at Elizabeth City, North Carolina, in 1832, but was home ported at Norfolk, Virginia, starting in 1833. She was 93' in length, 23.7' in breadth, and 7'6". in depth of hold. The *Walter Raleigh* was 147 56/95 tons. She had a wood hull; one deck; no masts; no galleries; a square stern; round tuck; and no figurehead. She was owned by Robert and James Souter of Norfolk, Virginia. Her enrollment was surrendered at Norfolk on September 15, 1835, with a notation that she had burned. (Note: Both the "Lytle-Holdcamper List" and Bruce Berman's *Encyclopedia of American Shipwrecks* show the *Walter Raleigh* as built in Norfolk and as lost in 1845. this vessel has also been listed under 1845-8x-US-SC/GA-1.)

References for entry 212 (SL Code™ 1835-8-US-SC/GA-1):
"Permanent Enrollment #115", (Norfolk, VA), December 11, 1833, NARS RG 41
Encyclopedia of American Shipwrecks, by Bruce D. Berman, (Boston, 1972), p. 150, #2036
Merchant Steam Vessels of the United States 1790-1868, ("Lytle-Holdcamper List"), edited by C. Bradford Mitchell, (Staten Island, NY, 1975), pp. 225, 305
Manuscript 3X5 index cards used in the preparation of the "Lytle-Holdcamper List", NARS RG 41

213: The schooner *Manuel*, Captain G.W. Folger, of and for Nantucket, from Georgetown, South Carolina, with a cargo of lumber, filled with water, rolled over, and sank, 54 miles north east of Georgetown Bar, South Carolina, in June of 1836. Her crew was picked up the next day in latitude 33°51' North, longitude 77°14' West, by the schooner *Convoy*, Captain Limett. (Note: 33°51' is the latitude of Little River, South Carolina.)

Reference for entry 213 (SL Code™ 1836-6-US-SC/GA-2):
"Charleston Mercury", (Charleston, SC), #37917, July 1, 1836, p. 3, c. 1

214: The schooner *David B. Crane*, bound from Darien, Georgia, to New York, reported seeing a schooner bottom up off Georgetown, South Carolina, on June 28, 1836.

Reference for entry 214 (SL Code™ 1836-6-US-SC/GA-3):
"Charleston Mercury", (Charleston, SC), #37921, July 7, 1836, p. 2, c. 6

215: Captain Hudgins of the schooner *Martha* saw a green bottomed, northern built vessel, bottom up, in latitude 33°50' North, longitude 77°40' West, on August 3, 1836. The vessel's rudder was gone and part of the shoe of her keel had been knocked off. The keel was about 60' long. The bottom appeared to be in perfect order. (Note One: 33°50' is the latitude of North Myrtle Beach, South Carolina.) (Note Two: See also next entry.)

Reference for entry 215 (SL Code™ 1836-8-US-SC/GA-1):
"Charleston Mercury", (Charleston, SC), #37949, August 8, 1836, p. 3, c. 1

216: Captain Delano of the brig *General Marion* reported that on August 29, 1836, he fell in with the wreck of a large schooner, bottom up, in latitude 33°50' North, longitude 77°15' West. The schooner was apparently eastern built, with an oak plank bottom, painted green, with ceiling pine or spruce timbers. The schooner had two anchors and chains over her bows. The starboard anchor had a wooden stock and the "larboard" (port) anchor, had an iron stock. Captain Delano cut a hole in her bottom and found her to be loaded with pine timber. He thought she had been in that situation for some time. (Note One: 33°50' is the latitude of North Myrtle Beach, South Carolina.) (Note Two: See also the previous entry.)

Reference for entry 216 (SL Code™ 1836-8-US-SC/GA-3):
"Charleston Mercury", (Charleston, SC), #37970, September 1, 1836, p. 3, c. 2

217: The brig *Improvement*, Captain Brock, which left New York on August 27, 1836, went ashore near the Georgetown, South Carolina, light-house on September 4, 1836. Every effort was reportedly being made to get her off.

Reference for entry 217 (SL Code™ 1836-9-US-SC/GA-1):
"Charleston Mercury", (Charleston, SC), #37985, September 20, 1836, p. 2, c. 6

218: The schooner *Dunton and Son* passed a wreck, bottom up, painted green, in latitude 32.5° North and 79° West on September 10, 1836. (Note: 33.5° is the latitude of Huntington Beach, South Carolina.)

Reference for entry 218 (SL Code™ 1836-9-US-SC/GA-2):
"Charleston Mercury", (Charleston, SC), #37980, September 13, 1836, p. 3, c. 3

219: The schooner *Martha Pyatt*, bound from Georgetown, South Carolina, to Charleston, South Carolina, was believed to have been lost in a terrible gale on August 18, 1837.

Reference for entry 219 (SL Code™ 1837-8-US-SC/GA-2):
"Southern Patriot", (Charleston, SC), #5877, August 28, 1837, p. 2, c. 5

220: The "Southern Patriot" of August 28, 1837, reported a vessel of about 140 tons, bottom painted green, as wrecked in latitude 33°20' North, longitude 77°55' West, on August 24, 1837. (Note: 33°20' is the latitude of DeBordieu Island, South Carolina.)

Reference for entry 220 (SL Code™ 1837-8-US-SC/GA-3):
"Southern Patriot", (Charleston, SC), #5877, August 28, 1837, p. 2, c. 6

221: The schooner *Three Sisters*, of Charleston, Captain Davis, loaded with lumber and bound from Charleston, South Carolina, to St. Augustine, Florida, was reported in the "Southern Patriot" Of

September 4, 1837, as wrecked fifteen miles south east of the lighthouse at Cape Romain, South Carolina.
Reference for entry 221 (SL Code™ 1837-9-US-SC/GA-2):
"Southern Patriot", (Charleston, SC), #5883, September 4, 1837, p. 2, c. 3

222: Captain Delahay of the schooner *Magnolia*, arrived at Charleston, South Carolina, from Georgetown, South Carolina, on January 23, 1838, reported having passed two cotton boats sunk near Holme's Landing, South Carolina. The cotton was floating all over the river. Captain Delahay picked up one bale marked W.M.
Reference for entry 222 (SL Code™ 1838-1-US-SC/GA-2):
"Charleston Courier", (Charleston, SC), #11985, January 24, 1838, p. 2, c. 3, 6

223: The brig *Phoebe*, bound from New York to Galveston, was wrecked on Georgetown Bar, South Carolina, on September 23, 1838. She was loaded with lumber, dry goods and $52,000 in specie. The vessel beat in over the breakers and sank, but the passengers, crew and specie were saved. This was probably the same brig that Captain Roby of the schooner *Waccamaw* reported seeing ashore on the Georgetown Bar on September 24, 1838. (Note: This may have been the brig *Phoebe*, 104 tons, which was built at Salisbury, Massachusetts, in 1815, and was registered at New York, New York, on August 30, 1838.)
References for entry 223 (SL Code™ 1838-9-US-SC/GA-2):
"Charleston Courier", (Charleston, SC), #12190, September 25, 1838, p. 2, c. 7
"Charleston Courier", (Charleston, SC), #12192, September 27, 1838, p. 2, c. 7
"Charleston Mercury", (Charleston, SC), #4601, September 25, 1838, p. 2, c. 7
"Charleston Mercury", (Charleston, SC), #4603, September 27, 1838, p. 3, c. 3
American Flag Merchant Vessels that received Certificates of Enrollment or Registry at the Port of New York, 1789-1867, National Archives "Special List #22", (Washington, DC, 1968), Volume 2, p. 557

224: The schooner *Two Sisters*, Captain Pennock, bound from Charleston, South Carolina, to Providence, Rhode Island, with a cargo of cotton and rice, went ashore in foul weather in Long Bay, South Carolina, in late October, 1838. Her position was also described as 38 miles from Georgetown, South Carolina. She got off after unloading her cargo on the beach and returned to Charleston leaking badly.
Reference for entry 224 (SL Code™ 1838-10-US-SC/GA-1):
"Charleston Courier", (Charleston, SC), #12227, November 8, 1838, p. 2, c. 2

225: The vessel *Harvest* stranded and filled on the South Breaker of Georgetown Bar, South Carolina, on February 22, 1839. She was a total loss. Her cargo was valued $30,000 and what was brought up from her was in a very damaged state.
Reference for entry 225 (SL Code™ 1839-2-US-SC/GA-1):
"Charleston Courier", (Charleston, SC), #12316, February 26, 1839, p. 2, c. 2

226: The schooner *Walter E. Hyer*, Captain Wright, bound from Charleston to Georgetown, South Carolina, got ashore on the Georgetown Bar on March 29, 1839, and was expected to be a total loss. The *Walter E. Hyer* was 84 tons. She was built in 1827 at

Brookhaven, New York, and was issued a certificate of enrollment at New York, New York, on July 27, 1827.

References for entry 226 (SL Code™ 1839-3-US-SC/GA-2):
"Charleston Courier", (Charleston, SC), #12343, April 1, 1839, p. 2, c. 2
American Flag Merchant Vessels that received Certificates of Enrollment or Registry at the Port of New York, 1789-1867, National Archives "Special List #22", (Washington, DC, 1968), Volume 2, p. 716

227: The schooner *Enterprise*, Captain John Miller, which sailed from Savannah for Baltimore on October 11, 1839, was driven ashore on the beach at South Island, South Carolina, and bilged the next day. The *Enterprise* was traveling in ballast and was attempting to make Georgetown Harbor, South Carolina, when she was lost. The crew and part of her rigging was saved.

Reference for entry 227 (SL Code™ 1839-10-US-SC/GA-3):
"Charleston Courier", (Charleston, SC), #12532, November 1, 1839, p. 2, c. 2

228: The sidewheel steamer *North Carolina*, Captain Davis, bound from Wilmington, North Carolina, to Charleston, South Carolina, was run afoul of by the steamer *Governor Dudley*, Captain Ivy, "25 to 30 miles Northward by Eastward of Georgetown," and sunk in eleven fathoms of water on July 26, 1840. The *North Carolina* was struck abreast of the saloon and against her quarter boards on the larboard side about 15 or 20 feet from the stern. The *North Carolina* bilged immediately but no lives were lost and part of the mail was saved. The passengers lost today's equivalent of between $300,000 and $400,000. Many lost their clothes. Several "gentlemen returning from Congress", had large amounts of money with them in their trunks, most of which was lost. The shock was so sudden that before half of the 30 or 40 passengers could get out of their berths, the cabins were filled with water, and most of them had to leap from the hurricane deck. The people were rescued and carried to Wilmington, North Carolina, by the *Governor Dudley*. Seven leather bags and two canvass mail bags were saved, but the remainder was lost. A mahogany table and other debris from the wreck later washed ashore on the front beach of North Island. A trunk belonging to the Honorable Mr. Nisbet of Georgia, was later picked up on Baldhead Beach. (Note One: The *North Carolina* was built of oak, birch and cedar at New York in 1837 and was 370 tons. She was composition fastened and had one deck. She had one 160 horsepower engine and her boiler was mounted below deck. She measured 160' in length; 24' in breadth; and 9'6" in depth of hold. She had her "cabin and plenty of houses on deck," and was described as a "good looking river boat but not fit to go to sea". She had been repaired and put in order in October, 1838, and was surveyed in September, 1838. Her first home port was at Wilmington. She was owned by Captain Potter.) (Note Two: The author has positively identified the *North Carolina* as one that was previously known to divers, but incorrectly thought to be worthless. He plans to file a salvage claim against the wreck in Federal Court.)

References for entry 228 (SL Code™ 1840-7-US-SC/GA-2):
"Charleston Courier", (Charleston, SC), #11533, July 25, 1840, p. 3, c. 2
"Charleston Courier", (Charleston, SC), #11534, July 27, 1840, p. 2, c. 6
"Charleston Courier", (Charleston, SC), #11535, July 28, 1840, p. 2, c. 4
"Charleston Courier", (Charleston, SC), #11537, July 30, 1840, p. 2, c. 3
"Charleston Courier", (Charleston, SC), #11550, August 14, 1840, p. 2, c. 6
"Charleston Courier", (Charleston, SC), #11537, September 2, 1840, p. 2, c. 3
"Charleston Mercury", (Charleston, SC), #5121, July 28, 1840, p. 2, c. 4
"Steam Vessels #1, 1850's" (bound manuscript, survey data, Marine Library of the Atlantic Mutual Insurance Companies of New York), entry for *North Carolina*
Merchant Steam Vessels of the United States 1790-1868, ("Lytle-Holdcamper List"), edited by C. Bradford Mitchell, (Staten Island, NY, 1975), pp. 87, 159, 286

229: The schooner *Nancy*, of Nantucket, bound from Ocracock (sic), North Carolina, for Georgetown, South Carolina, with a cargo of corn, was totally lost on the Day Breaker, Georgetown Bar, South Carolina, on January 24, 1841.

Reference for entry 229 (SL Code™ 1841-1-US-SC/GA-1):
"Charleston Courier", (Charleston, SC), #11689, January 28, 1841, p. 2, c. 2

230: The valuable river steamer *Osceola*, Captain Christian, in descending the Pee Dee River on March 11, 1841, was thrust against the shore by the violence of current at Wright's Bluff, South Carolina, and stove two of her planks. Captain Christian, finding it impossible to keep the *Osceola* afloat, put her ashore near Mrs. Goddard's plantation on the Pee Dee River, South Carolina. The *Osceola* was refloated through the efforts of her captain on March 28, 1841.

References for entry 230 (SL Code™ 1841-3-US-SC/GA-1):
"Charleston Courier", (Charleston, SC), #11726, March 15, 1841, p. 2, c. 5, 6
"Charleston Courier", (Charleston, SC), #11743, April 3, 1841, p. 2, c. 2

231: The brig *Detroit*, Captain Higgins, bound from New York to Georgetown, South Carolina, with a full cargo of merchandise, went ashore on the "outer Raft Tree Shoals" on August 26, 1841. (Note: From the report in the "Charleston Courier" of August 30, 1841, it appears that these shoals are located near Georgetown, South Carolina.) The schooner *Rice Plant* aided the *Detroit* by taking out portions of her cargo. The sloop *C. Vendeventer* was dispatched from Charleston to go to the *Detroit's* aid. The *Detroit* had cleared New York on August 17, 1841. (Note: This may have been the brig *Detroit*, 210 tons, built in 1836 at Guilford, Connecticut, which received a certificate of registry at the Port of New York on October 10, 1836. She may have gotten off. See also entry 236 of this book.)

References for entry 231 (SL Code™ 1841-8-US-SC/GA-1):
"Charleston Courier", (Charleston, SC), #11867, August 30, 1841, p. 2, c. 2
American Flag Merchant Vessels that received Certificates of Enrollment or Registry at the Port of New York, 1789-1867, National Archives "Special List #22", (Washington, DC, 1968), Volume 1, p. 173

232: The schooner *Christopher Columbus*, which had just arrived at Georgetown, South Carolina, from New York, with a cargo of hay, lime, bricks and soap, took fire from the lime on November 1, 1841, and it was necessary to scuttle her. It was feared that she would be a total loss. (Note: This may have been the schooner *Christopher Columbus*, 73 tons, built in 1833 at Washington, New Jersey, which received a certificate of enrollment at New York, New York, on September 22, 1842.)

References for entry 232 (SL Code™ 1841-11-US-SC/GA-1):
"Charleston Courier", (Charleston, SC), #11924, November 6, 1841, p. 2, c. 4
American Flag Merchant Vessels that received Certificates of Enrollment or Registry at the Port of New York, 1789-1867, National Archives "Special List #22", (Washington, DC, 1968), Volume 1, p. 130

233: A cotton flat, from Cheraw, South Carolina, was "forced ashore and filled" in a heavy wind at Georgetown, South Carolina, about December 6, 1841. Her cargo was landed in a damaged state.

Reference for entry 233 (SL Code™ 1841-12-US-SC/GA-1):
"Charleston Courier", (Charleston, SC), #11952, December 10, 1841, p. 2, c. 4

234: The steamer *Anson*, Captain Donnell, passed a piece of wreck north of Cape Romain, South Carolina, on March 31, 1842. The wreckage was painted white and about twenty-five feet long. It looked like one of the promenade deck carlines of a steam boat. About half an hour later Captain Donnell saw two boats inside of the inner breaker of Cape Romain. After crossing Cape Romain shoal he saw two or three other small pieces of wreck painted white.

Reference for entry 234 (SL Code™ 1842-3-US-SC/GA-3):
"Charleston Courier", (Charleston, SC), #12045, April 1, 1842, p. 2, c. 3

235: The steamer *Osceola*, Captain Christian, in descending the river near Society Hill, South Carolina, was snagged on May 10, 1842. She was expected to get off.

Reference for entry 235 (SL Code™ 1842-5-US-SC/GA-1):
"Charleston Courier," (Charleston, SC), #12088, May 23, 1842, p. 2, c. 5

236: The brig *Detroit*, bound from New York to Georgetown, South Carolina, was reported ashore on Georgetown Bar, South Carolina, with a steamer alongside attempting to tow her off, about January 6, 1843. The *Detroit* was afterwards reported off and safely arrived at Georgetown. (Note: This may have been the brig *Detroit*, 210 tons, built in 1836 at Guilford, Connecticut, which received a certificate of registry at the Port of New York on October 10, 1836. See also entry 231 of this book.)

References for entry 236 (SL Code™ 1843-1-US-SC/GA-1):
"Charleston Courier", (Charleston, SC), #12278, January 9, 1843, p. 2, c. 7
"Charleston Courier", (Charleston, SC), #12280, January 11, 1843, p. 2, c. 7
American Flag Merchant Vessels that received Certificates of Enrollment or Registry at the Port of New York, 1789-1867, National Archives "Special List #22", (Washington, DC, 1968), Volume 1, p. 173

237: The sloop *Martha Y. Howren*, Captain Howren, bound from Charleston for Georgetown, South Carolina, went ashore on the Georgetown Bar on January 28, 1843, and immediately bilged. The sloop and her cargo were expected to be a total loss. The crew was saved. The wreck was later reported as on the "Dry-Breaker" and as in the hands of authorized wreckers. A warning had even been posted to "unauthorized wreckers" who might have been tempted to attempt independent salvage of her.

References for entry 237 (SL Code™ 1843-1-US-SC/GA-3):
"Charleston Courier", (Charleston, SC), #12296, January 30, 1843, p. 2, c. 2
"Charleston Courier", (Charleston, SC), #12315, February 21, 1843, p. 2, c. 5 (quoted from: "Winyah Observer", February 18, 1843)

238: The 33 ton schooner *Highlander*, Captain Tomblin, which was had gone ashore on Long Bay, near Fraser's Island, South Carolina, was carefully examined by "respectable surveyors", during the first week in February, 1843. They reported themselves to be in favor of an effort to get her off. The vessel was sold where she lay for $315.00. Her cargo of potatoes was sold for about 15 cents per bushel. The new owner was reported making every effort to get her off. The *Highlander* was finally gotten off and arrived at Georgetown, South Carolina, on March 22, 1843.

References for entry 238 (SL Code™ 1843-2-US-SC/GA-1):
"Charleston Courier", (Charleston, SC), #12306, February 10, 1843, p. 2, c. 7
"Charleston Courier", (Charleston, SC), #12312, February 17, 1843, p. 2, c. 5 (quoted from "Winyah Intelligencer", February 15, 1843.)
"Charleston Courier", (Charleston, SC), #12315, February 21, 1843, p. 2, c. 5 (quoted from "Winyah Intelligencer", February 18, 1843.)
"Charleston Courier", (Charleston, SC), #12342, March 24, 1843, p. 2, c. 7

239: Captain Sherwood of the brig *Emily*, which arrived at Charleston, South Carolina, on March 18, 1843, reported that the before he had fallen in with a boat, about twenty miles south east of Cape Romain, South Carolina. The boat contained four Negroes, who stated that they were the crew of a small sloop belonging to M. Manigault, which was sunk in Bull's Bay, South Carolina, on March 16, 1843. The sloop was carrying a load of wood when it was lost. The men had been attempting to reach shore in the sloop's small boat when they were driven out to sea by the violence of the wind.

Reference for entry 239 (SL Code™ 1843-3-US-SC/GA-6):
"Charleston Courier", (Charleston, SC), #12338, March 20, 1843, p. 2, c. 2

240: The steamer *Utility*, bound from Georgetown, South Carolina, to Cheraw, South Carolina, while in the vicinity of Uhany Ferry, Pee Dee River, South Carolina, exploded her boiler and sank on March 29, 1843. No lives were lost, but two men were injured. She sank a short time after the explosion. The steamer *Osceola*, which was traveling with the *Utility*, rescued most of her cargo. Only a few hogsheads of sugar and about 50 bags of salt were lost. The *Utility* drew only 3.5' of water and was sunk up to her boiler deck. Her boilers were old but had been regarded as good and safe. She was said to have been a total loss.

References for entry 240 (SL Code™ 1843-3-US-SC/GA-7):
"Charleston Courier", (Charleston, SC), #12349, April 1, 1843, p. 2, c. 2
"Charleston Courier", (Charleston, SC), #12350, April 3, 1843, p. 2, c. 4

241: Captain Morse of the schooner *Marion*, who arrived at Charleston, South Carolina, from Jacksonville, North Carolina, on May 16, 1843, reported having fallen in with, off Little River, South Carolina, the stern of a vessel called the *Mary Emily*, of Lubec, Maine. A wreck with the stern torn off (and believed to have been the main portion of the *Mary Emily*) was fallen in with off Frying Pan Shoals, North Carolina, by the schooner *Harvest*. The *Harvest*, Captain Small, had arrived at Charleston on May 19, 1843, from Baltimore.

References for entry 241 (SL Code™ 1843-5-US-SC/GA-1):
"Charleston Courier," (Charleston, SC), #12387, May 17, 1843, p. 2, c. 7
"Charleston Courier," (Charleston, SC), #12388, May 18, 1843, p. 2, c. 3
"Charleston Courier," (Charleston, SC), #12390, May 20, 1843, p. 3, c. 2

242: The schooner *Erie*, Captain Wilson, collided with the steamer *C. Vanderbilt*, Captain Marshall, fifty miles south of Cape Fear, North Carolina, on July 26, 1845. The *C. Vanderbilt* received no material damage, but the *Erie* afterwards filled with water and capsized. The *Erie's* captain, crew and passengers made it to shore in the schooner's boats, but due to being overloaded had to leave three of crew on the wreck. Those three men were later rescued by the schooner *Surpass*, Captain Pugh, and were carried to Charleston, South Carolina. Captain Pugh reported the wreck as 25 miles north east of Georgetown, South Carolina, and described it as "full of water and capsized, having only a small portion of one of her quarters and the mainmast head out of water". The *Erie* had been bound from Mosquito Creek in Florida to Wilmington, North Carolina, in ballast, with sixteen crew and passengers when the collision took place.

References for entry 242 (SL Code™ 1845-7-US-SC/GA-1):
"Charleston Courier", (Charleston, SC), #13043, July 28, 1845, p. 2, c. 3
"Charleston Courier", (Charleston, SC), #13044 (sic), July 30, 1845, p. 2, c. 5

243: Bruce Berman's *Encyclopedia of American Shipwrecks* and the "Lytle-Holdcamper List" both show the sidewheel steamer *Walter Raleigh*, 157 tons, as burnt at Georgetown, South Carolina, on August 5, 1845, while the loss actually took place on August 5, 1835.

References for entry 243 (SL Code™ 1845-8x-US-SC/GA-1):
Encyclopedia of American Shipwrecks, by Bruce D. Berman, (Boston, 1972), p. 150, #2036
Merchant Steam Vessels of the United States 1790-1868, ("Lytle-Holdcamper List"), edited by C. Bradford Mitchell, (Staten Island, NY, 1975), pp. 225, 305

244: The "Charleston Courier" of October 16, 1846, reported that it was "feared" that the steamer *Utility* had been sunk in the Santee River, South Carolina, during the gale of October 13, 1846. (Note: This was probably the sidewheel steamer *Utility* which was issued "Permanent Enrollment #11" at Georgetown, South Carolina, on August 6, 1846. If so it was either raised or not sunk at all as it was mortgaged for $1000 on October 19, 1847. Furthermore the "Lytle-

Holdcamper" list shows that it was not abandoned or otherwise removed from documentation until 1850. That *Utility* had a sharp stern; a sharp bow; no billet head; one deck; and no masts. She had a wood hull and was built at Wilmington, North Carolina, in 1841. She measured 114'8" in length; 22'6.75" in breadth; and 7' in depth of hold. She was owned by Alexander McKenzie of Cheraw, South Carolina.)

References for entry 244 (SL Code™ 1846-10-US-SC/GA-4):
"Permanent Enrollment #11", (Georgetown, SC), August 6, 1846, NARS RG 41
"Charleston Courier", (Charleston, SC), #13411, October 16, 1846, p. 2, c. 4
Merchant Steam Vessels of the United States 1790-1868, ("Lytle-Holdcamper List"), edited by C. Bradford Mitchell, (Staten Island, NY, 1975), p. 219

245: The "Charleston Courier" of October 16, 1846, reported that it was "feared" that the steamer *Wateree* had been sunk in the Santee River, South Carolina, during the gale of October 13, 1846.

Reference for entry 245 (SL Code™ 1846-10-US-SC/GA-14):
"Charleston Courier", (Charleston, SC), #13411, October 16, 1846, p. 2, c. 4

246: The schooner *Judge Hitchcock*, of Dighton, Massachusetts, Captain Ludwick A. Hathaway, bound from Charleston, South Carolina, to Alexandria, Virginia, went ashore at Long Bay Beach, South Carolina, on October 13, 1846. The captain and crew were reported safe. Rogers and Black's *Marine Roll* of 1847 showed her signal letters and numbers as FZF 25044 and her port of entry as Fall River, Massachusetts. She was built in 1839 at Taunton, Massachusetts. She had one deck; two masts; a square stern; no galleries; and a billet head. She measured 69' in length; 19.5' in breadth; 6.75' in depth; and 81 54/95 tons.

References for entry 246 (SL Code™ 1846-10-US-SC/GA-15):
"Permanent Enrollment #34", (Fall River), NARS RG 41
"Charleston Courier", (Charleston, SC), #14419, October 27, 1846, p. 2, c. 2
"Record of Enrollments, 1844-1845", (bound manuscript, abstracts of enrollments), Volume 15, p. 51, NARS RG 41
Marine Roll, by Rogers and Black, (1847), p. 83
American Flag Merchant Vessels that received Certificates of Enrollment or Registry at the Port of New York, 1789-1867, National Archives "Special List #22", (Washington, DC, 1968), Volume 1, p. 391

247: The sidewheel steamer *Richland* exploded and was destroyed at Britton's Ferry, South Carolina, (35 miles from Winyah, South Carolina), on January 14, 1849. Fifteen lives were lost. Rogers and Black's *Marine Roll* of 1847 showed her signal letters and numbers as QYM 32460. She had a wood hull and was built in 1841 (or 1842) at Charleston, South Carolina, which was also her first home port. The *Richland* had a square stern; one deck; no masts; no galleries; and no figure-head. She measured 121' in length; 26' in breadth; 5'7" in depth; and 160 12/95 tons.

References for entry 247 (SL Code™ 1849-1-US-SC/GA-1):
"Permanent Enrollment #1", (Charleston, SC), March 4, 1842, NARS RG 41
"Permanent Enrollment #1", (Charleston, SC), March 9, 1843, NARS RG 41
"Permanent Enrollment #3", (Charleston, SC), March 16, 1843, NARS RG 41
"Permanent Enrollment #8", (Charleston, SC), December 30, 1843, NARS RG 41
Marine Roll, by Rogers and Black, (1847), p. 192
Manuscript 3X5 file card for steamer *Richland* used in preparation of "Lytle-Holdcamper List", NARS RG 41

Merchant Steam Vessels of the United States 1790-1868, ("Lytle-Holdcamper List"), edited by C. Bradford Mitchell, (Staten Island, NY, 1975), pp. 185, 293

248: The ship *Atlanta,* Captain Colby, bound from a northern port to Charleston in ballast, ran ashore on the north side of Cape Romain, South Carolina, on September 17, 1850. She was described as a large ship with painted ports, newly built in Newburyport, Massachusetts. On the fifth day, she was towed off and brought to Charleston by the steamer Charleston. She lost some of her anchors and some of her ballast, which was thrown overboard to lighten her.

References for entry 248 (SL Code™ 1850-US-SC/GA-1):
"Charleston Courier", (Charleston, SC), Volume 48, #14608, September 18, 1850, p. 2, c. 2
"Charleston Courier", (Charleston, SC), Volume 48, #14609, September 19, 1850, p. 2, c. 2
"Charleston Courier", (Charleston, SC), Volume 48, #14611, September 21, 1850, p. 2, c. 2
"Charleston Courier", (Charleston, SC), Volume 48, #14612, September 22, 1850, p. 2, c. 2, 6

249: The brig *Fox,* Captain Berry, bound from Bucksville, sprang a leak at sea shortly after crossing the bar at Georgetown, South Carolina, on September 23, 1850. She was turned around and run on the North Breaker. The crew was saved, but the vessel and cargo were a total loss.

Reference for entry 249 (SL Code™ 1850-9-US-SC/GA-2):
"Charleston Courier", (Charleston, SC), Volume 48, #14616, September 27, 1850, p. 2, c. 3

250: The sidewheel steamer *Wateree* was stranded and sunk in 9' of water at Allison's Landing, South Carolina, on the Pee Dee River on December 6 (or 7), 1850. She carried 970 bales of cotton and was insured by the Charleston Insurance and Trust Company. There were no lives lost. (The *Wateree* had a wood hull and was built in 1843 at Charleston, South Carolina, which was also her first home port. Rogers and Black's *Marine Roll* of 1847 showed her signal letters and numbers as QYO 32462. She was 169 20/95 tons; 111' in length; 26' in breadth; and 6'10" in depth of hold. She had a round stern; no galleries; no figure-head; and a round tuck. She was issued "Permanent Enrollment #11, at Charleston, South Carolina, on June 10, 1847.)

References for entry 250 (SL Code™ 1850-12-US-SC/GA-1):
Marine Roll, by Rogers and Black, (1847), p. 192
"Charleston Evening News", (Charleston, SC), #1589, December 9, 1850, p. 2, c. 2
"Permanent Enrollment #7", (Charleston, SC), November 28, 1843, NARS RG 41
"Permanent Enrollment #9", (Charleston, SC), December 30, 1843, NARS RG 41
"Permanent Enrollment #9", (Charleston, SC), May 2, 1846, NARS RG 41
Merchant Steam Vessels of the United States 1790-1868, ("Lytle-Holdcamper List"), edited by C. Bradford Mitchell, (Staten Island, NY, 1975), pp. 227, 305

251: The ship *Virginia* ran ashore on Cape Romain, South Carolina, on November 25, 1851. She was towed off on November 29, 1851, by the steamer *General Clinch* after "four days of hard work. Two thousand bags of salt were thrown overboard to lighten her. The *Virginia* sustained little or no injury.

References for entry 251 (SL Code™ 1851-11-US-SC/GA-2):
"Daily Morning News", (Savannah, GA), #274, November 29, 1851, p. 2, c. 3
"Daily Morning News", (Savannah, GA), #276, December 2, 1851, p. 2, c. 1

252: A ship was reported ashore in Warsaw Sound, Georgia, on March 3, 1853. It was believed that it was the ship *Italy*, of Bath, which had previously been reported adrift at sea with five or six men and no provisions. The steamer *Calhoun* was reported to have gone in search of the ship. [Note: The ship *Italy*, Captain Ryan, had been bound from New Orleans for Genoa, when she was ran ashore on Memory Rock (or Mantinilla Reef) in the Bahamas on December 24, 1852. There was $10,000 in insurance on her freight money, divided equally between the American (insurance company) office and the Atlantic (insurance company) office at Providence. Her cargo was said to have been worth $10,0000 and the vessel about $15,000 or $20,000. Wreckers managed to get 300 (or 400) bales of cotton from her, and were attempting to tow her to port, when the wind increased and they had to cut her loose on January 28, 1853. They reported that they had abandoned her about ten miles from Great Isaacs. She was later reported as a derelict in latitude 28°20' North, longitude 79°25' West, with all of her spars gone except her mizzenmast. Her rudder, boats and both anchors were also missing. Salvors boarding the derelict ship reported part of her cargo had been taken out along with all of her provisions. The bark *Henrietta*, of Searsport, Captain Treat, took 16 bales of cotton from the derelict *Italy* on February 3, 1853. The bark *P.R. Hazeltine*, Captain Cottrell, took 11 bales of cotton from her at the same time. The *Italy* was observed by the vessel *Retch Brothers* on February 13, 1853, in latitude 30°45' North, longitude 79°50' West, 124 miles from Charleston Bar, South Carolina. She was taken in tow by the United States Revenue cutter *Hamilton*, but was abandoned in the middle of the Gulf Stream in latitude 32°17' North about February 20, 1853. Two days later she was reported as on fire in latitude 30° North, longitude 70°40' West, and burned cotton and other wreckage was reported as observed in latitude 33° North, longitude 74°22' West. 33° North is the latitude of Cape Romain, South Carolina.]

References for entry 252 (SL Code™ 1853-3-US-SC/GA-1):
"Daily Morning News", (Savannah, GA), #42, March 4, 1853, p. 2, c. 1
"Charleston Daily Courier", (Charleston, SC), #16364, March 9, 1853, p. 4, c. 3
"Vessel Disasters, 1852-1853", (bound annotated clipping file, Atlantic Mutual Insurance Companies of New York, Marine Library), Volume 1, pp. 221, 226, 230, 239, 241, 246, 259, 265

253: The ship *Austria*, Captain Tessier, bound from Liverpool to Savannah, Georgia, with a heavy cargo of salt, went ashore in a very bad position on Cape Romain, South Carolina, on October 30, 1853. Her passengers were carried to Charleston, South Carolina, by the steamer *Charleston*, which had gone to her assistance. She went to pieces within three weeks. The *Austria* was consigned to Messrs. John Fraser & Company. She carried 100 tons of ballast. She was owed by John Fraser & Company; Captain Tessier; and

Shipwrecks, Pirates & Privateers:

others of Charleston. She was described as a fine ship capable of carrying 2700 bales of cotton. She was fully insured at Charleston.

References for entry 253 (SL Code™ 1853-10-US-SC/GA-13):
"Charleston Daily Courier", (Charleston, SC), Volume 51, #16563, November 1, 1853, p. 1, c. 1
"Charleston Daily Courier", (Charleston, SC), Volume 51, #16566, November 4, 1853, p. 2, c. 3
"Daily Morning News", (Savannah, GA), #247, November 3, 1853, p. 2, c. 2
"Vessel Disasters, 1853", (bound annotated clipping file, Atlantic Mutual Insurance Companies of New York, Marine Library), Volume 3, pp. 194, 203, 210, 216, 254, 257

254: The schooner *S.J. Moys* (or *S.J. Moye*), which took fire and was run ashore near Georgetown, South Carolina, prior to November 12, 1853, was reported to have burnt to the water's edge. Nothing was expected to be saved. She carried cotton; cedar staves; tobacco; spirits turpentine; and rosin. The schooner was insured by the Atlantic Mutual Insurance Companies of New York for $2000 and her cargo for $2007.

References for entry 254 (SL Code™ 1853-11-US-SC/GA-1):
"Charleston Daily Courier", (Charleston, SC), Volume 51, #16573, November 14, 1853, p. 2, c. 3
"Vessel Disasters, 1853", (bound annotated clipping file, Atlantic Mutual Insurance Companies of New York, Marine Library), Volume 3, p. 255

255: The sidewheel steamer *Robert Martin*, Captain C. Carroll White, burst her boilers at Ports Ferry, South Carolina, on the Pee Dee River, on November 19, 1853, and drifted 1.5 miles below the ferry, where she lay a complete wreck. Two people were injured and nine (or six) killed. The *Robert Martin* had a wood hull and was built in 1849 at Charleston, South Carolina, which was also her first home port. She was a cotton boat plying between Charleston and Cheraw, South Carolina. She measured 129'6" in length; 29'4" in breadth; 7'2" in depth; and 247 12/95 tons. She had a flush deck; a round stern; no galleries; no masts; and no figure-head. Captain White was a general partner in the limited partnership which owned the vessel.

References for entry 255 (SL Code™ 1853-11-US-SC/GA-2):
"Permanent Enrollment #11", (Charleston, SC), July 7, 1853, NARS RG 41
"Permanent Enrollment #12", (Charleston, SC), August 8, 1853, NARS RG 41
"Permanent Enrollment #14", (Charleston, SC), August 15, 1853, NARS RG 41
"Charleston Daily Courier", (Charleston, SC), Volume 51, #16579, November 22, 1853, p. 2, c. 2
"Charleston Daily Courier", (Charleston, SC), Volume 51, #16580, November 23, 1853, p. 2, c. 1
"Daily Morning News", (Savannah, GA), #263, November 22, 1853, p. 2, c. 1
Encyclopedia of American Shipwrecks, by Bruce D. Berman, (Boston, 1972), p. 142, #1690
Merchant Steam Vessels of the United States 1790-1868, ("Lytle-Holdcamper List"), edited by C. Bradford Mitchell, (Staten Island, NY, 1975), pp. 186, 294

256: The hermaphrodite brig *Nancy Pratt*, of and from Gloucester, Massachusetts, bound for Wilmington, North Carolina, with stone, was seen ashore, and probably bilged, on a "bank which is nearly dry at low water", off Bird Key, Cape Romain, South Carolina, on November 30, 1853. The steamer *Col. Myers*, Captain Paine, went to her aid, but was blown ashore in the heavy weather of December 8. Fortunately, the steamer got off safely and returned to Charleston. Captain Magee of the steamer *Nina*, described the brig as "an Eastern vessel, painted black with a red streak, and a new mainsail."

References for entry 256 (SL Code™ 1853-11-US-SC/GA-3):
"Charleston Daily Courier", (Charleston, SC), Volume 51, #16587, December 1, 1853, p. 2, c. 2
"Charleston Daily Courier", (Charleston, SC), Volume 51, #16589, December 3, 1853, p. 2, c. 3
"Charleston Daily Courier", (Charleston, SC), Volume 51, #16595, December 10, 1853, p. 2, c. 2, p. 4, c. 7

257: The schooner *H.M. Johnson*, Captain Butler, which struck the Georgetown Bar and put into Bull's Bay, South Carolina, for safety "was leaking badly, making upwards of a thousand strokes (of the pump) an hour". Captain Butler thought he was going to have to beach her, as his crew refused to risk attempting to sail her to Charleston.

References for entry 257 (SL Code™ 1854-1-US-SC/GA-6):
"Charleston Daily Courier", (Charleston, SC), Volume 52, #17633 (sic), January 26, 1854
"Charleston Daily Courier", (Charleston, SC), Volume 52, #16638, February 1, 1854, p. 1, c. 2

258: The schooner *Lucy Ann*, Captain Douglas, 27 days out of Boston, bound to Charleston, with ice, went ashore on the beach in Long Bay, thirty miles east of Georgetown and a quarter of a mile north of Murrel's Inlet, South Carolina, on January 28, 1854. She was totally lost with her cargo. The wreck was sold at auction by Messrs. Wareman and McGiney.

References for entry 258 (SL Code™ 1854-1-US-SC/GA-9):
"Charleston Daily Courier", (Charleston, SC), Volume 52, #16640, February 3, 1854, p. 1, c. 1
"Vessel Disasters, 1854", (bound annotated clipping file, Atlantic Mutual Insurance Companies of New York, Marine Library), Volume 5, p. 58

259: The British bark *Aquatic*, Captain Robert Wilson, bound from Matanzas to Cork, with a cargo of molasses, was run ashore in Long Bay, South Carolina, to the northward of Georgetown, South Carolina, on July 10, 1854. Her position was also given as on Pawley's Island Beach, South Carolina. The crew were said to have sick with yellow fever. She was of St. John's, New Brunswick, and was owned by McGivern & Seafield. The *Aquatic* was later reported as towed off.

References for entry 259 (SL Code™ 1854-7-US-SC/GA-1):
"Charleston Daily Standard", (Charleston, SC), #7, July 10, 1854, p. 2, c. 3
"Charleston Daily Standard", (Charleston, SC), #8, July 11, 1854, p. 2, c. 4
"Charleston Daily Standard", (Charleston, SC), #9, July 12, 1854, p. 2, c. 3
"Charleston Daily Standard", (Charleston, SC), #11, July 14, 1854, p. 2, c. 3

260: The brig *Joann*, Captain Tyler, bound from Bucksville, South Carolina, to Frankfort, Maine, with a load of lumber, filled with water and was abandoned on the bar of Georgetown, South Carolina, on August 14, 1854.

Reference for entry 260 (SL Code™ 1854-8-US-SC/GA-1):
"Charleston Daily Standard", (Charleston, SC), #47, August 25, 1854, p. 2, c. 5

261: The brig *E. Hinds*, Captain Barrington, which anchored off Georgetown, South Carolina, in a sinking condition, on September 7, 1854, was believed to have foundered at her anchors during the gale or hurricane of that date. The captain and most of the crew were sick and the brig was sinking when Captain H. Lachicotte, with the pilot boat *Margaret Davis*, went out to her at the imminent risk of losing his boat and all hands. Captain Lachicotte succeeded in taking off Captain Barrington and four of his crew, but one man refused to leave the brig without his sea chest. Night coming on and the gale increasing from east south east, the pilot boat was compelled to leave, and with the greatest difficulty got into the harbor. That night the *E. Hinds* parted her chains and went ashore on Cedar Island, South Carolina, to the northward of Cape Romain. The seaman who had remained aboard drifted ashore on a plank and although badly bruised, was saved. She was expected to be a total loss. The *E. Hinds* had been bound from Wilmington to Brunswick, Maine, when the loss took place, and she was loaded with lumber. (Note: This was probably the brig *E. Hinds*, 125 tons, built in 1847 at Pittston, Maine, which was issued a certificate of registry at New York, New York, on January 8, 1853.)

Reference for entry 261 (SL Code™ 1854-9-US-SC/GA-7):
"Charleston Mercury", (Charleston, SC), #9464, September 13, 1854, p. 2, c. 2
"Vessel Disasters, 1854", (bound annotated clipping file, Atlantic Mutual Insurance Companies of New York, Marine Library), Volume 7, pp. 67, 76
American Flag Merchant Vessels that received Certificates of Enrollment or Registry at the Port of New York, 1789-1867, National Archives "Special List #22", (Washington, DC, 1968), Volume 1, p. 182

262: The wreck of the schooner *Mary D. Hayman* was fallen in with eighteen miles north east of Georgetown, South Carolina, by the schooner *Sunny South*, Captain Smith, about September 15, 1854. The *Mary D. Hayman* was reported as lying partly on her side, house and deck load swept off, going to pieces, and no one on board. The *Mary D. Hayman* had been bound from Georgetown, South Carolina, to New York, with a cargo of naval stores. The Atlantic Mutual Insurance Company of New York had written $3,000 in insurance on the schooner and $2,624 in insurance on her cargo. Her cargo included two hundred and sixteen barrels of rosin.

Reference for entry 262 (SL Code™ 1854-9-US-SC/GA-46):
"Vessel Disasters, 1854", (bound annotated clipping file, Atlantic Mutual Insurance Companies of New York, Marine Library), Volume 7, pp. 92, 170

263: A letter from Waccamaw Beach, near Georgetown, South Carolina, written prior to October 13, 1854, stated that a wreck had come "ashore bottom up, split open in the head, head and stern both gone; she was covered with zinc underlaid with felt, and well done; she is built very strongly, closely ribbed, and between 90 and 100 feet log". It was believed with "no doubt" that it was the wreck of the brig *Horace Greeley*, Captain Smith. The *Horace Greeley* had sailed from Georgetown, South Carolina, on September 5, 1854, in company with the schooner *Mary D. Hayman*. (Note: Please see previous entry.)

Reference for entry 263 (SL Code™ 1854-10x-US-SC/GA-1):
"Vessel Disasters, 1854", (bound annotated clipping file, Atlantic Mutual Insurance Companies of New York, Marine Library), Volume 7, pp. 92, 170

264: The schooner *Augustus Moore*, Captain George Watts, bound from Portsmouth, North Carolina, to Charleston, South Carolina, went ashore on the bar of Georgetown, South Carolina, at two in the morning on March 20, 1855. Both the schooner and her cargo were a total loss. She was owned in Georgetown, South Carolina, by Mr. A. Morgan, and was fully insured. Her cargo consisted of 3,700 bushels of peas and 50 barrels of tar consigned to Messrs. James Gadsden & Company, and was insured by the South Carolina Insurance Company of Charleston. The vessel was not insured. The schooner drew 7' of water and the Georgetown pilot had told Captain Watts that there was 7'6" of water on the bar. She struck and pounded so heavily that her captain had to run her ashore to save the crew. The water swelled the peas so much that "they burst the vessel to pieces."

References for entry 264 (SL Code™ 1855-3-US-SC/GA-3):
"Charleston Mercury", (Charleston, SC), #9715, March 26, 1855, p. 2, c. 7
"Vessel Disasters, 1855", (bound annotated clipping file, Atlantic Mutual Insurance Companies of New York, Marine Library), Volume 9, pp. 72, 116

265: The ship *Harkaway*, Captain Breck, bound from Liverpool, with 4000 sacks of salt, went ashore on Cape Romain, South Carolina, on March 21, 1855. She was originally expected to be a total loss, but was got off by throwing a considerable quantity of salt overboard. She was reported leaking badly but she still made it safely to Charleston.

References for entry 265 (SL Code™ 1855-3-US-SC/GA-4):
"Charleston Mercury", (Charleston, SC), #9712, March 22, 1855, p. 2, c. 4
"Charleston Mercury", (Charleston, SC), #9713, March 23, 1855, p. 2, c. 3
"Charleston Mercury", (Charleston, SC), #9714, March 24, 1855, p. 2, c. 7
"Vessel Disasters, 1855", (bound annotated clipping file, Atlantic Mutual Insurance Companies of New York, Marine Library), Volume 9, p. 68

266: On February 22, 1859, the schooner *Haze*, Captain J. Bell, collided with an unidentified schooner in latitude 33°40' North; longitude 77° West. Then, in an effort to go into Charleston for repairs, the *Haze* mistook the Cape Romain light and struck in two fathoms of water and went ashore on February 26, 1859. The *Haze* was towed off by the steamer *Marion* and taken to Charleston. The *Haze* was a full model schooner with one deck and a half poop. She was built of oak and cedar in 1855 at Madison (or Mystic), Connecticut, and was copper and iron fastened. She was 320 tons and drew 11' of water. She had her centerboard taken out, and she was metalled in July of 1859. She was surveyed in March, 1857, at New York. She was surveyed again in 1859.

References for entry 266 (SL Code™ 1859-2-US-SC/GA-1):
New York Marine Register: A Standard of Classification of American Vessels, (New York, 1857), p. 231
"Vessel Disasters, 1859", (bound annotated clipping file, Atlantic Mutual Insurance Companies of New York, Marine Library), Volume 20, p. 63
American Lloyd's: Registry of American and Foreign Shipping, (New York, 1859), p. 345, #1811

267: The schooner *Samuel Adams*, Captain Prince, which left Charleston, South Carolina, on April 12, 1859, with 4,000 bushels of rough rice for the North Santee Pounding Mill, got ashore the same day on the North Santee Bar, South Carolina, where she knocked off her rudder and received other damage. She was got off and sailed for Georgetown, South Carolina, but was run ashore in Winyah Bay, South Carolina, to prevent her from sinking. The steamer *General Clinch* was sent to her to unload the rice.

Reference for entry 267 (SL Code™ 1859-4-US-SC/GA-2):
"Vessel Disasters, 1859", (bound annotated clipping file, Atlantic Mutual Insurance Companies of New York, Marine Library), Volume 20, p. 160

268: The schooner *Helen*, Captain Long, passed a wreck with "about 15' of her main or mizzenmast standing, and the top of her house about 2' above water" in latitude 33° North, longitude 76°05' West, on July 2, 1859. (Note: 33° is the latitude of Cape Romain, South Carolina.)

Reference for entry 268 (SL Code™ 1859-7-US-SC/GA-1):
"Charleston Daily Courier", (Charleston, SC), #18302, July 14, 1859, p. 4, c. 5

269: The schooner *Mary Louisa*, Captain Vultee, of and from New York for Saint Augustine, Florida, was stranded on the eastern shore of North Island, South Carolina, about fourteen miles from Georgetown, South Carolina, in late September 1859. She was got off after a few days and was towed to Georgetown. She carried an assorted cargo of merchandise which was insured through the Atlantic Mutual Insurance Company of New York. (Note: There was some suspicion expressed in contemporary newspaper accounts that her crew was made up of pirates or mutineers.)

References for entry 269 (SL Code™ 1859-9-US-SC/GA-1):
"Charleston Daily Courier", (Charleston, SC), #18381, October 14, 1859, p. 4, c. 6
"Vessel Disasters, 1859", (bound annotated clipping file, Atlantic Mutual Insurance Companies of New York, Marine Library), Volume 21, pp. 150, 157

270: The Savannah "Daily Morning News" of June 23, 1860, in an article datelined "Cape Island (Cape Romain, South Carolina), June 22" reported that the survey steamer *Walker* had been run into and sunk on June 21, 1860. About twenty people who had been on board were missing and were thought to have been lost.

Reference for entry 270 (SL Code™ 1860-6-US-SC/GA-1):
"Daily Morning News", (Savannah, GA), #148, June 23, 1860, p. 1, c. 1

271: The Savannah "Daily Morning News" of November 4, 1861, reported that two Federal steam transports, laden with cattle and provisions, were driven ashore a few miles north of Georgetown, South Carolina, during the storm of November 2, 1861. (Note One: This would place them in the vicinity of DeBordieu Island, South Carolina.).] (Note Two: See also entry 272 in this book.)

Reference for entry 271 (SL Code™ 1861-11-US-SC/GA-2):
"Daily Morning News", (Savannah, GA), November 4, 1861, p. 2, c. 1

272: The United States transport steamer *Osceola*, Captain Morrill, went ashore on the Day Breaker, off North Island, near Georgetown, South Carolina, in a severe gale on November 2, 1861. The transport carried potatoes, vegetables and thirty-nine head of cattle, some of which swam to shore. The officers and crew took to their boats and landed on North Island where they were captured by the Confederates. (Note One: The *Osceola* was described as "bilged in two hours," but her machinery was expected to be saved. She was afterwards reported as "being successfully overhauled," but the report may have been in error.) [Note Two: The steamer was owned in New York and had previously been engaged as a cattle boat between Cuba and Honduras. The *Osceola* was part of a Federal fleet of fifty or sixty vessels being sent South to capture a deep water port to be used as a depot. The vessel was built at Brooklyn, New York, in 1848, was schooner rigged with two masts and was copper sheathed. She was fastened with copper and treenails. The *Osceola* was said to be a poor sea risk and to have insufficient security against fire, so she was classed 5-A2 for insurance purposes. The *Osceola's* hull was built of oak, chestnut, etc., with composition fastenings and she had a large cabin on deck. The steamer measured 177 18/95 tons (or 173 tons), 120' along her keel, 117'8" in length, 22' in breadth and 7'4" in depth of hold, and she drew seven feet of water at her load line. The vessel's frame was of white oak and cedar. The steamer had one (also shown as two) iron propeller(s) seven feet in diameter. The *Osceola* had one smokestack and one flued boiler (17' X 6'5") which was mounted on her deck. She had "knees under her spar deck." The steamer's boiler was built in 1858 by Hogg and Delawater of New York. The *Osceola* was fitted "with vertical direct-acting engines, with two cylinders, each 24 inches in diameter and a stroke of piston of two feet; she was also supplied with one tubular boiler and her propeller was seven feet in diameter and made of iron." She was also shown as having had just one engine with one twenty-two inch cylinder with a twenty-six inch stroke. The vessel had a square stern, no galleries, and no figure head. She was owned by P.N. Spoford Esq. of New York.] (Note Three: "Lytle's list" shows the *Osceola* as having been stranded at Savannah, Georgia.)

References for entry 272 (SL Code™ 1861-11-US-SC/GA-3):
"Reports of Steamers, Volume B", (bound manuscript), National Archives, Record Group 92, entry 1432, p. 430
"Permanent Enrollment #55", (New York, NY), May 17, 1860, National Archives, Record Group 41
"Permanent Register #18", (New York, NY), August 3, 1860, National Archives, Record Group 41
"Permanent Register #19", (New York, NY), August 3, 1860, National Archives, Record Group 41
"Permanent Register #20", (New York, NY), August 5, 1860, National Archives, Record Group 41
"Daily Morning News", (Savannah, GA), Volume 12, # 258, November 4, 1861, p. 2, c. 1
"Daily Morning News", (Savannah, GA), Volume 12, #261, November 7, 1861, p. 2 c. 1
"Daily Morning News", (Savannah, GA), Volume 12, #265, November 12, 1861, p. 2, c. 3
"Charleston Daily Courier", (Charleston, SC), #19005, November 6, 1861, p. 2, c. 2
New York Times, (New York, NY), Volume 11, #3166, November 14, 1861, p. 2, c. 3, 4

Shipwrecks, Pirates & Privateers:

New York Times, (New York, NY), Volume 11, #3167, November 15, 1861, p. 1, c. 4
"Steam Vessels #1, 1850's", (bound manuscript, Atlantic Mutual Insurance Companies of New York), entry for *Osceola*
"Vessel Disasters, 1861", (bound annotated clipping file, Atlantic Mutual Insurance Companies of New York), Volume 28, pp. 191, 199
Official Records of the Union and Confederate Armies in the War of the Rebellion, (Washington, DC, 1882), Series 1, Volume 6, pp. 3, 186
Official Records of the Union and Confederate Navies in the War of the Rebellion, (Washington, DC, 1901), Series 1, Volume 12, pp. 288, 293
The Navy in the Civil War, (Charles Scribner's Sons, New York, NY, 1905), Volume 2 ("The Atlantic Coast" by Daniel Ammen), pp. 18, 33
Merchant Steam Vessels of the United States 1807-1868, ("Lytle List"), by William M. Lytle, (Mystic, CT, 1952), p. 146
List of American-Flag Merchant Vessels that Received Certificates of Enrollment or Registry at the Port of New York 1789-1867, compiled by Forest R. Holdcamper, (U.S. National Archives, Washington, DC, 1968), Special List #22, Volume 2, p. 536
Encyclopedia of American Shipwrecks, by Bruce D. Berman, (Boston, 1972), p. 138, #1524
Merchant Steam Vessels of the United States 1790-1868, ("Lytle-Holdcamper List"), edited by C. Bradford Mitchell, (Staten Island, New York, 1975), pp. 165, 287

273: The steamer *Governor*, Captain Phillips, under charter by the United States Navy as a troop transport, foundered in thirteen fathoms of water in a hurricane on November 2, 1861. She was carrying a battalion of four hundred "fine marines" under Major John G. Reynolds. Seven of *Governor's* crew were drowned or crushed to death. The remainder of the people were saved by the United States gunboats *Sabine*, Captain Ringgold; *Isaac Smith*; and *Rover*. The crew of the *Sabine* was awarded a gold medal by the "Life Saving Benevolent Association of New York." The *Governor* had a small supply of stores on board. Nearly all of the arms were saved, but the haversacks, knapsacks, canteens and 9000 cartridges of ammunition were lost. (Note One: The "Lytle-Holdcamper Steamship List" shows the United States transport *Governor* as wrecked off Hatteras, North Carolina, and gives the date as November 20, 1861, but the file card notes used in its preparation show the location as off Charleston. The *Ocean Atlas of the Carolina Margin* also lists her as wrecked off Hatteras and gives the date of loss as October 31, 1861. Most contemporary accounts give the date as November 2, 1861, and place the wreck further south. At least one contemporary account states that she foundered off Charleston, South Carolina.) [Note Two: The *Governor* was built by Samuel Sneeden at New York, New York, in 1846 of "white oak, etc. and fastened in an excellent manner." Her hull had been extensively repaired in 1858. She measured 644 81/95 tons, 230'3" in length, 28'3" in breadth, 10'3" in depth, and 7' in draft. She had one deck, no masts, a square stern and a billet head. She had condensing engines and her boiler was mounted on deck. She was issued a certificate of steam enrollment at the port of New York on March 28, 1846. She was owned by Albert Dailey and Company of New York. The *Governor* was described as a staunch vessel built to "run on the sound between New York and Providence, R.I." However, "never in her best days (was she) adapted to a sea voyage."] (Note

Three: Due to conflicting data, as to the actual location of this wreck, this entry has been given duel SL Codes.) (Note Four: Erik Heyl in his book *Early American Steamers* shows the *Governor* as 235'x28'2"x10'1"; 650 tons; vertical beam engine; cylinder 48" diameter with 11' stroke; and 30' diameter water wheels. Heyl has a drawing of the steamer based on an illustration in "Leslie's Weekly" and a painting at the Mariner's Museum at Newport News, Virginia.") [Note Five: In 1989, my friend Randy Lathrop and I dove on the wreck of an unidentified wooden hulled sidewheel steamer approximately 22.8 miles off Little River Inlet (South Carolina, North Carolina line). The wreck was in 78' of water at Loran-C coordinates 45333.5/59483.5. The wreck had been discovered by Captain Billy Long, a commercial fisherman, who had put divers (Blaine Garren, Randy McCormick and Hampton Shupen) down on the wreck shortly before Lathrop and I were asked to make our dive. Long's divers had tentatively identified the wreck as that of a blockade runner. However, Lathrop and I found New York State Militia and regular United States belt buckles. One buckle appeared to be a pre-Civil War type of buckle used by officers of the United States Marines. The numerous buckles, musket parts, sword handles, haversack hooks, knapsack fastenings, canteen necks and other items we observed, appear to be evidence that the wreck may be that of a Federal transport lost during or immediately after the war, and that it may even be the *Governor*. At the first Battle of Manassas (Bull Run), Major Reynolds had commanded a battalion of U.S. Marines, supporting the 14th Regiment of the New York State Militia, which could explain the New York militia buckles we found.] (Note Six: Local dive charter boats routinely carry divers out to this wreck.) [Note Seven: Some people believe that Captain Long's wreck may actually be that of the *Suwanee*, which was lost on December 4, 1866, while carrying arms and ammunition for the Mexican Republic, or even another vessel. The *Suwanee* (ex-*Pampero*) was a sidewheel, wooden hulled steamer, of 350 tons. She was built in Baltimore, Maryland, in 1850, and was first home ported at Washington, D.C. However, the *Suwanee* is shown in the "Lytle-Holdcamper List" as foundered without loss of life off Cape Romano, Florida.]

References for entry 273 (SL Code™ 1861-11-US-SC/GA-5)
"Vessel Surveys" (bound manuscript insurance surveys, by Haswell), entry for *Governor*, National Archives, Record Group 92
"Temporary Register," #295, (Boston, MA), Oct. 11, 1861, National Archives, Record Group 41
New York Times, (New York, NY), Vol. 11, #3163, November 11, 1861, p. 1, c. 1, 3, 4
New York Times, (New York, NY), Volume 11, #3164, November 12, 1861, p. 1, c. 3
New York Times, (New York, NY), Volume 11, #3165, November 13, 1861, p. 1, c. 3
New York Times, (New York, NY), Volume 11, #3166, November 14, 1861, p. 2, c. 3, 4
New York Times, (New York, NY), Volume 11, #3167, November 15, 1861, p. 1, c. 4, 5
New York Times, (New York, NY), Volume 11, #3180, December 1, 1861, p. 1, c. 3
"Daily Morning News," (Savannah), Nov. 18, 1861, p. 1, c. 1
"Charleston Daily Courier," (Charleston, SC), #19107, Nov. 21, 1861, p. 1, c. 4

Shipwrecks, Pirates & Privateers:

"Vessel Disasters, 1861," (bound annotated clipping file, Atlantic Mutual Insurance Companies of New York), Volume 28, pp. 184, 192, 199, 200

Official Records of the Union and Confederate Armies in the War of the Rebellion, (Washington, DC), Series 1, Volume 2, pp. 383, 386, 388, 391, 392

Official Records of the Union and Confederate Navies in the War of the Rebellion, (Washington, DC, 1901), Series 1, Volume 12, pp. 223, 232-249

The Navy in the Civil War, (Charles Scribner's Sons, New York, NY, 1905), Volume 2 ("The Atlantic Coast" by Daniel Ammen), p. 17

Graveyard of the Atlantic: Shipwrecks of the North Carolina Coast, by David Stick (University of North Carolina Press, Chapel Hill, North Carolina, 1952), pp. 51, 247

Battles and Leaders of the Civil War, edited by Robert U. Johnson and Clarence C. Buel, Volume 1 of 4 volumes (Century Co., New York, NY, 1884-87, reprinted by Thomas Yoseloff Inc. 1956), pp. 674, 676

Early American Steamers, by Erik Heyl, (Buffalo, New York, 1965), Volume 4, pp. 125, 126

List of American-Flag Merchant Vessels that Received Certificates of Enrollment or Registry at the Port of New York 1789-1867, compiled by Forest R. Holdcamper, (U.S. National Archives, Washington, DC, 1968), Special List #22, Volume 1, p. 288

Encyclopedia of American Shipwrecks, by Bruce D. Berman, Mariners Press, (Boston, MA, 1972), p. 122, #786

Naval History of the Civil War, by Howard P. Nash, (A.S. Barnes & Co., New York, NY, 1972), pp. 58, 59

Manuscript 3x5 file card for steamer *Governor* used in preparation of "Lytle-Holdcamper List," National Archives, Record Group 41

Merchant Steam Vessels of the United States 1790-1868, ("Lytle-Holdcamper List"), by William M. Lytle and Forrest R. Holdcamper, revised and edited by C. Bradford Mitchell, (Staten Island, New York, 1975), pp. 87, 167, 206, 265, 288

An Oceanographic Atlas of the Carolina Continental Margin, by J.G. Newton, (Duke University Marine Laboratory, Beaufort, North Carolina, 1971), p. 28

"Wreck Miscellanea," column by E. Lee Spence, in *ShipWrecks*, Volume 1, #2, p. 4

274: The fine blockade running schooner *Prince of Wales*, of Nassau, Captain W.F. Adair, bound from Nassau to a Confederate Port, was run ashore in an effort to save her crew after she was fired into by a Union gunboat on December 24, 1861. The shot took effect on the hull but did not injure anyone. The schooner's location was given as inside of the breakers at North Inlet and nine miles from the entrance to Georgetown, South Carolina. Captain Adair set the *Prince of Wales* afire to prevent the vessel and its cargo from falling into the hands of the enemy. The schooner carried one thousand sacks of salt, sundries, and oranges. (Note One: One report states that the *Prince of Wales* was burned by the *U.S.S. Gem of the Sea.*) (Note Two: Jim Batey and I found the wrecks of two wooden hulled sailing vessels while diving at North Inlet in 1966. We tentatively identified the larger hull as the wreck of the *Prince of Wales.*)

References for entry 274 (SL Code™ 1861-12-US-SC/GA-10):

"Charleston Daily Courier", (Charleston, SC), #19047, December 27, 1861, p. 2, c. 3

"Vessel Papers" (manuscript records), United States National Archives, Washington, DC, Record Group 109, files P-17, P-80

Official Records of the Union and Confederate Navies in the War of the Rebellion, (Washington, DC, 1901), Series 1, Volume 12, pp. 428-430, 459

Manifest, contained in miscellaneous documents, microfilmed by E. Lee Spence, at United States National Archives (Washington, DC, 1972), roll 2

History of Georgetown County, South Carolina, by George C. Rogers, (Columbia, South Carolina, 1970), p. 394

275: On February 14, 1862, the Federals burned a "very old worthless craft, without a cargo," which had been aground on a shoal in Bull's Bay, South Carolina.

References for entry 275 (SL Code™ 1862-2-US-SC/GA-1)

Official Records of the Union and Confederate Navies in the War of the Rebellion, (Washington, DC, 1901), Series 1, Volume 12, pp. 547, 548

Sunken Treasures of the Upper SC Coast, 1521-1865

276: On February 14, 1862, the Federals captured and sank the coasting sloop *Edisto*, with 1600 bushels of rice, in Bull's Bay, South Carolina.

References for entry 276 (SL Code™ 1862-2-US-SC/GA-2)
"Charleston Daily Courier," (Charleston, SC), #19089, January 17, 1862, p. 2, c. 3
"Daily Morning News," (Savannah, GA), #40, February 18, 1862, p. 1, c. 1
"Charleston Mercury," (Charleston, SC), Volume 80, #11377, March 4, 1862, p. 2, c. 1
Official Records of the Union and Confederate Navies in the War of the Rebellion, (Washington, DC, 1901), Series 1, Volume 12, pp. 547-550

277: On February 14, 1862, the Federals captured and sank the coasting schooner *Wandoo* (probably *Wando*) with eighteen hundred bushels of rice, in Bull's Bay, South Carolina.

References for entry 277 (SL Code™ 1862-2-US-SC/GA-3)
"Charleston Daily Courier," (Charleston, SC), #19089, January 17, 1862, p. 2, c. 3
"Daily Morning News," (Savannah, GA), #40, February 18, 1862, p. 1, c. 1
"Charleston Mercury," (Charleston, SC), Volume 80, #11377, March 4, 1862, p. 2, c. 1
Official Records of the Union and Confederate Navies in the War of the Rebellion, (Washington, DC, 1901), Series 1, Volume 12, pp. 547-550

278: On February 14, 1862, the Federals captured and sank the coasting schooner *Elizabeth*, with eighteen hundred bushels of rice, in Bull's Bay, South Carolina.

References for entry 278 (SL Code™ 1862-2-US-SC/GA-4)
"Daily Morning News," (Savannah, GA), #40, February 18, 1862, p. 1, c. 1
"Charleston Mercury," (Charleston, SC), Volume 80, #11377, March 4, 1862, p. 2, c. 1
Official Records of the Union and Confederate Navies in the War of the Rebellion, (Washington, DC, 1901), Series 1, Volume 12, pp. 547-550

279: On February 14, 1862, the Federals captured and burned the coasting schooner *Theodore Stoney*, with twenty-five hundred bushels of rice, in Bull's Bay, South Carolina. The *Theodore Stoney*, Captain Roberts, was described as a fine craft of fifty-four tons.

References for entry 279 (SL Code™ 1862-2-US-SC/GA-5)
"Charleston Daily Courier," (Charleston, SC), #19089, January 17, 1862, p. 2, c. 3
"Daily Morning News," (Savannah, GA), #40, February 18, 1862, p. 1, c. 1
"Charleston Mercury," (Charleston, SC), Volume 80, #11377, March 4, 1862, p. 2, c. 1
Official Records of the Union and Confederate Navies in the War of the Rebellion, (Washington, DC, 1901), Series 1, Volume 12, pp. 547-550

280: On February 14, 1862, the Federals captured and sunk the coasting schooner *Patriot*, Captain Wood, with 1,800 (or 1,850) bushels of rough rice, in Bull's Bay, South Carolina. (Note: She was afterwards reported safe.)

References for entry 280 (SL Code™ 1862-2-US-SC/GA-6)
"Charleston Daily Courier," (Charleston, SC), #19089, January 17, 1862, p. 2, c. 3
"Charleston Mercury," (Charleston, SC), Volume 80, #11377, March 4, 1862, p. 2, c. 1, p. 4, c. 3

281: On March 28, 1862, two armed boats from the U.S. bark *Restless* destroyed the schooner *George Washington*, Captain Finegan, with 3200 bushels of rice, 50 bushels of corn and 20 bushels of rice meal. The schooner was scuttled in two places and burned in the inland passage near Mill Island, South Carolina.

References for entry 281 (SL Code™ 1862-3-US-SC/GA-4)
"Charleston Daily Courier," (Charleston, SC), #19123, March 31, 1862, p. 2, c. 2
"Daily Morning News," (Savannah, GA), #73, April 1, 1862, p. 1, c. 3
Official Records of the Union and Confederate Navies in the War of the Rebellion, (Washington, DC, 1901), Series 1, Volume 12, pp. 666-668

282: Contemporary newspaper accounts reported that on March 28, 1862, two armed boats from the U.S. bark *Restless* burned the schooner *Julia Worden* (or *Julia Warden*), Captain Kroeg, in the inland passage between Bull's Bay, South Carolina, and Charleston. (Note: The newspaper reports are in conflict with the "Official Records" which show the *Julia Worden* simply as captured and not as destroyed.)

References for entry 282 (SL Code™ 1862-3-US-SC/GA-5)
"Charleston Daily Courier," (Charleston, SC), #19123, March 31, 1862, p. 2, c. 2
"Daily Morning News," (Savannah, GA), #73, April 1, 1862, p. 1, c. 3
Official Records of the Union and Confederate Navies in the War of the Rebellion, (Washington, DC, 1901), Series 1, Volume 12, pp. 666-668, 681, 682, 719, 793

283: On March 28, 1862, two armed boats from the U.S. bark *Restless* burned a schooner belonging to Mr. Thompson, in the inland passage between Bull's Bay, South Carolina, and Charleston.

References for entry 283 (SL Code™ 1862-3-US-SC/GA-6)
"Charleston Daily Courier," (Charleston, SC), #19123, March 31, 1862, p. 2, c. 2
"Daily Morning News," (Savannah, GA), #73, April 1, 1862, p. 1, c. 3

284: On March 28, 1862, two armed boats from the U.S. bark *Restless* burned Mr. Doar's sloop, the *Mary Louisa*, with two thousand and sixty bushels of rice and one hundred bushels of corn, near the lighthouse at Cape Romain, South Carolina.

References for entry 284 (SL Code™ 1862-3-US-SC/GA-7):
"Charleston Daily Courier", (Charleston, SC), #19123, March 31, 1862, p. 2, c. 2
"Daily Morning News", (Savannah, GA), #73, April 1, 1862, p. 1, c. 3
Official Records of the Union and Confederate Navies in the War of the Rebellion, (Washington, DC, 1901), Series 1, Volume 12, pp. 666-668

285: Just before sunset on April 10, 1862, the Federal gunboat *Keystone State* spotted the schooner *Liverpool*, of Nassau, ashore on the outside of the point of North Inlet, South Carolina. The schooner had been set on fire and deserted. The *Liverpool* was of 150 to 180 tons burden and was evidently deeply laden. (Note: Jim Batey, Ron Renau, and I found the wrecks of three wooden hulled sailing vessels while diving at North Inlet in 1966. We tentatively identified the two newer wrecks as *Liverpool* and the *Prince of Wales*. The third wreck was smaller and appeared much older.)

References for entry 285 (SL Code™ 1862-4-US-SC/GA-4):
Official Records of the Union and Confederate Navies in the War of the Rebellion, (Washington, DC, 1901), Series 1, Volume 12, pp. 677, 679
Personal knowledge of E. Lee Spence of dive he made with Jim Batey and Ron Renau, circa summer, 1966.

286: The schooner *Sir Robert Peel*, with a valuable cargo, was chased by the Federal blockading steamers while approaching the coast near Georgetown, South Carolina, in early April, 1862, and was burned by her own captain to prevent her falling into Federal hands. (Note One: This may have been the schooner *Sir Robert Peel*, W. Gyles master, 88 tons, which was built at Dartmouth in 1846 and was partly fastened with iron bolts. That vessel was

64'6"x17'5"x10'8".) (Note Two: A runaway slave, named Allen Davis, during an interrogation aboard the *U.S.S. James Adger* on April 28, 1862, mentioned a "brig" called the *Sir Robert Peel* as, at that time, being in Charleston.)

References for entry 286 (SL Code™ 1862-4-US-SC/GA-5):
"Charleston Daily Courier," (Charleston, SC), #19136, April 15, 1862, p. 2, c. 2
"Daily Morning Herald," (Savannah, GA), Volume 13, #86, April 16, 1862, p. 1, c. 1
"Vessel Papers" (manuscript records), United States National Archives, Washington, DC, Record Group 109, file S-130
Lloyd's Register of British and Foreign Shipping, from 1st July, 1863, to the 30th June, 1864, (London, 1863), entry S-494
Official Records of the Union and Confederate Navies in the War of the Rebellion, (Washington, DC, 1901), Series 1, Volume 12, p. 786

287: On April 26, 1862, the schooner *Chase*, of Nassau, was chased ashore by the United States steamer *Huron* near the middle of Raccoon Key (described as "the island on which Romain light stands") and set on fire by her own crew to prevent its capture. The heavy surf extinguished the fire and she was boarded the following day by a boat from the U.S. ship *Onward* who attempted to save her (and described her as registered as twenty tons but seeming much larger by American standards). The Federals were planning to burn her if their efforts to get her off proved unsuccessful. (Note: This was probably the schooner described in entry 1862-4-US-SC/GA-9, despite the differences in the descriptions of her location.)

References for entry 287 (SL Code™ 1862-4-US-SC/GA-8)
Official Records of the Union and Confederate Navies in the War of the Rebellion, (Washington, DC, 1901), Series 1, Volume 12, pp. 781, 795

288: The schooner *Sarah*, from Nassau, loaded with an assorted cargo, was run ashore and burned by her crew near the entrance to Bull's Bay, South Carolina, to prevent her capture by the United States gunboat *Onward* on May 1, 1862. The *Sarah's* tonnage was estimated as about one hundred tons. (Note: In the margin next to the entry for the schooner *Sarah*, G. Hore master, 95 tons, in "Lloyd's Register" for 1863/64 is the word "lost," but this may or may not have been the same vessel. That vessel was built at Lyme Bay, England, in 1819.)

References for entry 288 (SL Code™ 1862-5-US-SC/GA-1)
Official Records of the Union and Confederate Navies in the War of the Rebellion, (Washington, DC, 1901), Series 1, Volume 12, pp. 793, 794, 800
Lloyd's Register of British and Foreign Shipping, from 1st July, 1863, to the 30th June, 1864, (London, 1863), entry H-351

289: A flat belonging to Mr. J.I. Middleton, which was taken by the Federals during a foray up the Waccamaw River, South Carolina, on May 21, 1862, was sunk less than half a mile from where they took it. The flat was loaded with plunder when it was accidentally sunk.

Reference for entry 289 (SL Code™ 1862-5-US-SC/GA-4):
"Charleston Daily Courier", (Charleston, SC), #19172, May 29, 1862, p. 2, c. 3

Shipwrecks, Pirates & Privateers:

290: The brig *Joseph* was burned by the Confederates in the Waccamaw River within sight of the Federal gunboats which had run up near Georgetown, South Carolina on May 21 (or 22), 1862.

References for entry 290 (SL Code™ 1862-5-US-SC/GA-5):
Official Records of the Union and Confederate Armies in the War of the Rebellion, (Washington, DC, 1902), Series 1, Volume 14, pp. 512, 513
Official Records of the Union and Confederate Navies in the War of the Rebellion, (Washington, DC, 1901), Series 1, Volume 13, pp. 22, 23
History of Georgetown County, South Carolina, by George C. Rogers, (Columbia, South Carolina, 1970), pp. 399, 400

291: On June 26, 1862, an expedition under the command of Lieutenant F.M. Bunce of the *U.S.S. Monticello* found and burned two schooners, one lying high and dry, the other at the high-water mark, at the town of Little River, All Saints Parish, South Carolina.

References for entry 291 (SL Code™ 1862-6-US-SC/GA-1)
Official Records of the Union and Confederate Navies in the War of the Rebellion, (Washington, DC, 1898), Series 1, Volume 7, pp. 507, 720

292: The steamer *Scotia*, Captain Libby (or Lebby), bound from Nassau to Charleston, with one hundred and six tons of merchandise, went ashore on Bull's Breakers (South Carolina) on October 24, 1862. The *Scotia's* cargo consisted of sheets, blankets, woolens, etc. for the Confederate Army. Captain Libby believing it would be impossible to get the *Scotia* off, launched a small boat with two passengers. Leaving the crew behind, he abandoned her. When the Federals boarded the wreck and took the crew prisoner they threw the *Scotia's* men in irons as they were drunk and unmanageable. Captain Libby was described by the Federals as "an old offender." The Charleston papers thought that the *Scotia* had gone to pieces, but the steamer had actually been towed off and taken to Port Royal as a prize.

References for entry 292 (SL Code™ 1862-10-US-SC/GA-2)
"Charleston Daily Courier," (Charleston, SC), #19299, October 27, 1862, p. 2, c. 3
"Charleston Daily Courier," (Charleston, SC), #19301, October 29, 1862, p. 2, c. 2
Official Records of the Union and Confederate Navies in the War of the Rebellion, (Washington, DC, 1901), Series 1, Volume 13, pp. 409-415

293: The British steamer *Anglia*, Captain Newlands, which left Nassau on October 20, 1862, with a valuable general cargo, was kept off the coast so long (in trying to evade the Federal blockade fleet), that her captain, running short of fuel, ran her into the harbor at Bull's Island, South Carolina, on October 26, 1862, where she was afterwards reported as hard aground in front of Jack's Creek, four miles from the Cape Romain lighthouse. The Federals got her off.

References for entry 293 (SL Code™ 1862-10-US-SC/GA-3)
"Charleston Daily Courier," (Charleston, SC), #19299, October 27, 1862, p. 2, c. 3
"Charleston Daily Courier," (Charleston, SC), #19301, October 29, 1862, p. 2, c. 2
Official Records of the Union and Confederate Navies in the War of the Rebellion, (Washington, DC, 1901), Series 1, Volume 13, pp. 410-414

294: On November 2, 1862, the U.S. gunboat *Penobscot* chased the English schooner *Pathfinder*, of Nassau, ashore about two miles to the westward of Little River, South Carolina. The schooner was loaded with salt, boots, shoes, olive oil, liquors, cutlery, etc. The *Pathfinder* was set afire and destroyed. (Note: See also entry 1864-12-US-NC-4.)

References for entry 294 (SL Code™ 1862-11-US-SC/GA-1)
Official Records of the Union and Confederate Navies in the War of the Rebellion, (Washington, DC, 1899), Series 1, Volume 8, pp. 175, 190

295: The schooner *Lotus,* of Boston, Captain Thomas Quinn, with a cargo of sutler's stores, was run ashore on North Island Beach, one and a half miles from the Georgetown, South Carolina, lighthouse on January 15, 1863. While her cargo was being salvaged by the United States gunboat *Sebago,* it was discovered that the schooner carried a great many casks of liquor "concealed in barrels of potatoes and put up in various ways for smuggling". The *Lotus* was not a regular blockade runner as she had "legally" cleared from New York on December 23, 1862, bound for Port Royal, South Carolina, which was in Federal hands. The *Lotus* carried a crew of four men and a boy, and four passengers. (Note: This was probably the 132 ton schooner *Lotus* which was built in 1853 at Ellsworth, Maine. That vessel was issued a certificate of enrollment at New York, New York, on March 4, 1861. She was surveyed in May of 1858 and was listed in *American Lloyd's* for that year as A-2 1/2 for insurance purposes. She was a full model schooner and had one deck and a half poop and drew nine feet of water. She had iron fastenings and was built of mixed wood.)

References for entry 295 (SL Code™ 1863-1-US-SC/GA-1):
New York Marine Register: or American Lloyd's, (New York, New York, 1858), p. 272, #2364
Vessel log of the *U.S.S. Sebago,* January 16, 17, 19-21, 23, & 30, 1863, National Archives, Record Group 24
Official Records of the Union and Confederate Navies in the War of the Rebellion, (Washington, DC, 1901), Series 1, Volume 13, pp. 512, 513, 657
List of American-Flag Merchant Vessels that Received Certificates of Enrollment or Registry at the Port of New York 1789-1867, compiled by Forest R. Holdcamper, (U.S. National Archives, Washington, DC, 1968), Special List #22, Volume 2, p. 424

296: The English blockade running steamer *Wave Queen* (or *Queen of the Wave*), from Nassau, with an assorted cargo (including ammunition and clothing) on English account, was run ashore and burned by the *U.S.S. Conemaugh,* near the mouth of the North Santee River, South Carolina, about March 2, 1863, and was expected to be a total loss. It was her first and only attempt to run the blockade. Her cargo was valued at $250,000. Official Federal dispatches stated three thousand two hundred sheets of tin, twenty ounce bottles of quinine, twenty-three ounce bottles of morphine, fifteen pounds of opium, several bales of calico, two anchors, a complete binnacle, and twelve reams of paper were saved from the wreck. The wrecked steamer was set on fire and was later reported as broken up by the waves. The *Wave Queen* had an iron hull, but by March 8, 1863, the waves had already "broken her in two". She had been described as a "new Clyde built steamer" and as a "magnificent vessel". The wrecked steamer was afterwards blown up by the Federals in an effort to further destroy her. (Note One: Some sources show the date of the loss as early as February 24, and as late as March 24, 1863. Stephen Wise in his book *Lifeline of the Confederacy* shows her as a screw steamer built by Alexander Stephens and Sons at Kelvinghaugh, England, in 1861. Wise shows her as 775 tons burden and as 180'x30'x12.5'.) (Note Two: In 1967, Jim Batey and I located the wreck of a large steamer, with a riveted iron hull, in the breakers on the north side of the entrance to the North Santee River. The wreck was almost entirely buried in a large sand bar. That wreck, which I have tentatively identified as the *Wave Queen*, was located at approximately 33°08'12" North latitude and 79°14' West longitude.)

References for entry 296 (SL Code™ 1863-3-US-SC/GA-1):
"Charleston Mercury", (Charleston, SC), Volume 82, #11697, March 5, 1863, p. 2, c. 1
"Daily Morning News", (Savannah, GA), Volume 14, #55, March 6, 1863, p. 2, c. 2
"Daily Morning News", (Savannah, GA), Volume 14, #103, May 4, 1863, p. 2, c. 2
Times, (London, England), #24520, March 31, 1863, p. 12, c. 2
Times, (London, England), #24576, June 4, 1863, p. 7, c. 5
Official Records of the Union and Confederate Navies in the War of the Rebellion, (Washington, DC, 1901), Series 1, Volume 13, pp. 687-690, 736, 746
History of Georgetown County, South Carolina, by George C. Rogers, (Columbia, South Carolina, 1970), p. 408
Shipwrecks of the Civil War: The Encyclopedia of Union and Confederate Naval Losses, by Donald Shomette, (Washington, DC, 1973), p. 446
Lifeline of the Confederacy: Blockade Running During the Civil War, by Stephen R. Wise, (University of South Carolina, Columbia, SC, 1983), p. 628

297: The United States submarine *Alligator* was lost in a storm at sea on April 2, 1863. The *Alligator* had left Newport News, Virginia, under tow of the *U.S.S. Sumter* on April 1, 1863, and was bound to Port Royal, South Carolina, when the vessels got into a storm and the steamer was forced to cut the submarine loose. The submarine had been intended to be used to discover and explode mines in preparation for an assault on Charleston. The assault took place on April 7, 1863, and failed largely due to the Confederate mines. The *Alligator* was designed by the French inventor Brutus de Villeroy and launched by Neafie and Levy, Philadelphia, Pennsylvania, on April 30, 1862, under a subcontract from Martin Thomas. The vessel was completed in June of 1862. She was said to be about 30' long and 6' or 8' in diameter. "It was made of iron, with the upper part pierced for small circular plates of glass, for light, and in it were several water tight compartments." It had originally been fitted with sixteen paddles protruding from the sides to be worked by men inside, but on July 3, 1862, she was ordered to Washington Navy Yard to have her folding oars replaced by a propeller which was powered by a hand crank. It was said to be capable of seven knots. "The *Alligator* was to have been manned by sixteen men, besides one in submarine armor, who was the explorer, and a captain who was to steer the craft. An air pump in the center of the machine, to which were attached two air tubes, attached to floats, was to furnish air to the occupants, the machine being of course air tight. The entrance to it was through a man-hole at one end, which was covered with an iron plate, with leather packing." She was to have been submerged by the flooding of compartments. The *Alligator* was also described as a "semi-submarine boat," 46' (or 47') long and 4'6" in diameter, with a crew of seventeen. (Note: This entry is included because of the very real possibility that the loss actually took place in the waters covered by this book.)

References for entry 297 (SL Code™ 1863-4-US-x-1)
Official Records of the Union and Confederate Navies in the War of the Rebellion, (Washington, 1899), Series 1, Volume 8, p. 636
Official Records of the Union and Confederate Navies in the War of the Rebellion, (Washington, DC, 1921), Series 2, Volume 1, p. 32
Dictionary of American Naval Fighting Ships, (Washington, DC, 1959), Volume 1, p. 34
Civil War Naval Chronology 1861-1865, compiled by Navy History Division, Navy Department, (Washington, DC, 1971), Volume 3, p. 54, paragraph 26

298: The schooners *George Chisolm*, Captain Johnston, and *Antoinette*, along with several others, were reported destroyed by the Federals at Murray's Inlet (sic), South Carolina, on April 27, 1863. "One or more" of the vessels were described as "lately arrived" through the blockade from Havana. Some of the vessels were said to have been loaded with cotton. Their position was described as "high up in the Inlet, out of range of a steamer". (Note One: This report was later discredited as exaggerated, and it was said that only the *Gold Linen* was destroyed. For more on that vessel see next entry.)

References for entry 298 (SL Code™ 1863-4-US-SC/GA-11):
"Charleston Daily Courier", (Charleston, SC), Volume 61, #19454, April 30, 1863, p. 1, c. 2
"Charleston Daily Courier", (Charleston, SC), Volume 61, #19455, May 1, 1863, p. 2, c. 2
"Daily Morning News", (Savannah, GA), #103, May 4, 1863, p. 2, c. 2
Official Records of the Union and Confederate Armies in the War of the Rebellion, (Washington, DC, 1885), Series 1, Volume 14, pp. 3, 286

299: The large English schooner *Golden Liner* (or *Gold Linen*), of Halifax, just arrived and still loaded with a valuable cargo of flour, brandy, sugar and coffee, was captured and burned by a Federal expedition from the United States steamer *Monticello* and the United States schooner *Matthew Vassar* on April 27, 1863. The destruction was variously described as carried out "at" or "inside of" Murrell's Inlet, South Carolina. One report stated that the Federal force was headed by Acting master L.A. Brown, while another indicated it was headed by Lt. Braine of the *Monticello*. (Note One: David Stick in his book *Graveyard of the Atlantic*, incorrectly shows the *Golden Liner* as lost in the Cape Fear River.) (Note Two: See also previous entry.)

References for entry 299 (SL Code™ 1863-4-US-SC/GA-12):
"Charleston Daily Courier", (Charleston, SC), Volume 61, #19455, May 1, 1863, p. 2, c. 2

Shipwrecks, Pirates & Privateers:

Official Records of the Union and Confederate Armies in the War of the Rebellion, (Washington, DC, 1885), Series 1, Volume 14, pp. 3, 286

Official Records of the Union and Confederate Navies in the War of the Rebellion, (Washington, DC, 1898), Series 1, Volume 8, pp. 828, 829

Official Records of the Union and Confederate Navies in the War of the Rebellion, (Washington, DC, 1902), Series 1, Volume 14, p. 191

Graveyard of the Atlantic: Shipwrecks of the North Carolina Coast, by David Stick (University of North Carolina Press, Chapel Hill, NC, 1952), p. 247

History of Georgetown County, South Carolina, by George C. Rogers, (Columbia, South Carolina, 1970), p. 408

Shipwrecks of the Civil War: The Encyclopedia of Union and Confederate Naval Losses, by Donald Shomette, (Washington, DC, 1973), pp. 427, 428

300: On May 12, 1863, the United States steamer *Monticello* shelled five schooners while they were aground in Murrell's Inlet, South Carolina, setting one on fire and damaging the others.

References for entry 300 (SL Code™ 1863-5-US-SC/GA-1):

Official Records of the Union and Confederate Armies in the War of the Rebellion, (Washington, DC, 1902), Series 1, Volume 14, pp. 286-287

History of Georgetown County, South Carolina, by George C. Rogers, (Columbia, South Carolina, 1970), p. 408

301: The bark *Whistling Wind* (or *Windward*), Captain Thomas Butler, bound from Philadelphia to New Orleans, with a cargo of coal, was captured and burned on June 6, 1863, east of Cape Romain, South Carolina, by Lieutenant Charles W. Read, commanding the Confederate steamer *Clarence*. Lieutenant Read reported the bark as "insured by the Federal government for $14,000. Her chronometer and papers were taken off. Lt. Read recorded in the *Clarence's* log that he captured the bark in latitude 33°39' North, longitude 71°29' West. The *Whistling Wind* was a full model bark and was shown in "American Lloyd's" of 1858 as owned by C.E. Peters. She was rated A-2 for insurance purposes measured 349 tons (or 350), drew twelve feet of water. She was built in 1855 at Bluehill, Maine, of mixed woods and was iron fastened. She had one deck with a deck cabin and had been surveyed in 1858. The *Whistling Wind* was issued a certificate of register at the port of New York on April 18, 1863.

References for entry 301 (SL Code™ 1863-6-US-SC/GA-3):

New York Marine Register: or American Lloyd's, (New York, New York, 1858/59), p. 112, #1469

Official Records of the Union and Confederate Navies in the War of the Rebellion, (Washington, DC, 1895), Series 1, Volume 2, pp. 324, 331, 332, 354, 655

List of American-Flag Merchant Vessels that Received Certificates of Enrollment or Registry at the Port of New York 1789-1867, compiled by Forest R. Holdcamper, (U.S. National Archives, Washington, DC, 1968), Special List #22, Volume 2, p. 725

Shipwrecks of the Civil War: The Encyclopedia of Union and Confederate Naval Losses, by Donald Shomette, (Washington, DC, 1973), p. 221

302: The blockade running schooner *Rover* was driven ashore at Murrell's Inlet, South Carolina, on October 19, 1863, and was burned by her own crew, after her cargo had already been safely landed on the beach. The Federals landed seventeen men on the nearby beach, ten of whom (including an Ensign Tillson) were captured by Company B of the 21st Georgia Cavalry under Lieutenant Ely Kennedy.

References for entry 302 (SL Code™ 1863-10-US-SC/GA-2):

"Charleston Daily Courier", (Charleston, SC), Volume 61, #19606, October 26, 1863, p. 1, c. 3

Sunken Treasures of the Upper SC Coast, 1521-1865

"Charleston Mercury", (Charleston, SC), Volume 83, #11892, October 26, 1863, p. 2, c. 1
Official Records of the Union and Confederate Armies in the War of the Rebellion, (Washington, DC, 1890), Series 1, Volume 28, Part 1, pp. 736, 737
History of Georgetown County, South Carolina, by George C. Rogers, (Columbia, South Carolina, 1970), p. 411

303: The Federals destroyed a schooner, loaded with turpentine for Nassau, during a raid on Murrell's Inlet, South Carolina, on December 23, 1863.

References for entry 303 (SL Code™ 1863-12-US-SC/GA-5):
Official Records of the Union and Confederate Navies in the War of the Rebellion, (Washington, DC, 1902), Series 1, Volume 15, pp. 154, 155
History of Georgetown County, South Carolina, by George C. Rogers, (Columbia, South Carolina, 1970), p. 412

304: The sidewheel steamer *Dare*, bound from Bermuda to Wilmington, North Carolina, was chased ashore at North Inlet, near the south end of DeBordieu (aka DuBourdieu, or DeBordeau) Island, South Carolina, on January 7, 1864. (Note One: Her position was also described as "beached six miles east of the Pee Dee" River. The *Dare*, captain Thomas B. Skinner, was burned by her own crew to prevent her capture. Two Federal boats "filed to their utmost capacity with the baggage of the officers and other plunder" swamped drowning between three and "fourteen of the Yankee sailors". The Yankees had broken into the *Dare's* liquor and had all gotten drunk. Twenty-four (or 25) Federals were afterwards captured on the beach by Major William P. White and two other men.) [Note Two: The *Dare* was also known as the *Virginia Dare*, and is incorrectly shown in some records as the *Dan* and as the *Adair*. The *Dare's* iron hull was designated yard #52, and was built at Kelvinhaugh Yard, Glasgow in September, 1863, by Alexander R. Stephen and Sons. She was schooner rigged. Her builders charged £12,860 for her construction and £4,720 for her engines, making them a profit of £3,500. The *Dare's* first registered owner was David McNutt. The vessel was operated by the Richmond Importing and Exporting Company at the time of her loss. The *Dare* measured 179.46 tons register, 553 12/94 tons BM (or 552 6/94), 217 (or 218') in length, 23' in breadth, and 9'6" in depth of hold to top of floors.] (Note Three: She carried a cargo of seventy-five tons, 50 tons of which was for the State of Virginia, and a considerable portion of that was intended for the Virginia Military Institute. Most of her cargo was expected to be saved.) (Note Four: A signal lantern and a porthole on display with a model of the *Dare* at the "Ships of the Sea Museum" at Savannah, Georgia, were recovered by Master Diver Lawrence Wilde on June 11, 1962. Whether, the artifacts were actually recovered from the *Dare* is questionable, as a typed letter which was sent to the museum stated that the *Dare* lies "at the south end of Pawley's Island", which is factually incorrect. However, the blockade running steamer *Rose* was reportedly

Shipwrecks, Pirates & Privateers:

wrecked at the south end of Pawley's Island near the wreck of another unidentified steamer, and the museum's artifacts could have come from either of those two vessels. For more on the loss of the steamer *Rose* see her entry in this book.) (Note Five: In 1966, Jim Batey, Ron Renau, and I dove on the wreck of a steamer at North Inlet. That wreck's position closely matches the location given for the *Dare* in contemporary documents. We recovered a number of Civil War era bottles and other artifacts. Jim also found an extremely rare and valuable pewter inkwell just outside the broken iron hull of the wreck. A name and date had been scratched into the pewter. The inkwell was American made and dated from before the American Revolution, and may have been an heirloom or otherwise prized possession of one of the *Dare's* officers, or it may have come from a nearby wooden wreck, or even washed out of the adjoining creek. The inkwell was in excellent condition and was recently appraised at over $10,000. Portions of the wrecked steamer are exposed at low tide, so the wreck is easy to find.] (Note Six: Historian Stephen R. Wise in his book *Lifeline of the Confederacy: Blockade Running During the Civil War* gives the same date of loss, but incorrectly shows the *Dare* as having been wrecked off Lockwood Folly, North Carolina, on her first attempt through the blockade. Charles Foard's chart of Civil War wrecks of the Wilmington, North Carolina, area describes the *Dare* as wrecked at "North Inlet, South Carolina (Little River)."]

References for entry 304 (SL Code™ 1864-1-US-SC/GA-2):
Charleston Daily Courier, (Charleston, SC), Volume 62, #19664, January 13, 1864, p. 1, c. 2
Charleston Daily Courier, (Charleston, SC), Volume 62, #19665, January 14, 1864, p. 1, c. 2
Charleston Daily Courier, (Charleston, SC), Volume 62, #19669, January 19, 1864, p. 1, c. 3
Charleston Mercury, (Charleston, SC), Volume 84, #11959, January 15, 1864, p. 2, c. 1
Charleston Mercury, (Charleston, SC), Volume 84, #11961, January 18, 1864, p. 1, c. 4
Charleston Mercury, (Charleston, SC), Volume 84, #12082, June 8, 1864, p. 2, c. 1
"Vessel Papers" (manuscript records), United States National Archives, Washington, DC, Record Group 109, files D-51, V-34
Report of the Secretary of the Navy, Second Session, 38th Congress, 1864-1865, (Washington, DC, 1865), p. 725
Official Records of the Union and Confederate Armies in the War of the Rebellion, (Washington, DC, 1891), Series 1, Volume 35, Part 1, pp. 272, 273
Official Records of the Union and Confederate Navies in the War of the Rebellion, (Washington, DC, 1899), Series 1, Volume 9, pp. 388-393, 409, 410
A Chart of Wrecks of Vessels Sunk or Captured Near Wilmington, NC, Circa 1861-65, compiled by Charles H. Foard, (Wilmington, North Carolina, 1962)
Typed 3x5 file cards, ("Ships of the Sea Museum," Savannah, Georgia), catalog cards #65:39, #65:40
History of Georgetown County, South Carolina, by George C. Rogers, (Columbia, South Carolina, 1970), p. 413
An Oceanographic Atlas of the Continental Margin, J.G. Newton, O.H. Pilkey, & J.O. Blanton, (Duke University Marine Laboratory, Beaufort, North Carolina, 1971), p. 17 chart symbol #87, p. 20 entry #87
Pawley's Island, A Living Legend, by Prevost and Wilder, (Columbia, South Carolina, 1972), p. 49
Lifeline of the Confederacy: Blockade Running During the Civil War, by Stephen R. Wise, (University Microfilms International, 1983), pp. 368, 551
Merchant Sailing Ships, 1850-1875, Heyday of Sail, by David R. MacGregor, (Lloyd's of London Press, 1984), p. 236

305: On March 24, 1864, the iron steamer *Little Ada* (or *Ada*), of Glasgow, was boarded in the creek at McClellenville, South Carolina, by a Federal expedition intending to destroy or capture her during a day time raid. A Confederate battery opened up with three rifled guns (believed to have been 12-pounder Whitworths). One shot penetrating the steam drum and another through the boilers, destroying tubes, etc. "In fact, they had the range so perfectly that their shot completely riddled her". The Yankees then fled to escape capture or death. The *Little Ada* had a 6-pounder Whitworth gun mounted on her deck which she fired shell and shrapnel at the fleeing Yankees. The steamer was commanded by a Baltimore resident named Martin. A dispatch from the U.S. Consul at Glasgow had previously described the *Ada* as a "screw steamer of 220 tons, speed 12 knots". She was 112'x18'6"x10', drew 5'6" forward and 8' aft, and was rated at 208 tons burden and 94 tons register. The vessel was not destroyed, and was quickly repaired. She was owned by the Importing and Exporting Company of Georgia and was registered in the name of Henry Lafone. The vessel made two successful trips through the blockade before being captured at sea off Cape Romain, South Carolina, on July 9, 1864, by the *U.S.S. Gettysburg.*

References for entry 305 (SL Code™ 1864-3-US-SC/GA-5):
Official Records of the Union and Confederate Navies in the War of the Rebellion, (Washington, DC, 1902), Series 1, Volume 15, pp. 374-380
Lifeline of the Confederacy: Blockade Running During the Civil War, by Stephen R. Wise, (University of South Carolina, Columbia, SC, 1983), p. 586
Warships of the Civil War Navies, by Paul H. Silverstone, (Naval Institute Press, Annapolis, MD, 1989), p. 104

306: The fate of the steamer *Vesta*, Captain R.H. Eustace, which was wrecked near the South Carolina/North Carolina line on January 11, 1864, seems to have been sealed from the moment she left Bermuda. "For seven days she was chased over the seas by a number of Yankee cruisers; but succeeded in eluding them, and on the 10th (of January) made the coast in the vicinity of Wilmington. Being compelled to lay to she was decried by a Yankee cruiser, which gave chase; and in half an hour more than eleven Yankee vessels were pouncing down upon the suddenly discovered prey. The *Vesta*, although apparently surrounded, ran the gauntlet in splendid style, through one of the most stirring scenes which the war has yet witnessed on the water. Some of the cruisers attempted to cross her bows and cut her off; but she was too rapid for this maneuver, and at about half a mile's distance some of the cruisers opened their broadsides upon her, while five others in chase were constantly using their bow guns, exploding shells right over the decks of the devoted vessel. Fortunately, no one was hurt, and the vessel ran the gauntlet, raising her flag in defiance, suffering only from a single shot, which, though it passed amidships, above the water line, happily escaped the machinery." "But the trouble seems to have commenced with what the passengers, anticipated to be the triumphant escape from their captors; for the captain and the first officer, Tickler, are reported to have become outrageously drunk after the affair was over and the night had fallen. It is said that the captain was asleep on the quarter-deck, stupefied with drink, when he should have put the ship on land; and that at two o'clock in the morning he directed the pilot to take the ship ashore, telling him that the ship was above Fort Fisher, when the fact was that she was about forty miles to the southward of Frying Pan Shoals." In fifteen minutes she was run aground so hard, she could not be got off. The *Vesta* carried a cargo "of the most valuable description," including a "splendid uniform, intended as a present for General Lee from some of his admirers in London." Three fourth's of her cargo was "on government account, consisting of army supplies, and including a very expensive lot of English shoes." It had been her first attempt at running the blockade. One of her passengers was a paymaster for the Confederate Navy. The passengers and crew landed in lifeboats minus their baggage. The *Vesta's* fate was finalized when her inebriated captain ordered her fired and burned to the water's edge. The cruisers did not get up to the wreck until the afternoon of the next day when they were attracted to it by the smoke from the conflagration. Nothing of any account was saved from the wreck. Contemporary newspaper accounts stated that the wreck was at Little River Inlet at the South Carolina, North Carolina line. (Note One: Ship logs and official reports give a more precise location and show that the loss actually took place on the North Carolina side of the state line. Those reports show her as wrecked four miles south and westward of Tubb's Inlet, North Carolina. Her position is also given in some reports as at Little River Inlet, North Carolina. A Sea Grant publication put out by the University of North Carolina lists her as in ten feet of water off "*Vesta* Pier.") [Note Two: The *Vesta* was described as a "fine looking double propeller blockade runner," "exactly like the *Ceres*." She was "perfect in all appointments" and "worth about £300,000 to the Confederates." She had a long iron hull with an elliptical stern and was rigged as a hermaphrodite brig. Her smoke pipe and every thing forward was painted white, while the after part was painted a dark lead color. She was 500 tons (262 tons register) and drew eight feet of water. She was said to be "one of the finest steamers in the blockade running line" and measured 165'x23'x13'. The *Vesta* was built by J.&W. Dudgeon at London, England, in 1863, and was owned by Crenshaw, and Collie and Company. A penciled "Memo of loss by *Vesta*" in the Vessel File at the National Archives in Washington, DC, shows the *Vesta* as having lost 21 bales of blankets, 550 reams of paper, 127 cases of shoes, and 9 bales of cloth.]

Sunken Treasures of the Upper SC Coast, 1521-1865

References for entry 306 (SL Code™ 1864-1-US-NC-4)
"Charleston Daily Courier," (Charleston, SC), Volume 62, #19673, January 23, 1863, p. 2, c. 1
"Charleston Mercury," (Charleston, SC), Volume 84, #11966, January 23, 1864, p. 2, c. 1
Times, (London, England), #24798, February 18, 1864, p. 11, c. 2
"Memo of loss by *Vesta*," manuscript, United States National Archives, Washington, DC, Record Group 109, Vessel File, V-10-4
"Confederate Archives," NARS, Chapter 8-2-413, 437
Official Records of the Union and Confederate Armies in the War of the Rebellion, (Washington, DC, 1891), Series 1, Volume 33, p. 1
Official Records of the Union and Confederate Navies in the War of the Rebellion, (Washington, DC, 1899), Series 1, Volume 9, pp. 402-405, 409
Official Records of the Union and Confederate Navies in the War of the Rebellion, (Washington, DC, 1900), Series 1, Volume 10, p. 504
Graveyard of the Atlantic: Shipwrecks of the North Carolina Coast, by David Stick (University of North Carolina Press, Chapel Hill, NC, 1952), p. 247
A Chart of Wrecks of Vessels Sunk or Captured Near Wilmington, NC, Circa 1861-65, compiled by Charles H. Foard, (Wilmington, North Carolina, 1962)
"Vessel Papers" (manuscript records), United States National Archives, Washington, DC, Record Group 109, M909, roll 30, file V-10, frames 0921-0925
Spence's Guide to South Carolina, by E. Lee Spence, (Charleston, SC, 1972), p. 6
Wreck Diving in North Carolina, University of North Carolina, Sea Grant Publication, #78-13, p. 5
Lifeline of the Confederacy: Blockade Running During the Civil War, by Stephen R. Wise, (University Microfilms International, 1983), pp. 279, 368, 624
The Blockade Runners, by Dave Horner, (Florida Classics Library, Port Salerno, FL, 1992), Chapter 14, pp. 26, 217

307: The British blockade runner *Rose*, Captain W. M. Hale, was chased aground on the south end of Pawley's Island, South Carolina, by the United States gunboat *Wamsutta* on June 2, 1864. The *Rose* carried an assorted cargo which included barrels and cases of liquor, small stores, etc., but most was believed to have already been unloaded on the beach at North Inlet, South Carolina, prior to her being spotted and chased. The Federals captured her register and other papers. The Federals set the steamer on fire and she was completely destroyed. (Note One: The "Charleston Mercury" of June 8, 1864, reported the *Rose* as having a cargo of coal for the Confederate government, and gave her position as off "Butler's Island, near Georgetown, and near the wreck of the *Virginia Dare*." For more on the wreck referred to as the *Virginia Dare*, please see her entry in this book.) (Note Two: The *Rose* was a sidewheel steamer. Federal reports said she ran ashore near the wreck of another steamer, but did not say how near, or what the other wreck was called. It was the *Rose's* first attempt to run the blockade. The Federal troops were driven off by a company of seventy-five Confederates. Her crew lost all of their personal effects and baggage.)

References for entry 307 (SL Code™ 1864-6-US-SC/GA-1):
"Charleston Mercury", (Charleston, SC), Volume 85, #12082, June 8, 1864, p. 2, c. 1
Times, (London, England), #24909, June 27, 1864, p. 9, c. 6
Official Records of the Union and Confederate Armies in the War of the Rebellion, (Washington, DC), Series 1, Volume 15, Part 1, pp. 340, 409-411
Official Records of the Union and Confederate Navies in the War of the Rebellion, (Washington, DC, 1902), Series 1, Volume 15, pp. 467, 468, 513, 517
History of Georgetown County, South Carolina, by George C. Rogers, (Columbia, South Carolina, 1970), p. 413
Pawley's Island, A Living Legend, by Prevost and Wilder, (Columbia, South Carolina, 1972), p. 49
Lifeline of the Confederacy: Blockade Running During the Civil War, by Stephen R. Wise, (University of South Carolina, Columbia, SC, 1983), pp. 369, 609

308: The London *Times* of February 3, 1865, reported the steamer *Julia* as "lost while trying to get out of Charleston". The *Julia* had been caught in a gale while escaping from Charleston in December of 1864, and was forced to seek shelter in the Santee River where she accidentally ran aground. She was soon discovered and captured by small boats from the United States gunboat *Acadia*. The *Julia* was an iron hulled, sidewheel steamer built by Simons and Company at Renfrew, Scotland, in 1863. She was 210'x23.2'x9.8', 117 tons register and 735 tons burden. The steamer was owned by Donald McGregor and she had made one previous run through the blockade.

References for entry 308 (SL Code™ 1864-12-US-SC/GAx-1):
Times, (London, England), #25099, February 3, 1865, p. 9, c. 2
Lifeline of the Confederacy: Blockade Running During the Civil War, by Stephen R. Wise, (University of South Carolina, Columbia, SC, 1983), p. 580

309: On March 1, 1865, while the United States gunboat *Harvest Moon*, was going up the river to Georgetown, South Carolina, a torpedo (Confederate mine) exploded near her, shattering her wheel house and injuring her hull so badly that she quickly sank in Winyah Bay. Her ward room steward was killed, but the remainder of her officers and men were saved. [Note One: The *Harvest Moon* was a sidewheel steamer measuring 193' in length, 29' in breadth, and 10' in depth of hold, with a draft of 8'. She was serving as Admiral Dahlgren's flagship when she was lost. The vessel was launched at Portland, Maine, on November 22, 1862, and was completed in 1863. Her first home port was at Boston. She was purchased at Boston on November 16, 1863, by Commodore J.B. Montgomery from Charles Spear for $99,300. She was commissioned at Boston Navy Yard on February 12, 1864. The *Harvest Moon* had a wood hull with a vertical beam engine (41" diameter cylinder with a 10' piston stroke). She averaged nine miles an hour and could make a maximum of fifteen miles per hour. She was armed with one 20-pounder Parrott rifle, four 24-pounder howitzers, and one 12-pounder rifle. She carried a complement of 72 men.] (Note Two: The *Harvest Moon's* logbook is in the National Archives, and apparently includes some data on salvage efforts as covers the period February 12, 1864, through April 20, 1865. She "was abandoned, after taking out machinery, etc.) (Note Three: Drew Ruddy, Steve Howard, John Coleman and I visited this wreck in the mid 1960's. We tied up to her stack which stuck out of the water. Ruddy, who was then about fifteen and still a novice diver, was extremely safety minded and recited a long list of signals and things to do if anyone got into trouble on the wreck. As he went to go overboard, he tripped and fell head first into the murky waters. Seconds later he reappeared. His head was covered with sticky black mud, and he quipped "if you get in trouble, just stand up." The wrecked gunboat was almost entirely buried in mud and sand. Her stack stuck out of the water which, due to heavy silting, was only about three feet deep. Ruddy later held the record for deep diving in a mechanical suit, and made international news when he found the Bank of Rome safe on the wreck of the *Andrea Doria*.)

References for entry 309 (SL Code™ 1865-3-US-SC/GA-1):
"Steam Vessels #1, 1850's," (bound manuscript, Atlantic Mutual Insurance Companies of New York), entry for *Harvest Moon*
"Savannah Daily Herald," (Savannah, GA), #41, March 7, 1865, p. 2, c. 1
Times, (London, England), #25136, March 18, 1865, p. 14, c. 1
Records of General Courts Martial and Courts of Inquiry of the Navy Department, 1799-1867, Court of Inquiry, #4319, NARS M-273, roll 167, frames 0647-0695
"Vessel Papers" (manuscript records), United States National Archives, Washington, DC, Record Group 109, file H-106
"Description and Disposition of U.S. Vessels, Navy Dept.," (bound manuscript), Volume 1, National Archives, Record Group 45, entry 287
History of the Confederate States Navy From its Organization to the Surrender of its Last Vessel, by J. Thomas Scharf, (New York, New York, 1887), p. 705
Official Records of the Union and Confederate Armies in the War of the Rebellion, (Washington, DC, 1895), Series 1, Volume 47, Part 1, pp. 1008, 1009
Official Records of the Union and Confederate Navies in the War of the Rebellion, (Washington, DC, 1903), Series 1, Volume 16, pp. 282-284, 366, 371, 386
Official Records of the Union and Confederate Navies in the War of the Rebellion, (Washington, DC, 1921), Series 2, Volume 1, p. 99
The Navy in the Civil War, (Charles Scribner's Sons, New York, NY, 1905), Volume 2 ("The Atlantic Coast" by Daniel Ammen), p. 148
Logbooks of the United States Navy Ships, Stations and Units 1801-1947, p. 126
Merchant Steam Vessels of the United States 1790-1868, ("Lytle-Holdcamper List"), edited by C. Bradford Mitchell, (Staten Island, NY, 1975), p. 92
Warships of the Civil War Navies, by Paul H. Silverstone, (Naval Institute Press, Annapolis, MD, 1989), p. 84

310: The Confederate States gunboat *Pee Dee* (or *Peedee*, or *Pedee*) was burned and sunk along with several other vessels about March 15, 1865, by the Confederates to prevent their falling into the hands of the rapidly advancing Federal Army. The *Pee Dee's* location was given as just below the railroad bridge on the west side of the Great Pee Dee River, South Carolina. [Note: The *Pee Dee* was described as the best wooden ship constructed by the Confederacy. She had a single engine, twin propellers, and was schooner rigged. Her hull was 170' in length, 26' in breadth, 10' in depth of hold. The *Pee Dee* was armed with two 3-inch pivot guns (bow and stern) and a 9-inch Dahlgren mounted as a pivot gun amidships (one report said she was to have been armed with four 32-pounders and two pivots). She was built in January of 1865 at the Confederate Navy Yard at Mars Bluff, just above the railroad trestle on the Pee Dee River. In 1926 the Ellison Capers and Maxcy Gregg Florence chapters of the United Daughters of the Confederacy salvaged the ship's propellers which are now displayed on the grounds of the Florence Museum in Florence, South Carolina. In 1954 the remainder of the vessel was salvaged and displayed at the South of the Border tourist center in Dillon County, South Carolina. The *Pee Dee* was commanded by Lieutenant Oscar Johnson. Her guns may have been salvaged immediately after the war. The other vessels, which were scuttled and burned, were all sunk at the shipyard above the railroad bridge. They included a "Tender," described as a new boat 128' in length and 22' in breadth.]

References for entry 310 (SL Code™ 1865-3-US-SC/GA-4):
Manuscript letter from William Radford to the Chief of the Bureau of Construction and Repair, (August 17, 1865), National Archives, Record Group 45, Subject File AX, Box 87, (0-1910), #15
Manuscript letter from R.L. Law to Gideon Welles, (October 20, 1865), NARS Microfilm M-89-roll 246, p. 14
"Vessel Papers" (manuscript records), United States National Archives, Washington, DC, Record Group 109, file P-100
Official Records of the Union and Confederate Navies in the War of the Rebellion, (Washington, DC, 1903), Series 1, Volume 16, p. 511
Official Records of the Union and Confederate Navies in the War of the Rebellion, (Washington, DC, 1921), Series 2, Volume 1, p. 262
Theodosia and Other Pee Dee Sketches, by James A. Rogers, pp. 3-5 *Civil War Naval Chronology 1861-1861*, compiled by Navy History Division, Navy Department, (Washington, DC, 1971), p. VI-281
Warships of the Civil War Navies, by Paul H. Silverstone, (Naval Institute Press, Annapolis, MD, 1989), p. 218

311: The United States steamer *Commodore McDonough* sprang a leak, filled rapidly, and sank about 10:30 a.m. on August 22 (or 23), 1865, while being towed from Port Royal, South Carolina, to New York (also shown as bound from Charleston to Baltimore). [Note One: The *Commodore McDonough* was a wooden hulled side wheel ferry boat of 532 tons, with an inclined engine (38" diameter cylinder with a 10' piston stroke). She drew 8'6" of water and could make eight knots. Her battery was last reported as consisting of one 100-pounder rifle, one 9-inch Dahlgren smooth bore, two 50-pounder Dahlgren rifles, and two 24-pounder howitzers. She had been purchased by Rear Admiral H. Paulding from the Union Ferry Company at New York for $42,409.40. The total cost of her repairs while in government service was $27,790.48. Under normal circumstances she carried a complement of 75 men.] (Note Two: The actual location of the wreck has not been determined at this time and the loss is included in this list solely to alert the reader that she may have been lost in the area covered by this book, and may even be the wreck found by commercial fisherman Captain Billy Long and mentioned in entry 273 as possibly being the *Governor*.)

References for entry 311 (SL Code™ 1865-8-US-NCx-1)
"Savannah Daily Herald," (Savannah, GA), Volume 1, #190, August 28, 1865, p. 3, c. 5
Official Records of the Union and Confederate Navies in the War of the Rebellion, (Washington, DC, 1921), Series 2, Volume 1, p. 63
Warships of the Civil War Navies, by Paul H. Silverstone, (Naval Institute Press, Annapolis, MD, 1989), p. 100

Final Entry: Two vessels that fall outside of the time period covered by this book, still deserve mention because they both played significant roles in the Civil War, and were later sunk in the waters covered by this book.

The British blockade runner *Princess Royal*, which was captured off Charleston and converted to a Federal gunboat, was lost off Cherry Grove, South Carolina, on January 10, 1874. The $1,000,000 cargo she carried when captured had been owned by

George Alfred Trenholm. (Trenholm was the historical basis for Margaret Mitchell's Rhett Butler character in *Gone With The Wind*.) The 619 ton screw steamer was built at Glasgow, Scotland, in 1861. She was sold to private parties after the war and was registered under the name *Sherman* (official #22267 ex #43681) at Philadelphia on September 23, 1865. The wreck is frequently referred to as the "General Sherman." The *Princess Royal's* captured log shows her as 494 tons register.

The Confederate steamer *Planter,* which made history after being high-jacked out of Charleston Harbor by its black pilot, Robert Smalls, was wrecked on Cape Romain, South Carolina, on July 1, 1876, while going to the rescue of another vessel. The sidewheel, wooden hulled, 313 ton, *Planter* (official #19658) was built in 1860 at Charleston, South Carolina.

References for Final Entry
"Charleston Daily Courier", (Charleston, SC), Volume 61, #19379, January 30, 1863, p. 2, c. 2
"Charleston Daily Courier", (Charleston, SC), Volume 61, #19380, January 31, 1863, p. 2, c. 2
"Charleston Daily Courier", (Charleston, SC), Vol. 61, #19406, March 3, 1863, p. 2, c. 2
New York Times, (New York, NY), Vol. 12, #3550, February 9, 1863, p. 1, c. 1, 2
New York Times, (New York, NY), Vol. 12, #3551, February 10, 1863, p. 1, c. 3, 4
"Log of the *S.S. Princess Royal*", December 6, 1862, to January 10, 1863, contained in the collection of the Philadelphia Maritime Museum, listed as logbook #67.296
Merchant Steam Vessels of the United States 1790-1868, ("Lytle-Holdcamper List"), edited by C. Bradford Mitchell, (Staten Island, NY, 1975), pages 198 and 297 for *Sherman,* and pages 175 and 290 for *Planter*

Rare silver wedge and pieces of eight from the author's private collection.
Photo by Charles King.

One hundred year old bottle of "Whyte & MacKay" Scotch recovered intact from a shipwreck in 86' of water. Photo by Randy Lathrop.

Civil War era sword and beer bottle. Photo by Jo Pinkard.

These wine glass shards were found by the author in a South Carolina river.
Photo courtesy of the South Carolina Institute of Archaeology & Anthropology.

The author aboard a modern car ferry he had just salvaged.
1980 photo by Kevin Rooney.

The author on the stern of his 116' salvage vessel "Sea Raven." Note the two Propwash Deflection Units (PDU's) in the up or travel position. PDU's, used while a vessel is anchored over a wreck, allow the salvor to direct the vessel's propwash downwards to wash sand and mud off the site and/or to blow the clearer surface waters down to the divers. The port unit is designed to blow straight down, while the one on the starboard side is meant to be used at an angle to allow for a different effect. 1987 photo by Chip Knudsen.

APPENDIX A
SL Codes™ Explained

      The references for each entry in this book have been keyed to an *SL Code*™. *SL Codes*™ are alpha-numeric reference codes used to organize shipwreck data in various versions of *Spence's List*™. You do not need to understand them to use or enjoy this book. However, for the more serious researcher the following information is provided. *SL Codes*™ are based on an easy to understand system. *SL Codes*™ are divided into five sections and are designed to answer five different questions at a glance. Each of the five sections of the *SL Code*™ is separated by a dash. The *SL Code*™ for the wreck of the steamer *Dare* is 1864-1-US-SC/GA-2. The first section tells the year of loss (1864); the second the month of loss (In this case, January, which is designated numerically as 1.); the third is the general coastal area (US for the country); the fourth pinpoints the region (Each region has been assigned a particular code. In this case the wreck lies the region designated as SC/GA. A partial listing of country and regional codes used in assigning *SL Codes*™ for other areas follows for informational purposes only.); and the fifth section would be a sequential number in case the *SL Code*™ data in the first four sections is identical for two or more wrecks (In this case it is, so it has been assigned the number 2.). When data for any part of the file number is not known, or when there is unresolvable conflicting data, the cataloger simply enters an arbitrary or best guess followed by an "x" for that section. Wrecks or other entries taken from a source which failed to give the month are shown by the number for the most logical month followed by an "x," or if there is no clue at all to the month, December may be arbitrarily selected, and 12x placed in the month section. *SL Codes*™ containing sections with an "x" are meant as preliminary designations until better information can be located. In some cases a vessel may be accessed through more than one *SL Code*™. This is intentionally done in cases of multiple sinkings, updating of *SL Codes*™, or in cases where existing published data might otherwise be confusing and cause you to look in the wrong spot. If you think of *SL Codes*™ as being assigned to "data packages" rather than being assigned to individual or particular wrecks, it may be less confusing. In fact, in some cases such data packages will not refer to a wreck at all, but may instead contain data on something else which might be of interest to researchers. An entry may give a detailed listing of all of the vessels that sailed in a particular fleet (and some of those vessels may also have separate individual listings) or an entry may simply give data on the passage of a law involving salvage. In any case, whenever possible, multiple listings will be cross referenced. When an *SL Code*™ containing one or more x's is updated with a more accurate *SL Code*™, the old *SL Code*™ may or may not remain in future editions of *Spence's List*™ for cross referencing, but the main body of the data may appear only under the new more accurate *SL Code*™. When organizing entries by *SL Codes*™, section two is considered a subsection of section one, section three a subsection of section two, etc. It should also be noted that, for organizational purposes, an "x" in any section of an *SL Code*™ causes that particular section to treated as a further subsection. Therefore, an entry with an "x" in its *SL Code*™ would be placed after an entry with an otherwise identical (up to that point) *SL Code*™ without an "x" in that section. Advantages of this system should quickly become obvious.

Researchers using this book (or any other volume in the *Spence's List*™ series of books.) should use the *SL Code*™ in citing the source. It is not correct or fair to the original compiler for users of this list to show the "references" given with the entry as "their" source. By including the *SL Code*™ in the citation, future readers will be able to locate additional information, not only by returning to the original list, but by looking up the same *SL Code*™ in future revisions of the list. The correct form of citation for information on the *Dare*, taken from this particular list would be: *Shipwrecks and Sunken Treasures: The Upper Coast of South Carolina, 1521-1865*, by Edward Lee Spence, (© 1994), pages 139-140, #304, *Spence's List*™ entry #1864-1-US-SC/GA-2. Or, for less formal purposes, you might simply record the same citation as: *SL Code*™ 1864-1-US-SC/GA-2. "SL" is simply an abbreviation for *Spence's List*™. Although not used in this book, *SL Codes*™ for the East and Gulf coasts of the United States are: ME/NH - Maine, New Hampshire; MA/RI/CT - Massachusetts, Rhode Island, and Connecticut; NY/NJ/DE - New York, New Jersey, and Delaware; MD/VA - Maryland and Virginia; NC - North Carolina; SC/GA - South Carolina and Georgia; FL - Florida; AL/MS/LA - Alabama, Mississippi and Louisiana; and TX - Texas.

Compilation of the data contained in this book took many years and cost many thousands of dollars. To protect that investment in time and money, actual and punitive damages, etc., will be sought in the event of any copyright infringement.

Dr. E. Lee Spence with one of the two cannon (both dated 1798) salvaged from the "Pirate Wreck" he discovered on Cape Romain. Photo by Steve Howard.

ABOUT THE AUTHOR
by Charles King

S purred on by childhood tales of pirates and adventure, shipwreck expert, Edward Lee Spence, found his first shipwrecks at the age of twelve. He has since found hundreds of wrecks and has worked on everything from Spanish galleons and pirate ships to blockade runners and Great Lakes freighters.

Always an adventurer, Spence has traveled to a wide range of countries including such places as Hong Kong, Vietnam, the Philippines, the Bahamas, the Cayman Islands, the Dominican Republic, El Salvadore, Jamaica, Haiti, Mexico, Colombia, Honduras, Costa Rica, Panama, Nicaragua, Canada, England, Holland, Italy, Germany, Spain, and France. He has explored castles, palaces, shipwrecks, ancient ruins, secret tunnels, and subterranean and underwater caves.

He has been shot at, buried in cave-ins, trapped in fishing nets, pinned under wreckage, run out of air, lost inside a wreck, and bitten by fish while pursuing his quests.

Finding himself the target of an extortionist, Spence "borrowed" over a million dollars worth of original prints by famed wildlife artist John James Audubon in an unsuccessful effort to save the life of his child. Afterwards, he voluntarily turned himself in along with the art which was the only concrete evidence against him. Charged with theft, he was unjustly imprisoned, but was finally pardoned. Legally, the pardon means he was never convicted.

A man of action, Spence has saved the lives of others on more than a dozen occasions, sometimes at great risk to his own. He freely admits to having worked undercover for our government. However, he says it was many years ago when he was "young, invisible, and bulletproof." He refuses to say which agency.

His tools of discovery have ranged from primitive grappling hooks to highly sophisticated side-scanning sonars. Over the years, he has worked out of tiny sailboats, beautiful yachts, and ocean going research vessels.

He first made local and national news when he was a teenager. His work has since been written up in *Life*, *People Weekly*, the *London Sun* and hundreds of other periodicals all over the world. You may have seen him on the *Today Show* or heard him on Talk Net Radio.

Having extensively researched ships lost in hurricanes, Spence was not surprised when his home on Sullivan's Island, South Carolina, was destroyed by Hurricane Hugo.

Spence's initial, but very brief announcement in 1989 of the identity of the "Real Rhett Butler," made international news. He had discovered (what one of the editors for *Life* magazine later characterized as "overwhelming evidence") that Margaret Mitchell based her famous *Gone With The Wind* character on a 19th century Charlestonian named George Alfred Trenholm. This book represents the first time that detailed information relating to that discovery has been made available to the public.

Spence has actually located several steamers and sailing ships once owned by Trenholm. Trenholm's blockade running activities earned him today's equivalent of over one billion dollars in less than five years time. Spence is currently working on a book specifically on Trenholm.

Although long considered one of the "founding fathers" of underwater archeology, at age 47, Spence is still a relatively young man.

In June of 1992, Spence was appointed chief of underwater archeology for Providencia, an archipelago owned by the country of Colombia and covering more than 43,000 square miles in the Western Caribbean. As part of the arrangement, Spence's company was granted the exclusive salvage rights to the entire area for 25 years. His primary target was a treasure fleet which was lost in 1605 with over 250 tons of silver, gold, and precious jewels. His share would have made him richer than Ross Perot.

When word leaked out that Spence had discovered the location of one of the fleet's richest galleons, he suddenly found himself threatened with trumped up charges of treason. The charges were absolutely absurd, but definitely not laughable, as they could have meant the death penalty. When Spence didn't immediately flee the country and seemed to be winning major political support, he was told that one of the drug cartels wanted his salvage rights and was going to have him killed. The man who warned Spence was one of the wealthiest and most powerful men in the archipelago. Knowing that the man didn't make idle threats, and had previously shot and killed a top government official in front of witnesses, Spence wisely said good-by to Colombia. He has no immediate plans to return. However, he does miss the island and his friends, and regrets that his dreams of building a shipwreck museum and a marine oriented university on the island had to be abandoned.

Spence is a member of Mensa and the even more elite Intertel, both organizations are widely known as societies for geniuses. He has a Doctor of Marine Histories and has served as a consultant for numerous "for-profit" and "not-for-profit" organizations, including the College of Charleston and the National Endowment for the Humanities. He has served as an editor for several internationally distributed magazines on shipwrecks and treasure, and is actively working on more than a dozen new books relating to shipwrecks and treasures of various eras and localities.

Not only an historian, cartographer, and an underwater archeologist, Spence is a successful treasure hunter. He has raised hundreds of thousands of valuable artifacts (with a total estimated retail value well in excess of $50,000,000) from the ocean floor. He says most of it went to the government and to his partners.

On September 14, 1995, the South Carolina *Hunley* Commission asked Spence to donate his rights to the Civil War submarine *Hunley* to the State. He did so in writing, with the South Carolina Attorney General signing for its receipt. Spence's rights were based on his 1970 discovery of the tiny vessel. The *Hunley* was the first sub in history to sink an enemy warship.

As an historian, Spence believes the biggest key to success on any expedition is the archival research that precedes it. Spence calls historical research "his drug of choice" and says, "In today's world, time is the most expensive part of an expedition. Man-hours spent in the archives can cut hundreds of thousands of dollars worth of time from the field phase of most projects."

• • •

About the Author

Captain Steve Howard on the deck of the salvage vessel "Derelict II" helps the author with a ceramic jar found on a Civil War blockade runner.
Photo by Kevin Rooney, courtesy of Shipwreck Archeology Inc.

The author with a bronze cannon salvaged from a French warship.
Photo by Ray Lunsford.

INDEX

Sunken Treasures of the Upper SC Coast, 1521-1865

This tankard, valued at over $100,000, dates from the late 1600's and is the oldest intact piece of American pewter ever discovered. It was found by Jim Batey and the author, as teenagers, while diving near an unidentified wreck in a South Carolina river. A musket ball hole in the back side may be the only remaining evidence of a drunken sea brawl. The tankard is now on display at the Colonial Williamsburg Museum. Photo by the L. Spence.

About the Author